C000185277

BEYOND THE EMPIRE

A GUIDE TO THE ROMAN REMAINS IN SCOTLAND

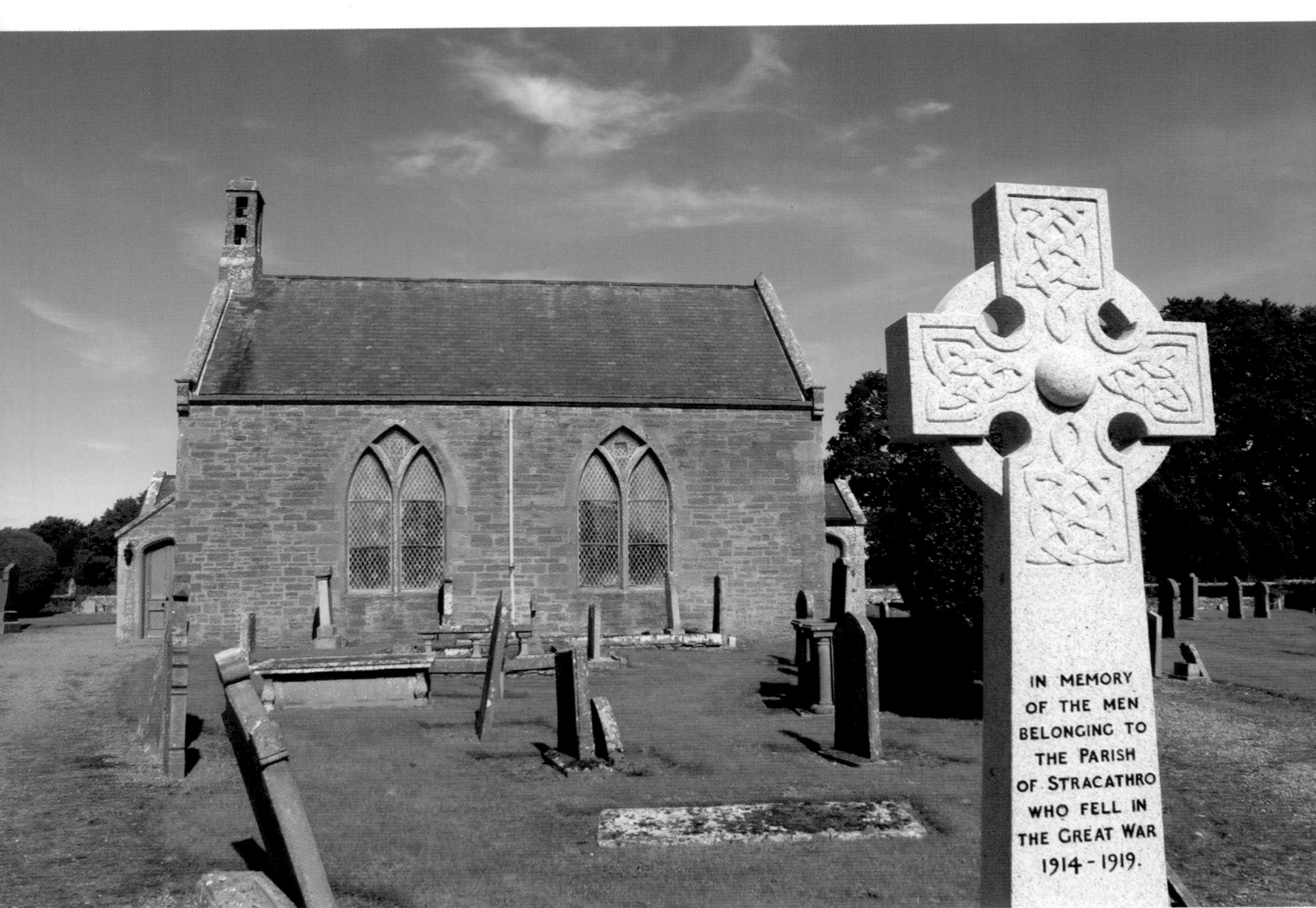
IN MEMORY
OF THE MEN
BELONGING TO
THE PARISH
OF STRACATHRO
WHO FELL IN
THE GREAT WAR
1914 - 1919.

Stracathro parish church which sits on top of the most northerly Roman fort in the world (*see* Chapter 21).

BEYOND THE EMPIRE

A GUIDE TO THE ROMAN REMAINS IN SCOTLAND

Andrew Tibbs

ROBERT HALE

First published in 2019 by
Robert Hale, an imprint of
The Crowood Press Ltd
Ramsbury, Marlborough
Wiltshire SN8 2HR

www.crowood.com

British Library Cataloguing-in-Publication Data
A catalogue record for this book is available from the British Library.

ISBN 978 0 7198 2927 7

Dedication
For patience and understanding; for Paul and Archie.

Typeset by Julie Laws, Stroud, Gloucestershire
Printed and bound in India by Parksons Graphics

Contents

ACKNOWLEDGEMENTS

WRITING A GUIDE BOOK SUCH AS THIS is dependent on the efforts of many people, including long-gone antiquarians and more recent scholars and archaeologists. Without their efforts to learn about Roman Scotland, their surveys, excavations, analysis and hypotheses, our knowledge of this country 2,000 years ago would be much poorer, and volumes such as this could not exist. Such academic efforts are frequently brought together in a number of publications, including the *Proceedings of the Society of Antiquaries of Scotland*, the *Journal of Roman Studies, Britannia, Discovery and Excavation in Scotland*, and Canmore, the National Record of the Historic Environment in Scotland, all of which are excellent resources to which I owe a debt of gratitude.

Scotland has always been lucky to have some eminent scholars and archaeologists researching its Roman past, and I want to note particularly the people whose work has helped inform this guide: Professor David Breeze, Dr David Woolliscroft, Professor Bill Hanson, Gordon Maxwell, Dr Birgitta Hoffmann and Dr Rebecca Jones, who deserves a special mention for her excellent work on Roman encampments.

It would be remiss of me not to acknowledge the support and help that I've had from my various colleagues at Durham, in particular Professor Richard Hingley and Dr Rob Witcher, who have answered numerous questions, under the guise of PhD research, inadvertently helping with this book. A special mention also goes to Professor Elizabeth Archibald.

Briefly, I need to thank Mike Tibbs for help with processing the images and the photograph of Dun Troddan broch, and finally my partner Dr Paul Bennett, whose endless patience, support and views have proved invaluable as ever, as have his editing skills.

It has been a challenge to keep up to date with the latest research on Roman Scotland, and the sites detailed in this book. Any errors in the interpretation or details are mine alone.

Some site data, particularly grid references and classifications, have been taken from Canmore, the National Record of the Historic Environment. The fort plans, and some camp outlines have been drawn from various sources, including excavation reports, aerial photography and LiDAR imaging by the author. The remaining camp outlines have been adapted from previous research undertaken by Dr Rebecca Jones, for which I am grateful.

PART ONE: INTRODUCTION

Beyond the Empire brings together all of Scotland's known, and sometimes suspected, Roman sites in one volume. It has been written for the ordinary person who might be curious about Scotland's role in and beyond the Roman Empire, and will hopefully provide a good grounding for finding out more. Research into Roman Scotland has been carried out for hundreds of years, and a book of this size cannot possibly do justice to all that research, or to the many sites. It does not pretend to offer a complete overview of Roman activity in the area. Instead, it aims to give a taster of what archaeologists know about each site – sometimes that can be quite a lot and occasionally it can be very little.

The idea for this book grew out of a series of lifelong learning courses – 'Beyond the Empire: The Romans in Scotland' and 'Marching on Edinburgh: The Romans in the Lothians' – which I was teaching at the University of Edinburgh for several years. Many of the students were unaware of the impact the Romans had on Scotland. They did not know that it was never absorbed into the Empire, that it remained a military zone, that the army went beyond the Forth–Clyde isthmus and got as far as the Moray coast, and that one of the biggest Roman fortifications in the UK was located at Inchtuthil, in Perthshire.

Archaeology has changed drastically since the earliest excavations began, in the 19th century. Digging is no longer the preserve of the educated elite, with the wealthy landowner taking a stroll down to the site every now and then to see what artefacts had been recovered. Today, excavation is a much more complex and expensive process because archaeologists can extract more data than ever before. Sites can tell archaeologists much about how the Romans lived, who they worshipped, what they ate and what happened when fortifications were abandoned. With modern technologies, archaeologists can create a profile of what lies beneath the soil before they have even put a trowel in the ground. While this volume is an attempt to give a snapshot of life on the edge of the Roman Empire and beyond, knowledge is constantly evolving. Undoubtedly, as more and more new techniques are developed and deployed in the field, archaeologists will learn more about the army, discover new fortifications and perhaps find out that few sites are even Roman.

At the very least, I hope this book will encourage readers to find out more about the Roman archaeology in their own back garden, and hopefully inspire them to visit places they have not seen or heard of before.

Chapter 1

A BRIEF TIMELINE OF ROMAN SCOTLAND

1020–700 BC: The Iron Age in Rome

***c.* 500 BC–AD 43**: The Iron Age in Britain begins around 800 BC, but iron tools do not become commonplace in Scotland until some time around 500 BC. While the citizens of Rome are constructing architecturally advanced buildings such as the Temple of Jupiter, in Scotland the buildings are simpler, tower-like structures known as 'brochs'. Dun Troddan was built around 500 BC, the same time as the temple in Rome was begun

55 BC: Julius Caesar attempts to invade Britain but has limited success

54 BC: Caesar invades with a larger force and establishes diplomatic ties with tribes in the southeast, in anticipation of bringing Britain into the Empire, before returning to Gaul

AD 43: Verica, a tribal leader in the south of England, is deposed and begs the Emperor Claudius to intervene. Claudius invades, accepting the surrender of eleven tribal leaders

43–60: The Roman Army begins to annex southern Britain

60: Tribal revolt led by Boudica sees the destruction of the fledgling Roman settlements at Verulamium (St Albans), Camulodunum (Colchester) and Londinium (London)

69: Vespasian, formerly the commander who began the conquest of Britain under Claudius, becomes Emperor

69–96: The Flavian period

***c.* 70–80**: Construction begins on the fortifications that make up the Gask Ridge frontier

71–73/74: Quintus Petillius Cerialis appointed governor of Britain

73/74–77/78: Sextus Julius Frontinus appointed governor of Britain

74–77: Wales falls to the Empire and northern England is annexed

77/78–83/84: Gnaeus Julius Agricola becomes governor

A replica of the Temple of Jupiter on the set of the television series *Rome*.

The broch at Dun Troddan, constructed between 500 BC and AD 100.

80: Agricola secures Scotland as far north as the River Tay

81–96: Titus Flavius Caesar Domitianus Augustus (Domitian) is made Emperor

83/84: The Battle of Mons Graupius, the final showdown between Agricola's troops and the Caledoni, takes place somewhere in Scotland

86: Legio II Adiutrix is transferred from Britain to the Danube because the Dacians have invaded the Empire and killed the provincial governor

87/88: Inchtuthil fortress is abandoned

97: Tacitus begins to write his eulogy to his father-in-law, Agricola

117–138: Publius Aelius Hadrianus (Hadrian) becomes Emperor

122: Hadrian visits Britain and orders the construction of the wall that would bear his name

138–161: Fulvius Aelius Hadrianus Antoninus Augustus Pius (Antoninus Pius) becomes Emperor

139/140: Antoninus Pius orders the re-invasion of Scotland, establishing new fortifications and reoccupying many old sites

142: Construction of the Antonine Wall begins

145–211: Lucius Septimius Severus Augustus (Septimius Severus) becomes Emperor

158: Orders are given to refurbish fortifications along Hadrian's Wall

163–165: The Antonine Wall is abandoned

181–184: Hadrian's Wall is breached by northern tribes attacking

197–205: Northern tribes wage war on the Romans but are bribed into behaving because of a lack of soldiers to quell the rebellion

208–211: The Emperor Septimius Severus personally leads an invasion force into Scotland. He defeats the Caledoni and bribes them before they renege on this and continue guerrilla attacks on the Roman army

211: Septimius Severus, over-wintering in York, dies. His sons return to Rome to fight for the throne

Late 3rd/early 4th century: Kingdom of the Picts emerges, possibly a loose confederacy of tribes

305–306: Constantius leads a military campaign in Scotland, reaching the end of the land. Constantius dies at York and his son, Constantine, is declared Emperor

305, 360s, 390s: Some evidence indicates that there may have been attempted Roman invasions of Scotland at these times

310: An anonymous Roman text refers to both the Caledoni and the Picts

360: The army is dispatched to Scotland to deal with uprisings by the Scots and the Picts

364: The Scots and Picts continue to invade the northern part of the Empire

367: The Picts are described as being two groupings – Dicaledonae and the Verturiones. The 'barbarian conspiracy' involves the Picts and Scots raiding from the north and the Franks and Saxons attacking Gaul, although there is no evidence for these actions being coordinated

383: The end of Roman rule in the north and west, according to most archaeologists, although some coins have been found on Hadrian's Wall that imply later occupation

410: The 'official' date marking the end of Roman rule in Britain, when the Emperor Honorius, dealing with a crumbling empire, tells the citizens of Britain to arrange their own defences against invaders

731: The Venerable Bede, an English monk based at Jarrow by Newcastle, writes *Historia Ecclesiastica*, which gives an early account of the Antonine Wall

16th century: Timothy Pont produces a map and account of the fortifications that make up the Antonine Wall

1707: Sir Robert Sibbald, the Astronomer Royal, publishes an account of numerous Roman remains in Scotland

1726: Alexander Gordon publishes his map of the Antonine Wall, including an account of Arthur's O'on

1732: Having walked the entire length of the monument, the Rev. John Horsley publishes his work on the Antonine Wall, giving detailed descriptions of the various components

1755: William Roy undertakes his survey of Roman sites in Scotland and begins to record the Antonine Wall

Agricola: The Great General?

Almost of the information that archaeologists have about Agricola comes from one source, *De vita et moribus Iulii Agricolae*, or *On the Life and Character of Julius Agricola,* a tract eulogizing the general and detailing his campaigning, particularly in Britain. It was written by Publius Cornelius Tacitus, who had married Agricola's daughter in AD 77, and begins with a disclaimer, in which the author admits that he is setting out to 'honour my father-in-law'. This has led many scholars to suggest that the work is biased, showing the great general in too favourable a light.

Agricola was governor of Britain under Vespasian for seven years, an unusually long period during which he may have been expected to complete the conquest of Scotland. According to Tacitus, Agricola went on to conquer the north of Britain, crushing the native Caledoni at the battle of Mons Graupius. Soon after, the Emperor Domitian, seemingly jealous of his achievements, recalled Agricola to Rome.

Unlike the works of Tacitus, the archaeological record tells us very little about Agricola. Although it was common practice for the army to record dedications to the Emperor and governor when constructing or refurbishing buildings, Agricola is mentioned in only a couple. One example is a lead water pipe excavated at the legionary fortress at Chester, which had the following inscription:

> This lead pipe was made when Vespasian and Titus were Consuls for the ninth and seventh times respectively, and when Gnaeus Julius Agricola was governor of Britain.

An inscription from the fort at Hardknott Castle in the English Lake District reads 'Assemble with Agricola' and may date to his early campaigns. However, the stone was not found during excavations, so some archaeologists think it could equally refer to another governor called Agricola who was here in the AD 160s.

A third inscription referring to Agricola was found in five fragments in 1955, near the forum at Verulamium:

> For the Emperor Titus Caesar Vespasian Augustus, son of the deified Vespasian, Pontifex Maximus, in the ninth year of tribunician power, acclaimed Imperator fifteen times, having been consul seven times, designated consul for an eighth time, censor, Father of the Fatherland, and to Caesar Domitian, son of the deified Vespasian, having been consul six times, designated consul for a seventh term, Prince of Youth, and member of all the priestly brotherhoods, when Gnaeus Julius Agricola was legate of the emperor with pro-praetorian power, the Verulamium basilica was adorned.

Having analysed the use of certain words, epigraphy experts have dated the inscription to around AD 79.

According to Tacitus, Agricola was solely responsible for the conquest of north Britain, and for many years, antiquarians and early scholars charted the early Roman occupation of Scotland using his writings. However, modern scientific analysis of the archaeological evidence is beginning to tell a different story. Antiquarians and early scholars believed Agricola was responsible for the founding of the Roman fort at Carlisle as he progressed north, but research in the latter part of the 20th century has challenged this. Dendrochronological analysis of timbers excavated within the fort site, which had been seasoned but not put in place, indicated that the trees had been cut down in around AD 72 – that is to say, before Agricola became governor. It therefore seems plausible that Agricola's predecessor, Cerialis, could have been the one who actually conquered the north, although not all archaeologists agree with this interpretation. It appears that Tacitus may have been selective in his writings, being dismissive of Cerialis, but David Shotter has suggested that perhaps he was responsible for the early frontier on the Gask Ridge.

Chapter 2

ROMAN FORTIFICATIONS AND STRUCTURES

SCOTLAND WAS ALMOST UNIQUE WITHIN THE Roman Empire. While the rest of Britain was swallowed up by the Romans, Scotland sat on the edge - sometimes within the Empire, sometimes outside it, but never fully assimilated by the imperial machine. When it was occupied, Scotland remained a military zone with no towns or large settlements, and apparently little commercial activity. While the overwhelming majority of Roman sites in Scotland are related to the military – forts, fortlets, camps and towers – there is, however, a small amount of evidence for civilian activity, such as the *vicus* at Inveresk or the possible temple of Arthur's O'on by Falkirk. This section gives an overview of the main types of structure built by the Romans in Scotland.

The Roman Army

Without a doubt, it was the army that made Rome great, enabling the Empire to spread across most of the known world; Scotland was the one exception that was never held. At the time of the initial invasion of Scotland, the army was divided into two parts: the *legio* and the *auxilia*, with additional support from the navy, the *Classis Britannica*.

Legio

Originally, the *legio*, or legion, consisted of 6,000 paid soldiers, although they were often smaller in number due to illness, death, deployment elsewhere, and so on. The soldiers came from Rome or the provinces and would have served for around 25 years before retirement and the coveted Roman citizenship. In charge of the legion was a *legate*, usually a senator from Rome and below him were the six *tribunes*, who were there to gain experience of the army but were not professional soldiers.

The legion was divided into 10 *cohorts* (of around 480 men), each of which was made up of six *centuries* – 80 men commanded by a *centurion*. However, by the late 3rd century, legions had evolved into forces of 1,000 men as a response to the changing threats from outside the Empire. Within the legion, soldiers would have had specialisms, including surveying, standard bearing, engineering and administration.

Auxilia

The *auxilia* was essentially made up of paid mercenaries recruited from across the Empire, and used as a frontline fighting force for the army. They were divided into *alae* for the cavalry and *cohortes* for the infantry. Some groups of auxiliaries had specialisms such as archery, or were experts in using slingshots. Like legionaries, the *auxilia* were divided into *cohorts* of 500 or 1,000 men (at full strength), and were commanded by a *praefectus* or a *tribune*, respectively. Most forts were garrisoned by auxiliaries.

Classis Britannica

The Roman navy in Britain was established in AD 43 to aid with Augustus' original invasion, and continued its role supporting and transporting the army into the late 1st century, when it appears to have taken the name *Classis Britannica*. The early headquarters may have been at Boulogne, where a significant number of inscriptions have been found; there was also a heavy presence at Dover. The role of the fleet in supporting the Flavian invasion of Scotland, and during the later invasion by the Emperor Septimius Severus, is recorded in the classical texts, although the wider role of the *Classis Britannica* in Scotland has gone unrecorded. Inscriptions recovered from along Hadrian's Wall indicate that soldiers from the fleet helped to construct the frontier, so it is possible that the *Classis Britannica* helped to build fortifications in Scotland. There are no more mentions of, or finds relating to, the *Classis Britannica*, which seems to imply that the fleet may have been disbanded by the mid-3rd century.

Legionary Fortress

The fortress was the central hub of military operations in any particular region. Similar in layout to a fort, but on a larger scale, its additional buildings included accommodation for the tribunes, workshops, a hospital and possible storage rooms along the main internal roads. A fortress normally covered an area in excess of 20 hectares and was constructed from stone, although there is evidence that some may have started as turf and timber constructions, before being replaced in stone.

There is only one legionary fortress in Scotland, at Inchtuthil in Perthshire. The fortress was constructed in the late 1st century and was intended to be a base for the army in central Scotland, forming a central component of the defences on the edge of the Empire. However, the fortress was never completed and was abandoned less than 20 years after construction began, with the army relocating its headquarters to the nearest legionary fortress, at York.

Fort

Garrisoned by auxiliary soldiers, the fort was a permanent structure and the local base of operations. Usually playing-card shaped, each fort had a similar layout, although in Scotland there are some exceptions such as Loudon Hill, which appears to be half a fort. The fort had a central range of buildings consisting of the *praetorium* (the home of the commanding officer), the *principia* (the headquarters building) and usually two *horrea* (granaries). The *principia* not only functioned as the administrative building for the site, but also housed the treasury, as well as the regimental standards and statues of the imperial cult, which were kept in a rear room.

On the front and rear sides of the central range were four buildings, usually interpreted by archaeologists as stores, and on either side of these were the *centuriae* (barrack blocks), where the soldiers slept. The buildings were surrounded by a rampart (a bank of earth acting as a perimeter wall), with towers in the corners and at the entrances, and, in some instances, additional towers between these. The fort would have been surrounded by a series of ramparts and ditches; in a very few rare examples, there are as many as four or five of these.

The majority of Scottish forts were constructed with turf foundations and wooden buildings, which were, in some instances, subsequently replaced with stone structures. Archaeologists have found that, when some forts were abandoned, the buildings were knocked or burnt down, and the ramparts pushed into the ditches, probably to stop the enemy making use of the site. However, this did not happen everywhere.

Adjacent to many of the fortifications was an enclosure known as an annexe, a large area surrounded by a rampart and ditch, which was usually attached to the main defences of the site. Found almost exclusively in Scotland, the purpose of the annexe is not known, but evidence indicates a variety of possible uses, including industrial workings and even horse rearing at Newstead.

Fortlet

A fortlet was a smaller version of a fort, but usually without the central range of buildings. Most fortlets in Scotland follow the same pattern: an internal space

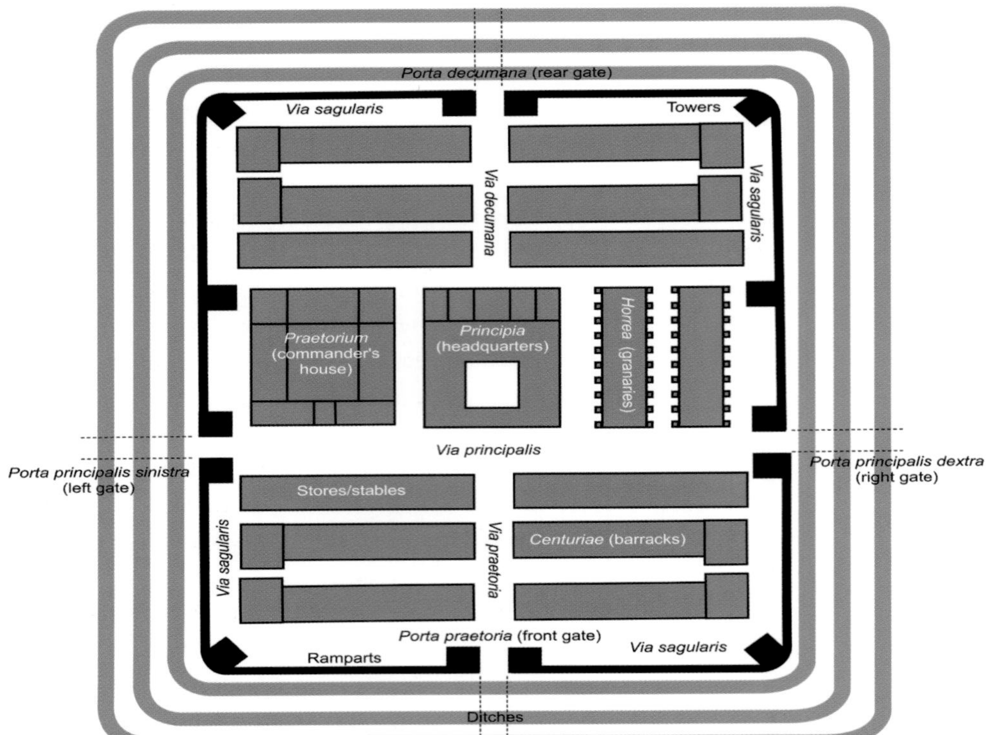

Layout of a typical auxiliary fort.

containing buildings (probably barracks), separated by a road. These were surrounded by a rampart and ditch, over which there was a causewayed road; some fortlets were surrounded by several ditches, and some may have had an annexe attached to them. While there are some examples constructed from stone, those in Scotland were usually constructed out of turf and timber. Fortlets were generally positioned between the forts, or used to guard areas of strategic importance, such as river crossings or road junctions.

Camps

Camps make up the majority of Roman sites in Scotland, with over 160 known examples, and many more that are unconfirmed. These were temporary structures thrown up in a few hours and were probably only in use overnight or for a few days, providing secure shelter as the army moved from one place to another. Their shape in Scotland is often described as playing-card, consisting of at least two turf ramparts and ditches surrounding an internal space, within which tents would have been pitched for accommodation and administrative purposes. Surviving records from Roman writers show how plans were expected to be laid out. However, this is much more difficult to see in the archaeological record because of the temporary nature of the structures involved – tent postholes have proved elusive in excavations.

Reconstruction of a stone *porta decumana* (looking out of the fort) from Weissenburg, Germany.

Archaeologists have identified four types of camp: arching (for soldiers on the move), practice (for training purposes), construction (occupied when building permanent fortifications) and siege (used as a base when attacking a nearby hillfort). Not all archaeologists agree with these definitions, but it seems logical that there would have been distinctive camps for soldiers on the move and for those who were building other fortifications, for example.

Towers

Towers are located across Roman Scotland, with some of them probably acting as signal stations, while others (such as those along the Gask Ridge) would be securing the adjacent road and surrounding countryside. Towers in Scotland consisted of a wooden structure surrounded by a defensive ditch, which was rounded.

Vicus (Settlement)

There is surprisingly little evidence for *vici* in Scotland despite the number of soldiers that must have been stationed in the region. The most extensive example is from Inveresk in the Lothians, although this settlement probably dates to the Antonine period. Evidence from elsewhere in the Roman Empire indicates that, wherever the army went, civilians (such as families of soldiers and traders) followed and established themselves outside the forts. This is how towns such as Londinium and York grew into urban centres, but it does not seem to have happened on the same scale in Scotland. For example, no *vici* have been identified outside of the forts on the Antonine Wall. There is a long history of Romans trading with those beyond the frontiers, and this could explain some of the random artefacts which have been found beyond the forts, such as the coins unearthed at Fort Augustus, on the shores of Loch Ness.

Harbours

Archaeologists know from the Roman writers that the fleet had an integral role in supporting the army, helping to transport troops and supplies and also undertaking reconnaissance – according to Tacitus, Agricola sent the fleet to sail around Britain to prove that it was an island. However, no Roman harbours have been confirmed in Scotland, despite the fact that a number of sites, such as Cramond, Inveresk and Dun, are located on the coast and would have made ideal locations for sea-going traffic. Perhaps ships were simply hauled up on to the beach to be unloaded, but it seems more than likely that, if they were offloading large amounts of supplies, then a harbour or dock structure would have been constructed to make the job quicker and easier. It may be that the evidence is out there waiting to be discovered, or that it has been obliterated by later development. Archaeologists are still trying to locate such features.

A replica tower from Burgsalach, Germany. Similar structures have been found on the Gask Ridge, Perthshire.

Chapter 3

ARCHAEOLOGICAL TECHNIQUES

Before a trowel goes in the ground, archaeologists build a picture of a site using a variety of resources and techniques. Archaeology may be renowned for its excavations, but digging is often not deployed as soon as people think, as there are a range of methods that are just as effective. In fact, excavation is the last tool archaeologists use, because it can lead to the destruction of the site and of archaeological evidence.

Historical Records

Historical records are an important tool when it comes to studying Roman Scotland. Many important records have survived, from the 16th-century eye-witness accounts of 'Romayne' remains being uncovered at Inveresk, to *The Old Statistical Account* and *The New Statistical Account of Scotland*, descriptions of every Scottish parish gathered by local ministers in the 18th and 19th centuries, with details of upstanding remains of Roman forts and camps. Archaeologists also have good descriptions of sites from early antiquarians and surveyors such as General William Roy, the founder of the Ordnance Survey, who recorded many archaeological features, including some of the earliest descriptions of the Antonine Wall, in accurate detail.

The importance of these old accounts in helping to identify previously unknown Roman sites is invaluable. There are a number of accounts in this book that describe sites that have long since been lost, such as the possible camp at Paisley, which may lie underneath the modern town, or the 18th-century description of a fort at Bona on Loch Ness, which has been lost for centuries under the waves. Nonetheless, many of these accounts are still to be investigated by archaeologists using modern techniques, which may confirm their existence or not.

Epigraphy

Epigraphy is the study of inscriptions, and there are numerous examples from Scotland, mainly written on altars and distance slabs found along the Antonine Wall, detailing which detachment built that section of the barrier. The Bridgeness slab is a prime example of this. Epigraphy can tell observers a lot about the soldiers based in Scotland, including who they were and where they came from. This is especially useful when it comes to the auxiliary forts as the garrisons were usually named after a group of people from a particular geographic location; so, for example, the evidence indicates that the fort at Castlecary was occupied by the 'First Cohort of Tungri' and the 'First Loyal Cohort of Vardulli'.

Another useful source of information is the study of carvings, which gives an extra layer of detail to the interpretation of sites. The triumphal monument of Trajan's Column in Rome, carved to celebrate the Emperor Trajan's victory in the Dacian Wars (in modern-day Romania), is one useful resource. Covered with scenes from the war, its detail can help to shed light on what was going on in Scotland. The towers shown on the column have been recreated in Germany, and archaeologists analysing a series of postholes excavated from the centre of the Gask Ridge site have concluded that towers in Scotland may have looked similar. This demonstrates the importance of the study of carvings in the interpretation of archaeological sites.

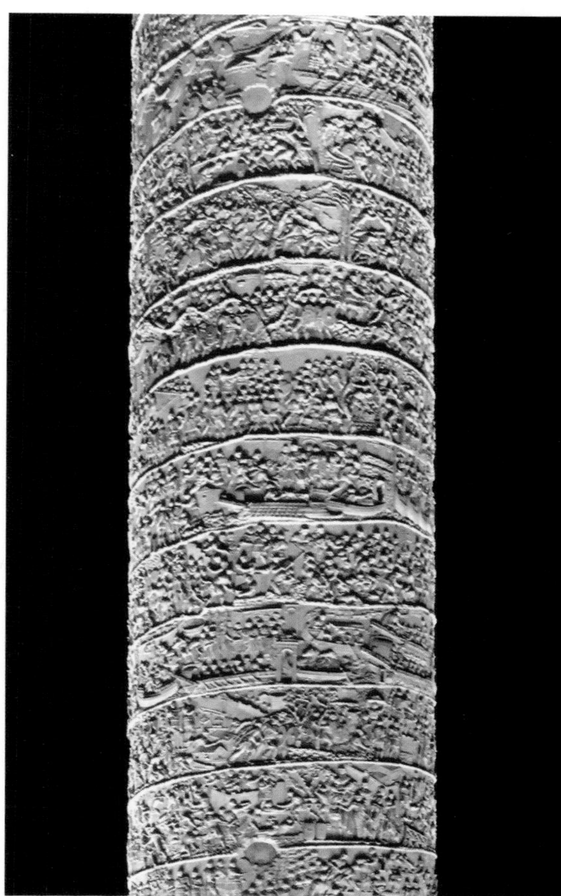

Trajan's Column in Rome, one of the most important sources of information on the Roman army.

Aerial and Satellite Imagery

Aerial photography has been the most successful tool for detecting Scottish Roman sites. Indeed, Dr Rebecca Jones has noted that over 93 per cent of camps discovered in the 20th century were identified through aerial reconnaissance or a retrospective examination of photographs taken from the air. Intensive searches by the likes of Crawford, St Joseph, Maxwell and Woolliscroft have vastly increased the body of knowledge about Roman Scotland, although a significant number of these sites have yet to be explored on the ground through geophysical survey or excavation.

Geophysical Survey

Geophysics is the modern archaeologist's best friend, allowing observation beneath the soil without necessarily needing to excavate. There are a number of geophysical techniques used in archaeology. Magnetometry is a technique broadly similar to metal detecting but much more powerful. All objects, including rocks and bricks, have a magnetic field and a magnetometer can pick these up, particularly when they form a structure, or if the stones have been burnt, as this changes the strength of their magnetic field. Another technique is resistivity, where an electrical current is passed through the ground, measuring the resistance of the soil. If there is an obstruction underneath the soil, such as the foundations of a building or a rampart, there is more resistance and this shows up during the survey.

LiDAR

LiDAR ('light detection and ranging') is a relatively new technique used by archaeologists. It involves scanning a site from the air using a plane or drone with a laser bouncing off the ground, recording any lumps and bumps and creating an image that displays archaeological features.

Excavation

Excavation is a methodical process of uncovering archaeological remains to reveal a buried site, but it is not without its challenges. It can be an expensive process, as finds need to be preserved and then studied and displayed, or archived. It can also be labour-intensive, particularly if a site is large or in danger of destruction from development, and this can also cost a lot of money.

Excavation is also a process of destruction; once a layer has been dug, it is lost for ever. Early excavators often dug through features such as timber foundations because they were not aware of the imprints left behind by rotten wood. As a result, there are a number of excavated forts where nothing is known about the earlier timber structures.

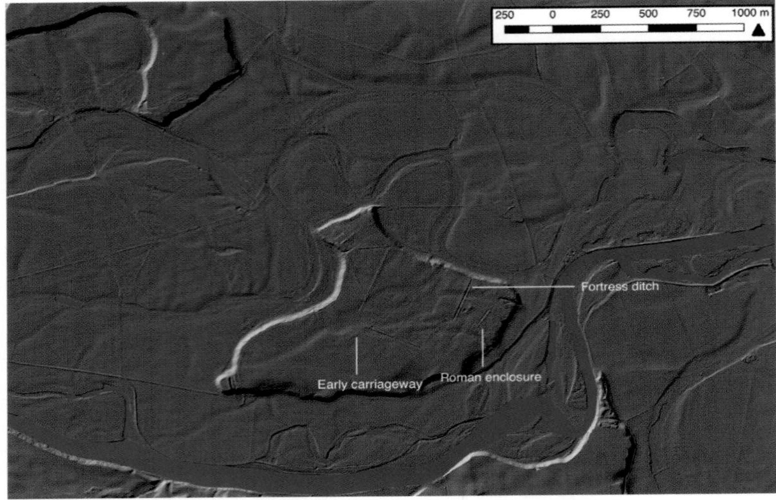

LiDAR image of the fortress defences at Inchtuthil, along with the 19th-century carriageway. The River Tay gives an indication of the old water channels.

Artefacts

Artefacts can tell archaeologists a great deal about a site. The study of coins (numismatics), pottery and inscribed remains (such as altars and distance slabs) can often give archaeologists an idea of when a site was occupied or abandoned. They can also tell us what sorts of people occupied a site: was a fort purely for soldiers, or did the commanding officer have family with him, for example? Roman artefacts in native settlements, as at Traprain Law, indicate to archaeologists that the indigenous population had a good relationship with the invaders. Even artefacts that may not be datable can point to the origins of a feature; for example, fragments of pottery found at the bottom of a ditch might show that it was dug by Roman soldiers.

Aerial photograph of the fort at Birrens, taken with a drone. The northern rampart and ditch defences are clearly visible at the bottom of the image.

Chapter 4

VISITING THE SITES

Scotland has some outstandingly well-preserved Roman remains, such as the earthwork defences of Ardoch and Birrens, and the bath houses at Bearsden and Bothwellhaugh. There are a good number where faint traces of ramparts and ditches can be seen, along with the occasional platform on which the fortifications were built. There are also many sites that have no remains visible above ground. This does not mean, however, that there is nothing to see, because the landscape holds clues to the Roman advancement on Scotland. Standing by the camp at Dun, for example, it is easy to see why the Romans chose the site, overlooking Montrose Bay. Take a walk through Inchtuthil to appreciate the vastness of the fortress and understand how the army used it to control the surrounding landscape, or perch on the edge of the fortlet remains at Durisdeer, and see how the Romans managed the route through the hills.

Maps and Locations

Some, but not all, of the sites are marked on the Ordnance Survey Explorer maps, and a handful are on the Landranger series. The maps included within this volume have been especially prepared to show the outline of some sites, and the general location of others, but not all of the sites are easy to locate or safe to access. Where possible, directions have been included to make visiting the sites easier, but it is recommended that you also take an Ordnance Survey map with you, as well as appropriate clothing and footwear.

The Scottish Outdoor Access Code

The majority of sites featured in this book are on private land but can be accessed under the Scottish Outdoor Access Code in most circumstances.

The Code gives people a legal right to access most of Scotland's outdoor spaces for educational or recreational purposes, but reminds visitors that they should respect the interests of others, take care of the environment, and take responsibility for their own actions. This includes sticking to paths where they are available, not damaging the environment, and taking home litter.

Most of the sites detailed in this book are undeveloped, often in rural locations and not necessarily set up for visitors, so there may not be footpaths or signposts, and the terrain will vary greatly, from bogs and abandoned tracks to heather and grassland. Visitors to the sites should come properly equipped, with maps, waterproofs and appropriate footwear.

Some sites are located within the National Parks. As additional rules may apply to visiting those sites, it is worth consulting the various websites.

For more information on the Scottish Outdoor Access Code, visit www.outdooraccess-scotland.com

Dogs

Dogs are allowed to accompany people accessing land, but the Code lays down a few basic rules:

- Dogs should be kept under control and any waste should be picked up and removed.
- Dogs should not be taken into fields with young farm animals such as lambs or calves.
- Dogs should be kept on a tight lead around other animals.
- Dogs should be taken through crops only if there is a clear path or right of way.

PART TWO: THE EAST OF SCOTLAND

Chapter 5

EDINBURGH AND THE LOTHIANS

EDINBURGH AND THE LOTHIANS (EAST Lothian, Midlothian and West Lothian) played a crucial role in the various Roman invasions of Scotland, being at the end of Dere Street, the main eastern road north from the legionary fortress at York. West Lothian is rich in Roman remains, and is the location for the Antonine Wall, which ends near Bo'ness. In East Lothian there is a distinct lack of sites beyond those at Inveresk. Perhaps this was a strategic decision influenced by the substantial native site at Traprain Law. Stuck in between is Midlothian, an area of temporary encampments but relatively few permanent forts, and the City of Edinburgh itself.

Ask most residents of Scotland's capital if there were any Romans in the city, and they will probably claim there was a fort under Edinburgh Castle, but there is no evidence to support this at all. Most people are also unaware of the Roman fort sitting on the shores of the Firth of Forth. The visible remains of the fort at Cramond are one of Edinburgh's hidden secrets and well worth a visit.

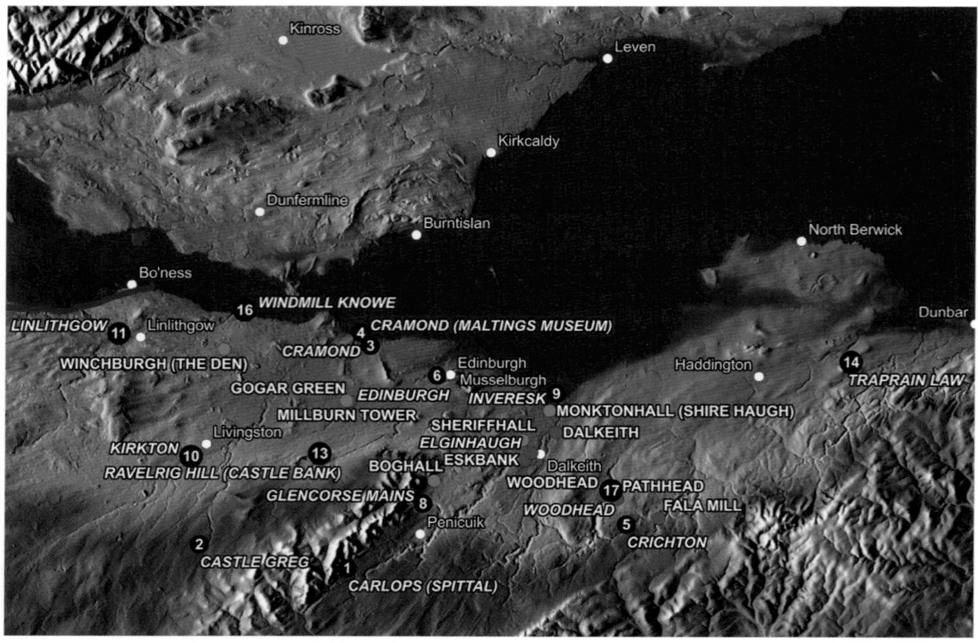

Carlops (Spittal)

Camps | NT 171 572

There is at least one camp at this site, although a second is suspected. The larger camp is around 17 hectares, while it appears to have been reduced in size at some point to 12 hectares. There is also some evidence for an annexe on the northeast side of the site.

Key Dates

1984: The camp is discovered from the air
1985: Limited excavations confirm the presence of at least one camp
1996: Further aerial photographs reveal the annexe

Exploring

The site sits alongside the A702, northeast of the village of Carlops, with the minor road to Nine Mile Burn running northwards through the camp. The Roman road is visible as a raised mound running towards the hamlet.

Castle Greg

Fortlet | NT 050 592

The fortlet at Castle Greg is one of the better-preserved sites in Roman Scotland. Located on the edge of the Pentland Hills, the site was excavated in the 19th century, although there are earlier accounts of finds from the sites, including coins from the reigns of Vespasian, Domitian, Hadrian, Antoninus Pius and Marcus Aurelius. Despite the range of coins, the fortlet has been dated to the 1st century because of the style of construction. Geophysical surveys in 2012 and 2013 revealed the internal roads, possible ovens and one curious feature: at the northeastern corner, the defensive ditch continued well beyond the fortlet, which archaeologists originally thought was an annexe, although this has since been questioned.

A fortlet was usually constructed at a strategically important site, guarding resources, a river crossing or an arterial route. However, the purpose of the site at Castle Greg is not clear, as there are no rivers or confirmed Roman roads, although there is a possible road heading southwest towards the A70.

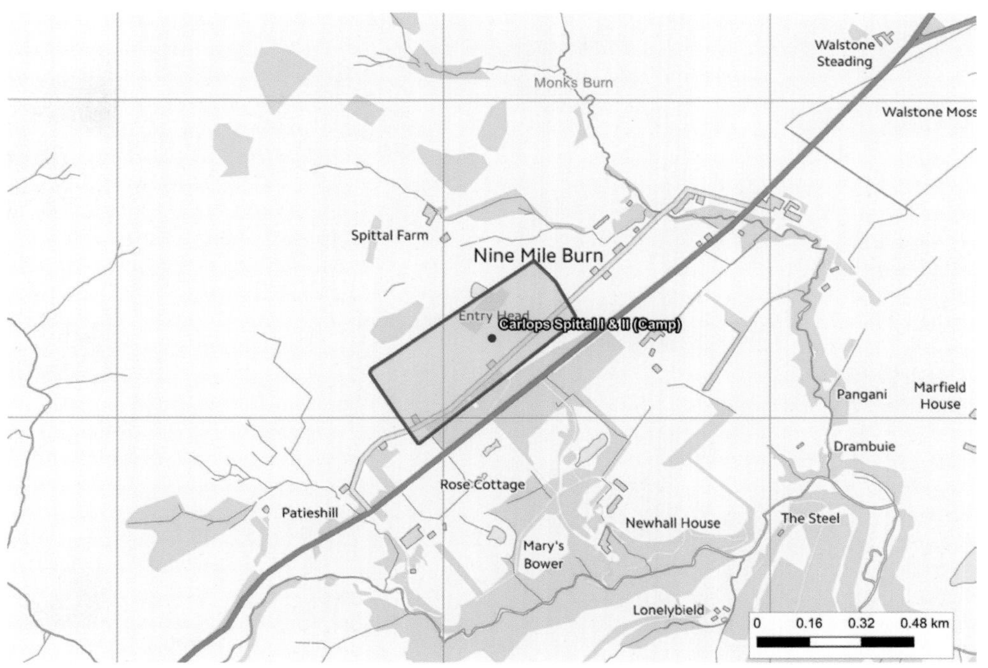

Key Dates

1830: Roman coins are unearthed from within the fortlet

1846: Pottery is uncovered during excavation of the site

1998: Aerial photographs show the defences, including the parrot-beak style entrance

2009, 2012, 2013: Geophysical survey reveals the external and internal roads, possible buildings and ovens

2014: Topographical survey of the site is undertaken

Exploring

The fortlet is easily reached from West Calder, on the A71. Heading south on the B7008, the fortlet is about a mile before the junction with the A70. Parking is possible at the dirt track just after the allotments. Walk past the first small plantation as the track curves south. Come off the track at the beginning of the second plantation and follow the line of trees southwards. The fortlet is about half a mile on from this.

Cramond

Fort and Vicus | NT 189 769

Cramond may have been made famous by Muriel Spark's girls of Marcia Blane, who would go sailing on Sundays with their teacher Miss Jean Brodie, but less well known is its Roman fort on the shores of the Forth. Archaeologists have also found evidence of a large civilian population living next to the fort in Roman times, as well as some evidence hinting at grand funerary monuments in the vicinity.

The fort is on the eastern side of the River Almond, where it flows into the Firth of Forth, creating a natural shelter in the river. It was strategically placed to act as a supply base for the eastern end of the Antonine Wall, which terminates at nearby Bo'ness. With the modern village sitting on top of the fort, the Roman levels can lie up to eight metres underneath, so knowledge of Roman Cramond has been gained from pockets of development and excavation, giving archaeologists pieces of an incomplete jigsaw from which to ascertain the history of the site. The river has been affected by more recent industrial activity,

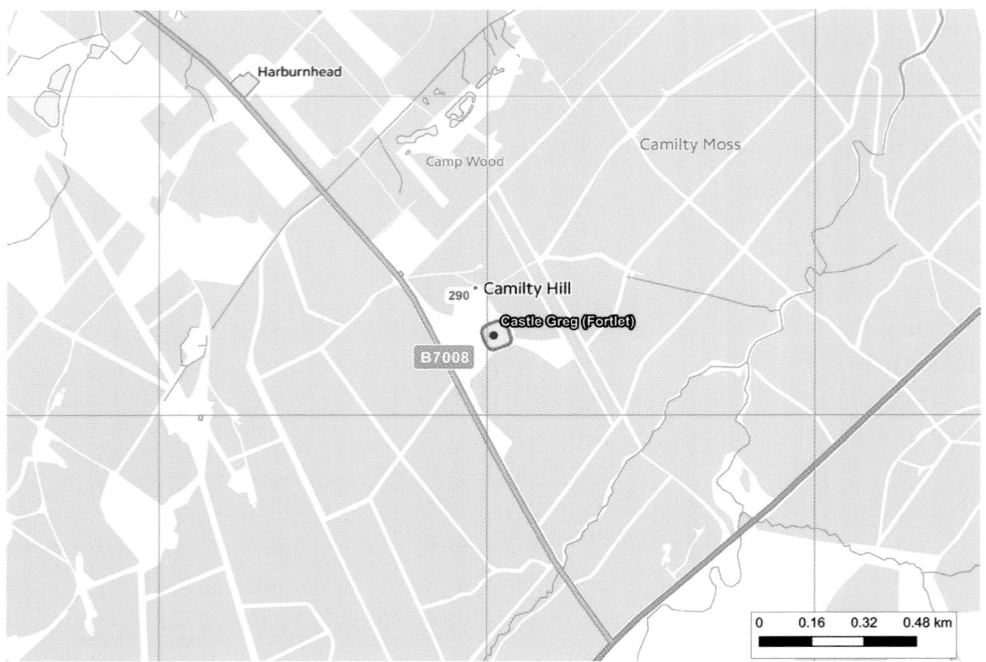

with numerous mills influencing the flow and course of the Almond. As a result, what would have been a fast-flowing body of water has become much slower and calmer. War-time defences, along with the industrial development, have also affected the shore, most notably with some of the golden sands being replaced by a concrete promenade during the last century.

From the parts of the site excavated so far, there seem to be four different periods when the fort was occupied. It was initially constructed during the Antonine period, around AD 140. There was a second phase of occupation during this period before the site was re-occupied during the Severan era, and then once again in the 4th century. As archaeologists have gathered this evidence from pockets across the village, there is still some debate as to how representative this is of the overall fort. A geophysical survey in 2008 uncovered evidence of a number of additional ditches, which some have speculated could be from the Antonine occupation. However, they have yet to be excavated and could turn out to be from a fort dating from the Hadrianic or even Flavian period.

Despite the closeness of the fort to the shore, no evidence of Roman activity has been found in this in-between area. In 2001, the Edinburgh Archaeological Field Society and the city archaeologist excavated the area and found flint tools and hazelnuts that were carbon-dated to the Mesolithic period, or, more specifically, 8699 to 8200 BC. However, there is no confirmed evidence for a harbour on the waterline, although the Romans may have beached their ships on the shore.

The fort was not discovered until the middle of the 20th century, although there were occasional finds, including masonry, before this in the grounds of Cramond House. In the 18th century, General Roy had noted a Roman road heading towards the village from the direction of Davidson's Mains (now under northwest Edinburgh). In the 1930s, the remains of a hypocaust were discovered underneath a house on Glebe Road. Twenty years later, volunteers from the Moray House College of Education (which had a campus in the village) began a series of excavations,

The visible remains of the fort foundations at Cramond.

The site of the settlement that was just outside the fort at Cramond, now a play park. The north manse garden is on the other side of the wall on the right.

mainly centred on the kirk and its hall. Throughout the 1950s and 1960s, the excavations uncovered parts of the defences, the *intervallum* road that ran around the inside of the rampart, the *vicus* or civilian settlement, the *praetoria*, the home of the commanding officer, and the *principia*, the HQ building underneath the kirk.

The Bath House

In 1975, as the car park next to the Cramond Inn was being developed, part of a Roman building was uncovered. Excavation of the site revealed it to be the extremely well-preserved bath house of the fort, with the walls standing to a height of 14 courses (around

1.5 metres) in places. The site was covered over again, but further work almost 20 years later revealed that the bath house was actually filled with about 2 metres of medieval rubbish. Despite this, the archaeologists managed to figure out that there were at least four phases of construction. Some of the bath house remains unexplored, so it may have been much bigger than was first thought. The Council decided to cover over the site, and it now exists as an overgrown hollow on the southern side of the car park.

The Cramond Lioness

In the late 1990s, there was still a service crossing the Almond at Cramond, with a ferryman punting visitors from one bank to the other. In 1997, he noticed that he was frequently colliding with a large stone object in the water. The tide and shifting sands gradually began to reveal the object as a stone ornament. In the end, the ferryman contacted the authorities and an excavation was undertaken. The statue that was uncovered depicts a crouching lioness devouring a naked, bearded man (believed to represent natives), with two snakes underneath depicting the survival of the soul. The actual purpose of the statue is unknown, but some believe that it might have been part of a funerary monument. However, no cemetery has been found at Cramond to date. Another idea is that the statue may have been lost overboard when being shipped to the site, or it could have been thrown into the river when the fort was abandoned and destroyed. While archaeologists do not know where the lioness came from, or what it was part of, this account by John Philip Wood writing in 1792 may shed some light on it:

> On the subject of Roman antiquities, I have only to add, that, within my remembrance, there was to be seen a large sepulchre [funerary monument], formed of flat stones, on the east side of the road leading from Lauriston to Nether Cramond, on the line of the military way, a little below the east entry to [the village of] King's Cramond; but this monument is now completely destroyed.

The Cramond Lioness can now be seen on display at the National Museum of Scotland in Edinburgh.

Eagle Rock

For centuries, the ferry would take visitors across the Almond to visit Hunter's Craig, an outcrop now better known as Eagle Rock. Facing Cramond, the rock features a carving that is now almost indistinguishable; even back in 1794, the early accounts mentioned how worn it was. Today, the details are difficult to make out, but there a number of suggestions as to what it depicts; it could be a carving of an eagle (a sacred symbol for soldiers) or of Mercury (the Roman god of trade), or possibly even a local spirit thought to bring good luck and fortune to those sailing to and from Cramond. The old accounts seem to describe a figure holding a container full of food or flowers, and making a sacrifice at an altar. The ferry has long since disappeared, so the only way the site can be visited is on foot.

Exploring

The fort is easily explored on foot, with plenty of interpretation signs around the site. Cramond Kirk is constructed on the site of the *principia*, and is worth a look around. If you go through the graveyard and out of the rear gate, you will be in the heart of the fort. Parts of the defences are underneath the modern extension to the Kirk Hall, while to the right of this building (through the gap in the wall) is the site of the *vicus*. To the left, there is a path through the woodland, which leads to a sign detailing the Mesolithic finds. Follow the path and it takes you to the car park with the bath house underneath. This area has been fenced off and is overgrown. On the opposite side of the car park are steps down to the shoreline; turn left and you will come to the mouth of the Almond. Eagle Rock is in the distance on the opposite side of the river. Follow the wall and head

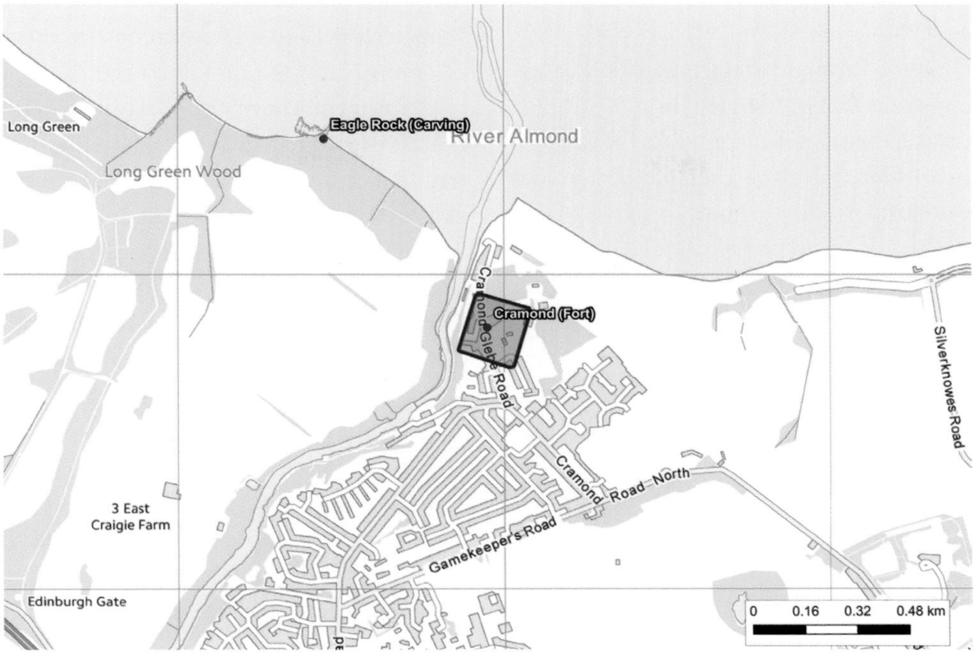

upriver until you come to the steps opposite the ferryman's cottage; this is roughly the point where the Cramond Lioness was found.

Cramond is accessible by car or Lothian Bus 41, which runs from the city centre to Glebe Road, and from there it is a short walk. Alternatively, you can drive and park on top of the bath house. A further option is to park at Silverknowes and take an easy half-hour stroll along the waterfront to the village.

Eagle Rock is more difficult to access since the demise of the ferry. It can be reached by a long walk east from South Queensferry, following the path that begins under the Forth Bridge.

The Maltings Museum, Cramond

6 Riverside, Cramond, EH4 6NY
cramondheritage.org.uk
Opening Times (seasonal): Sat & Sun 14:00–17:00
April–September

The Maltings is a small treasure trove of the history of the village, in particular the Roman fort. The whitewashed museum building is located up the steps which lead to the Cramond Inn, opposite the ferry steps. It is run by volunteers and the opening times are seasonal, but it is worth visiting.

Crichton

Fort (Possible) | NT 40 61

Crichton has long been suspected as being the site of a Roman fort, given its location next to Derek Street. Indeed, the area was considered so strategically important in the Middle Ages that a stronghold was constructed here in that period. James Curle and George Macdonald were two early archaeologists who believed that there would be a Roman site in the location, with the latter noting a souterrain found at Crichton Mains (NT 400 619) that used Roman stones – although he could not explain where they had come from. Field walking in the 1970s from around the souterrain failed to find any more artefacts, however. Many archaeologists are convinced that there must be a camp or a fort out there; they just have to find it.

Key Dates

1816: A number of Roman artefacts are found at the nearby indigenous fort of Longfaugh
1918: Macdonald makes the case for a fort at Crichton
1932: Curle proposes that there should be a Roman fortification in the neighbourhood

Exploring

The ruins of Crichton Castle are located just to the south of the village of the same name, near Pathhead (EH37 5XA). It is managed by Historic Scotland and open seasonally to the public.

Edinburgh

There are well over 100 recorded Roman finds within the boundaries of the city of Edinburgh, including the fort at Cramond, temporary camps, patches of road, numerous coins, statues, pottery and a milestone, but most were probably found out of context or not where they were dropped by Romans.

A number of coins have been found around the city, including one of Constantine the Great (306–337) at Castlehill, and one of Vespasian at the Pleasance in 1782, although none of this is firm evidence that the Romans were occupying the area that is now Edinburgh city centre. That is not to say that they were not in the area, and there have been some significant finds offering a glimpse of what might be under the city streets. In 1815, during the construction of Regent Bridge, which runs from Calton Hill to Princes Street, *The Prehistoric Annals of Scotland* record that 'a quantity of the fine red Samian ware, so peculiar to the Roman ruins, was found near the Calton Hill.'

According to *The New Statistical Account of Scotland*, written a few years later, 'when cutting the new line of road over the Calton Hill in 1817, a Roman urn was dug up entire. It was exactly the same shape, pattern and materials as the one broken in Inveresk churchyard since.'

Both accounts seem to be referring to the same set of finds – Samian urns are not very common in Scotland. In 1845, in the same area, a stretch of Roman road was seen during construction on the site of Trinity Hospital, now underneath Waverley station.

Another account, by Sir John Clerk in 1742, describes a Roman arch that was pulled down; either within it or near by was an urn that contained coins of Faustian Minor (160–212). In 1822, a stretch of 'ancient causeway' was discovered during the expansion of the Nor' Loch, now underneath Princes Street Gardens. Two coins were also found near the Heart of Midlothian, outside St Giles' Cathedral on the Royal Mile. The account went on to say that they were found near some Roman sculptures although no records of this find exist.

In 1851, Sir Daniel Stuart noted a carving of Septimius Severus on a house in the Nether Bow (now part of Victoria Street), which was apparently found close by. The artefact has since been lost, but some commentators believe that it was actually a medieval carving.

Edinburgh Castle

Most people expect Castle Rock or Calton Hill in the centre of the city to have been the location of a Roman fort, but the truth is that there is no archaeological evidence to support this. Edinburgh has grown significantly since Roman times, so it is likely that any traces of ancient remains have been destroyed by development. Castle Rock is exactly that – a rock with very little soil on top – which is why so many patches of bedrock are visible around the castle. With the medieval buildings being built on to the rock, anything older would have been destroyed. There is some suggestion that St Margaret's Chapel, the oldest structure in the castle, was built using Roman stones, but archaeologists looking more recently have been unable to find any evidence for this.

Main Guard, Edinburgh Castle

Possible Building | NT 251 735

In the late 1980s, an area inside the central part of Edinburgh Castle was stripped back to reveal the

Arthur's Seat from Edinburgh Castle.

> ### The Ingliston Milestone
>
> **Roman Milestone | NT 130 727**
>
> Scotland's only Roman milestone has a bit of mystery attached to it, as its original location is unknown. It would certainly have been placed on one of the roads heading towards a Roman settlement, showing the distance between sites. Two parts of the milestone were discovered before 1697; it is not known where they were found, but it may have been near the village of Ingliston. A third stone, now in the possession of the National Museum of Scotland, was subsequently examined and is also believed to have formed part of the milestone. The milestone would have been about 1.37 metres high, with an inscription indicating it was erected around 140–144. The surviving fragments can be seen in the National Museum of Scotland.

foundations of walls that some archaeologists have speculated are Roman. However, there is no evidence to confirm this.

Elginhaugh

Fort | NT 21 673

Elginhaugh is one of the most extensively excavated Roman forts in Britain. Because it has been examined so thoroughly, archaeologists have acquired a significant amount of information about how soldiers lived and operated in the northernmost reaches of the Empire. In common with many Scottish sites, the fort was discovered from the air in 1979, and confirmed by a small excavation later that year. It was not until 1986 that William Hanson at Glasgow University began a large-scale excavation of the site.

Covering an area of 1.2 hectares, the fort was surrounded by a turf rampart and three or four ditches, with the internal buildings constructed from timber. One exception to this was a stone building adjoining the northeast rampart, which the excavators thought may have been a workshop built from non-flammable materials. There were also towers above each of the four gates, and at each fort corner.

During excavations, a hoard of 45 *denarii* was discovered, with the coins ranging in date from the Republican period to the late 1st century AD. The most recent dated to AD 77–78, while another came from AD 86, implying that the site is from the Flavian period. Further work in 2009 on the annexe recorded a series of ditches, a gateway and a well, indicating that it may have been subdivided into different areas, an arrangement that is so far unrecorded elsewhere in Scotland. A coin of Trajan (AD 97–117) was found in one of the ditches and may indicate that parts of the site were in use ten years later than archaeologists originally believed.

Key Dates

1979: The fort, followed by the annexe and bath house, is originally spotted during aerial reconnaissance
1986: Extensive excavations of the fort are undertaken in advance of development
1987: Parts of the annexe are excavated
2007: Watching brief recovers some Roman pottery and tiles
2009: Excavation on the annexe in advance of development reveals ditches and a well

Exploring

The site has largely been lost to modern development, with only a small part of the northern side of the fort and annexe (to the immediate west) having been spared. The site is just off the A7, and can be found by taking the B6392 (Gilmerton Road) east towards Dalkeith from the roundabout where the A7 meets the A772. The site is between Gilmerton Road and Melville Gate Road, just before the former passes over the River North Esk.

Glencorse Mains

Fortlet (Possible) | NT 233 627

Archaeologists originally thought this was a camp, but investigations in 2007–08 discovered three sides of a 1.2-hectare site, leading to the conclusion that it may have been a more permanent structure. Further work in 2012 failed to find any datable artefacts, so, until further work is undertaken, the site at Glencorse will have to remain a possible, rather than a confirmed, fortlet.

Key Dates

1976: The site is identified from the air and suspected to be a camp
1988: Further details of the site are revealed through aerial images
1998: Re-evaluation of the aerial images indicates the site is a fortlet rather than a camp

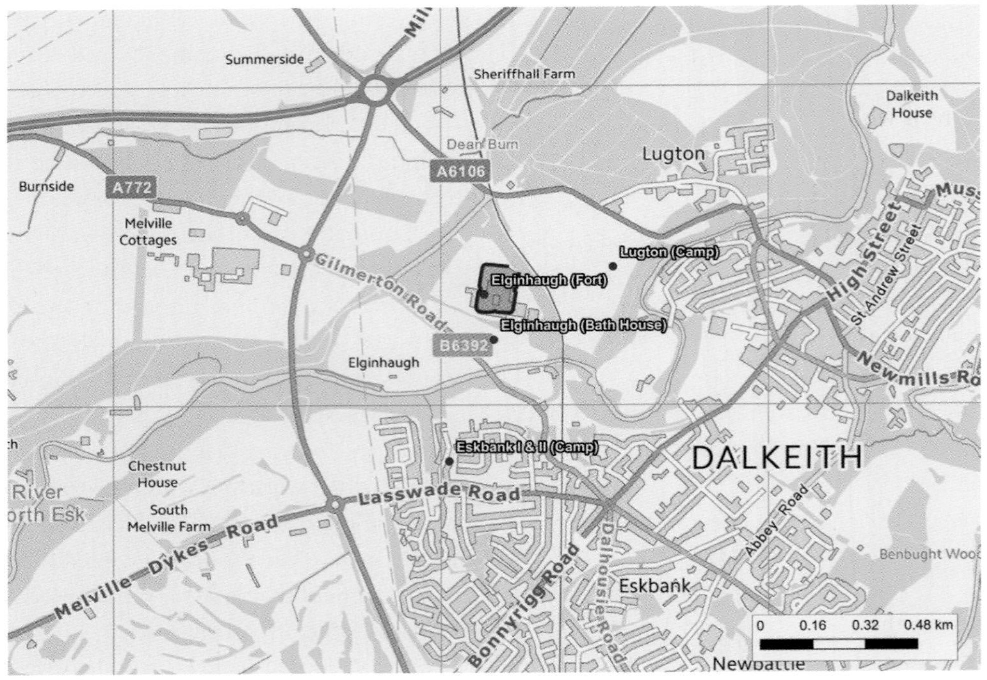

The view of Arthur's Seat from the centre of Inveresk fort, now covered by a modern cemetery.

Inveresk

Fort & Settlement | NT 342 720
Camp I & II | NT 348 712
Possible Camp III | NT 348 720

One of the oldest recorded Roman sites in Scotland, Inveresk is home to a plethora of activity: one fort, two camps, a large settlement, a temple, a funerary monument, a possible harbour and even a possible amphitheatre. However, like Cramond, most of the Roman remains have been built on and any knowledge has had to be gained from pockets of development.

Located near where the Esk flows into the Forth, the fort was founded in AD 139/140 under Governor Quintus Lollius Urbicus. Originally built from timber, then in stone, the fort is larger than average at 2.7 hectares (the fort at Cramond is only 2.3 hectares). Some archaeologists have speculated that it is bigger because it housed a cavalry unit and more space was required for the horses. The majority of the fort is now covered by the cemetery of St Michael's Church.

One of the earliest accounts of the discovery of Roman remains in Scotland comes from Inveresk, when Thomas Randolf, the English ambassador to Scotland wrote to Elizabeth I's secretary:

> For certayne ther is founde a cave bysyds Muskelbourge, stondinge upon a number of Pillers, made of tyle stones curieusyle wrought, signifying great antiquetie, and strayngc monuments found in the same. Thys comyethe to my knowledge, bysyds the common report by th' assurance of Alexander Clerke, whoe was ther to see yt, wch I wyll do myself wthin these three or four days. (7 April 1565)

Randolf subsequently visited Inveresk and reported back:

> The cave founde bysyds Muskelbourge semethe to be some monumente of the Romaynes by a stone that was founde with these words graven upon hym – Apolloni Granno Q L Sabinianus Proc. Aug. Dyvers short pillers sette upright upon the grounde, covered with tyle stones large and thyuck, torninghe into divers angles, and certayne places lyke unto chymnes to awoide smoke. Thys is all that I can gether thereof.

Around 1765 and 1783, masonry was found during the construction of a bowling green near the church, including a hypocaust ascribed to a bath house. Local resident James Wedderburn gave an early description of cropmarks, noting that crops grew poorly in an area near the Pinkie Burn during dry weather. In

1878, while houses were being built, a pine cone finial, a symbol of mortality, was unearthed. Usually associated with cemeteries, on this occasion it was found with pottery but no evidence of human remains. It can now be seen in the National Museum of Scotland. Various artefacts were found during the 19th and 20th centuries, including a carved stone inscribed 'CHVIIII', which some archaeologists have identified with the fabled Ninth Legion. However, despite all the remains found, there was no firm evidence of a Roman military site until 1939 when OGS Crawford flew over the site and noted a number of Romanesque cropmarks; the site was confirmed as a Roman fort a few years later.

In 1945, grave workers uncovered fragments of a Roman column from an unknown building. This led the Society of Antiquaries of Scotland, under Ian Richmond, to begin excavating the cemetery and grounds of the adjacent St Michael's House. Floors, internal walls, buildings and a street were uncovered. Richmond concluded that the fort was possibly garrisoned by a 500-strong cavalry unit, although he did not recover any artefacts that supported this view, instead basing his conclusions on the size of the site. This work was reviewed in the 1980s by William Hanson, who noted that Richmond had declared the area to the west of the modern cemetery as being void of Roman activity. Hanson noted that the ground level in that area was higher than that of the cemetery, indicating that there had been earlier activity there, and he confirmed this by excavation. The site was subsequently excavated more extensively in 1991 by Alan Leslie, who identified up to three phases of excavation. Further excavations uncovered the southern rampart, roads and internal buildings.

Little is known about the Roman settlement or *vicus* but several developments have helped to build up a picture of Roman Inveresk. Between 1996 and 2000, the Inveresk Gate housing development was built, less than a hundred yards from St Michael's Kirk. Although some Roman activity had been revealed when the site was landscaped in 1827, it was only excavated before the housing development was built. This work revealed a series of defensive ditches, which were only used for one year, as well as a box tile of the type usually used to heat bath houses, although there was no other evidence of such a building. Three phases of occupation were identified. The earliest consisted of buildings constructed of wattle and daub and probably shingle roofs. The second phase saw the boundaries of the earlier buildings maintained, although they were built using timber posts (something which was widespread in the Antonine period). By the third phase, the ditch had been filled in and buildings built from stone.

A second housing development located in the grounds of Eskgrove House, where an old wall needed repair, led to an excavation to clear the area around the foundations. A number of sandstone blocks (which may have been Roman) were unearthed, along with pottery, glass, butchered bones and hypocaust tiles – there is a known bath house around 30 metres away. Analysis of the bones has given archaeologists an idea of the diet of the *vicus* inhabitants, which seems to have included meat from cattle, sheep, pigs, wild boar, and red and roe deer – the latter only found in wooded area. There was also evidence of seafood having been consumed, with shells from oysters, mussels, whelks, limpets, winkles and cockles.

The Amphitheatre

In advance of another housing development in 1995, an area to the northeast of the fort was explored, revealing a site with three phases of occupation. Relating to the third phase was a series of postholes arranged in a semi-circular shape, possibly creating a fence, while to the rear other postholes intersected, to create the base of a rectangular structure. Some archaeologists have speculated that this arrangement of a semi-circular fence with a square building was an amphitheatre, with a stand for spectators. The only other amphitheatre in Scotland can be found at Newstead in the Borders, although that one was constructed from turf, like the example at Cirencester, in Gloucestershire, England.

There is limited evidence from the pottery discovered of an Antonine date, although this style of amphitheatre is similar to the design used in the Flavian period. However, to date there is no other evidence of Flavian activity at Inveresk. Archaeologists disagree about the existence or otherwise of an amphitheatre here, with some arguing that the remains of the rectangular building are similar to those left by granaries (although there are no known granaries with a fence surrounding them). It does not help that only half the possible amphitheatre fence was found. Others have speculated that it may have been a cavalry training ground, because the fence appears to have been quite flimsy and would not have been particularly useful during the games taking place there.

The site of the supposed amphitheatre, now covered by modern housing.

An example of a turf amphitheatre at Cirencester.

The Temple of Mithras

In 2010, during construction of a new cricket pavilion by Lewiscale Park (a short distance east of the fort and south of the possible amphitheatre), the foundations of a Roman temple or *mithraeum* were uncovered. It was essentially an underground chamber with a sunken floor, within which were two large altars that were deliberately buried face down, something which is incredibly rare. The first was dedicated to the sun god Sol, with the following inscription:

SOL C(AIUS) CAS(SIUS) FLA(VIUS)
'To Sol, Caius Cassius Flavius, Centurion'

The second is inscribed as follows:

D A E O
INVICTO MY
C CAS
FLA
'To the Invincible god Mithras'

Replica altars found at the site of the *mithraeum* at Carrawburgh on Hadrian's Wall. The altar to the sun god Sol is on the left.

The remains of the stone *mithraeum* at Carrawburgh on Hadrian's Wall.

The Sol altar had an image of the god carved in it, with holes where the sun's rays, eyes and nose were. At the back was a recess where a candle would be placed, with the light shining through the holes.

The temple was dedicated to the cult of Mithras, which worshipped the bull and was based on Greek mythology. This was the first time such a site had been found in Scotland – the nearest known site is at the fort at Carrawburgh on Hadrian's Wall. The cult is usually associated with the army, but archaeologists know very little about it, and what actually went on in the temple. The altars are currently being preserved, after which they are expected to go on display at the National Museum of Scotland in Edinburgh.

Exploring

The best place to begin a tour of Roman Inveresk is from St Michael's Kirk. From the church, head west into the cemetery and go through the first wall, following the road, and then through the second gap. The little building on the left is almost on top of the HQ building in the centre of the fort, which was orientated towards Arthur's Seat. Go back to the entrance of the cemetery to the war memorial, then follow the lane running parallel with the cemetery (past St Michael's House, where the mid-20th-century excavations took place). At the end of the lane is the western limit of the site.

To see the other main sites, head through the gate opposite the kirk and down the path towards the river. On the left is the Inveresk Gate development. At the bottom of the hill, turn left and follow the river for about 300 metres until you get to a wall with a bench by it. On the other side of this is the Eskgrove House site, next to the doocot. Follow the path again for about half a mile, passing under the railway bridge. Just after, the path bends to the left; head up the steps to the left (slightly overgrown) and at the top take the track towards the houses.

The track runs through the two Roman camps (not on the map), which were identified by St Joseph in the 1960s, as well as a Neolithic cursus monument that is no longer visible. Head on to the main road and turn left. In 2007, a Roman tombstone was discovered near the railway bridge. Originally dedicated to a soldier named Crescens, it is now in the National Museum The pine cone finial was discovered during the construction of housing on the left, just after crossing the railway line.

Head into the village and cross the road by the National Trust for Scotland's Inveresk Lodge Garden, and go down Double Dykes lane, taking the left-hand path at the end. This takes you into the park where the *mithraeum* was discovered (now under the cricket pavilion at the far end). To the left of the pavilion, the path heads down a ramp, opposite which is the modern housing development covering the possible amphitheatre. Head left and go through the park gates – buses stop opposite, outside Musselburgh Grammar School – or turn left and head up the hill back to St Michael's Kirk. An original piece of preserved hypocaust that has been exposed for several centuries is located nearby in a private garden.

Inveresk is easily accessed by car by following the signs to the village from the A1 (heading eastwards from Edinburgh) or follow the signs to Musselburgh

The site of the camps at Inveresk.

and then those to Inveresk. Parking is limited in the village, with several spaces outside the kirk, but there are additional spaces at the nearby Tesco at Musselburgh, from where the kirk can be reached by footpath.

There are frequent buses from the city to Inveresk and Musselburgh, with the number 40 stopping at Musselburgh High School.

Kirkton (Livingston)

Possible Fortlet | NT 039 666

A possible fortlet has been identified from the air, located next to the confluence of the Killandean Burn and River Almond. Unfortunately, the site has now been swallowed up by modern development.

Key Dates

1993: Aerial reconnaissance detects cropmarks resembling the corner of a small fortlet

Linlithgow

Linlithgow Palace – Possible Fort | NS 98 77

Birthplace of Mary, Queen of Scots, the current ruins on the site belong to the 15th century, although the site has been home to various royal residences. Its importance partly stems from its location between the royal strongholds of Edinburgh and Stirling castles, and, while there is no confirmed Roman military fortification on the site, it seems like a logical place to have built one. It was not a huge surprise, therefore, when a rounded corner was spotted as a cropmark

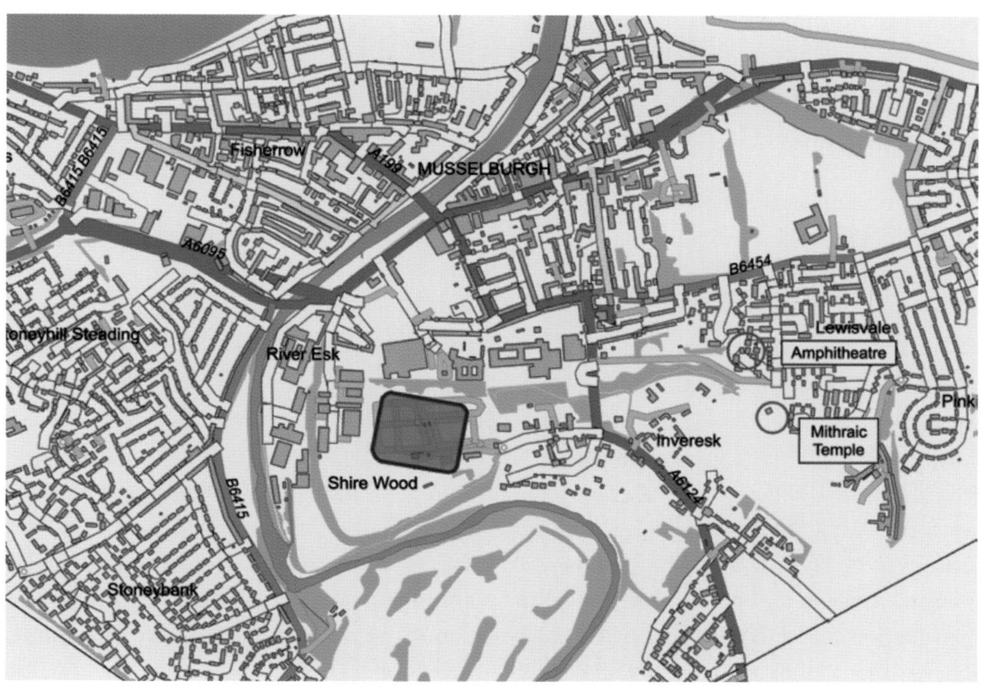

to the southwest of the palace in 1989. A number of finds have been made near the palace including *amphorae* from the local cemetery as well as other pottery fragments, a bell and a coin hoard dating to the reign of Antoninus Pius. To date, there has been no further work on the cropmarks, so archaeologists cannot yet confirm whether or not a Roman fort lies underneath the palace.

Key Dates

1781: Roman coins are discovered in an urn at Burgh Muir
1862: Roman pottery is recovered from the town cemetery
1992: Roman *amphora* fragments are recovered from the area around the north side of the palace
1892: A Roman bell is found near the palace
1990: Aerial survey detects possible cropmarks indicating a camp or fort may be underneath the palace

Exploring

The cropmarks were recorded outside the southwest corner of the palace, between the walls and the track.

Linlithgow Palace is located in the centre of the town and easily reached by road or rail. It is managed by Historic Scotland and open to the public all year round.

National Museum of Scotland

Chambers Street, Edinburgh EH1 1JF | Free Entry
www.nms.ac.uk | @NtMuseumsScot
Opening Times: daily 10:00–17:00

Home to the national collection, the National Museum of Scotland looks after a vast wealth of artefacts, representing the breadth of Scottish archaeology and history.

Beginning life in the 1780s as part of the Society of Antiquaries of Scotland, the then National Museum of Antiquities was first located in what is now the National Portrait Gallery on Queen Street in Edinburgh. (The Gallery is certainly worth a visit, not least to see the frieze of famous Scots in the entrance hall, which includes Agricola.) In the 1990s, various collections were brought together on the Chambers Street site, with the Iron Age and Roman collections housed in the lower levels of the new building. Highlights include the Cramond Lioness, the Traprain Hoard, the Bridgeness distance slab, the Ingliston milestone and the Mithraic altars from Inveresk, when they go on display. There really is no better place to begin an exploration of Roman Scotland.

Ravelrig Hill

Castle Bank – Possible Fort & Beacon | NT 145 669

The General's Watch – Possible Beacon | NT 154 667

18th-century accounts detail two Roman sites on Ravelrig Hill. One is described as being surrounded by two ditches and faced with stone sounding similar to indigenous, vitrified forts. All traces of the sites have been destroyed by quarrying.

Key Dates

1793: *The Old Statistical Account of Scotland* details two Roman sites on the hill

Traprain Law

Native Hillfort & Settlement | NT 580 747

A Tribal Centre

Beyond the forts and camps of Inveresk is a Roman wilderness, with East Lothian apparently devoid of Roman activity. There are the usual occasional finds of coins and other artefacts but none in any great concentration, which might indicate a presence in the area. Archaeologists speculate that this is because the region was a client kingdom of Rome – in other words, the local tribe had been bribed by the Romans to be loyal to the Empire. Very little is known about the Votadini, the local tribe, other than their name appearing on a 2nd-century map. The map is vague about the scale of their territory, which may have extended as far south as northeast England and as far north as Fife, but archaeologists believe that the capital was focused on Traprain Law. Originally known as Dumpelder Law, this is a substantial mound of volcanic rock near Haddington. While there is no evidence precisely linking the tribe to Traprain Law, it is a logical assumption given that the mound is 221 metres high, with an area on top of 16 hectares, and has magnificent views of the Fife coast, East Lothian, Edinburgh and beyond. It would have been the largest tribal centre in this part of Scotland.

Excavated at least eight times since the early 20th century, Traprain Law is a complex site that has been in use for about 4,000 years. The earliest occupation seems to have taken place in the Neolithic period, although there is evidence of burial and ritual activity from the Bronze Age. A dense settlement existed from 1000–600 BC, after which the story is less clear, with fewer datable artefacts found from before the AD 80s. By the 1st century AD, the occupants appear to have been enjoying good relations with Rome, evidenced by a number of Roman artefacts found on site, including pottery, glass and even tweezers. A number of random coins have also been found, leading some archaeologists to argue that Traprain Law was the site of a Roman temple, similar to that which exists in the hillfort of Maiden Castle in Dorset.

The Traprain Law Treasure

Weighing a hefty 2.4kg, the Traprain Law Treasure is the largest hoard of Roman treasure discovered outside of Rome. It was originally excavated in AD 191 and consists of over 250 fragments of silver recovered from a pit underneath the floor of a building. Most of the artefacts were everyday objects such as tableware, including goblets, bowls and jugs, all cut up into smaller pieces before being hidden. It is likely they may have been destined for smelting and eventual recasting into new objects. Amongst the hoard were a number of coins issued by the Emperors Valens, Arcadius and Honorius, giving a date range of AD 410–425. A number of Christian motifs feature on some of the objects, including the Rho and fish symbols and an inscription of 'Jesus Christus' on the rim of one bowl. Archaeologists have suggested that these symbols indicate that the objects may have come from an early Christian community or a church, although some of the items were everyday household objects such as silver spoons.

Archaeologists have proposed a number of explanations as to why the hoard ended up on a windswept hill in East Lothian. It could have been booty from a raiding party, or payment to defend the area against the Saxons, who were beginning to invade Britain in the 5th century. Some classical texts record that, after Scotland was abandoned in the 2nd century, the Romans were bribing tribes to the north of Hadrian's Wall to stop them invading, and this may have been happening in East Lothian.

The Treasure is on display at the National Museum of Scotland and can be seen as part of the 'Scotland's Early Silver' exhibition.

Exploring

Although steep and windswept, Traprain Law can easily be visited, and is only a 10-minute drive from Haddington. Turn off the A1 at Haddington and follow the signs for Hailes Castle. As you approach the track to the castle, Traprain Law is ahead of you (it cannot be missed). Carry on until the Law is on your right; park in the car park and follow the small path heading to the summit.

Warklaw Hill

Possible Beacon | NT 199 673

Several early accounts claim that there is a beacon on the hill, dating to the Roman period, but there are no traces of it today.

Key Dates

1807: Chalmers notes a Roman site somewhere in the vicinity of the hill
1845: *The New Statistical Account of Scotland* describes the Roman station on Warklaw Hill

Windmill Knowe

Possible Tower | NT 096 789

Sir Robert Sibbald described a camp here in 1710, but later writers claimed that Sibbald probably saw the remains of the windmill site rather than a Roman fortification. The site was landscaped a number of years ago and there remains nothing to be seen.

Key Dates

1710: Sibbald records that there are Roman remains at Windmill Knowe

1855: Ordnance Survey fail to find any evidence of a Roman site

Woodhead

Camps | NT 384 638

Located near the camps at Pathhead, and next to Dere Street, these two sites were first identified as crop-marks before being confirmed by excavation in the 1970s and 1980s. The smaller camp is 1.5 hectares, but the size of the larger one is unconfirmed as the southern defences have not been spotted. Archae-ologists have suggested that the site may have been a construction camp for the 1st-century fort at Elgin-haugh, although that site is some 7km to the north of Woodhead.

Key Dates

1976: Kenneth Steer discovers the camp from aerial photographs

1980: Gordon Maxwell, during aerial reconnais-sance, notes further cropmarks and the possibility of another, smaller camp

1983: Excavation of the original site confirms the camp

Exploring

The camps are located near to Pathhead, and the main road into Scotland. Both sites are on a ridge overlooking the Tyne Water. The camps can be visited from Vogrie Country Park, which is west of Pathhead on the B6372, where there is a woodland track that passes by the western boundary of the larger camp.

The Other Sites

Boghall (Possible Camp | NT 245 650)

Only parts of this camp have been identified from the air, and no investigations have taken place on the ground, so little is known about the site.

Dalkeith (Smeaton) (Camp | NT 345 691)

Close to the camp at Eskbank and the fort at Elgin-haugh, this 12-hectare site was identified by St Joseph

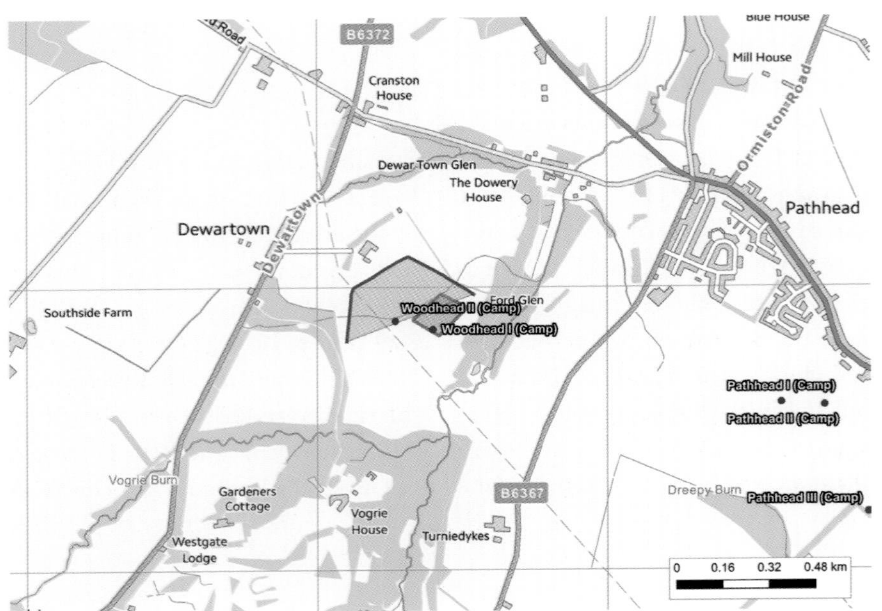

during his aerial photograph surveys. Parts of the defences have been identified, while the eastern and southeastern corners have remained elusive, despite excavations on the site in advance of the construction of the Dalkeith bypass. Two ovens were uncovered during those excavations, one within the western ditch, and the other just beyond. Following radiocarbon dating of burnt material found within the ovens, the one in the ditch gave a Roman date and the one just outside dated to the 5th to 7th centuries. The second date range was a surprise, given that there were no other nearby structures, suggesting this was a single oven located in the middle of an empty and possibly abandoned field.

A fragment of Antonine-period Samian pottery was excavated from near the surface of the defensive ditch, with layers of silt underneath. This indicated that many years had passed (enabling the silt to build up) before the pottery fragment was lost, implying that the Antonine period on the site was later than the initial invasion.

Eskbank (Camp | NT 320 668)

Not all of the defences of this camp have been located, but what has been traced indicates that this is potentially one of the larger sites in Scotland. Following the initial discovery in the 1960s, a number of excavations have failed to locate the elusive, missing sections.

Fala Mill (Camp | NT 430 619)

Located next to the A68, which probably follows the line of Dere Street, the main road into Scotland, this camp covers an area of 3.3 hectares. It has not been further explored.

Gogar Green (Camp | NT 176 717)

Two possible sites were identified by Gordon Maxwell from the air in 1980, both positioned next to each other – one at Gogar Green and the other at Milburn Tower (*see* below). The camp, around 7.5 hectares, was excavated in advance of construction of the city bypass in the mid-1980s. With the bypass, and commercial development, cutting across the camp, most of the site has been destroyed.

Lugton (Camp | NT 325 674)

Set in a loop in the North Esk, the site is close to the camp and early fort at Eskbank. It is particularly small, at 0.5 hectares.

Millburn Tower (Possible Camp | NT 173 718)

Located next to the camp at Gogar Green, only parts of the defences have been identified. It is possible that the rest of the site has been destroyed by the construction of the city bypass and the surrounding industrial development.

Monktonhall (Shire Haugh) (Possible Camp | NT 34 71)

The New Statistical Account of Scotland records a Roman camp visible on the Shire Haugh, but no trace of the site survives today.

Pathhead (Camp I | NT 396 635, Camp II | NT 397 635, Camp III | NT 399 632)

Close to the probable line of the Roman road, Dere Street, lie three temporary camps at Pathhead. Identified from the air, two were excavated by St Joseph who clarified that the first was 20.5 hectares and the second 5.3 hectares. The third camp is substantially bigger, at 56 hectares, making it comparable with similar sites at Newstead and St Leonards, both in the Scottish Borders. The implication is that the three were occupied at the same time during the Severan campaigns.

Sheriffhall (Possible Camp | NT 318 685)

An 18th-century account claims that a camp was located at Sheriffhall, more specifically at a farm known as Campend. There are no traces of the site today.

Winchburgh (The Den) (Possible Camp | NT 073 761)

A possible camp was recorded at this site by St Joseph in the 1970s. The site has never been examined.

Chapter 6

FIFE

Archaeologists have traditionally argued that Fife was left alone by the Romans, and there are indeed no known forts and relatively few confirmed camps in the area. Perhaps the Romans never needed to occupy the region because it was controlled by the Votadini, whom they paid to be loyal to the Roman Empire (*see* Traprain Law, Edinburgh and the Lothians). Despite the lack of permanent fortifications, there are nonetheless some tantalizing glimpses of Roman activity in Fife – several coin hoards have been found, along with brooches, pottery and glass, as well as a hoard of silver (with similarities to the Traprain Law Treasure). The finds imply that there was probably a bit more of a Roman presence in Fife than archaeologists have typically assumed.

Auchtermuchty

Camp | NO 242 118

Partially buried under the eastern end of the town, the camp at Auchtermuchty is one of only two confirmed

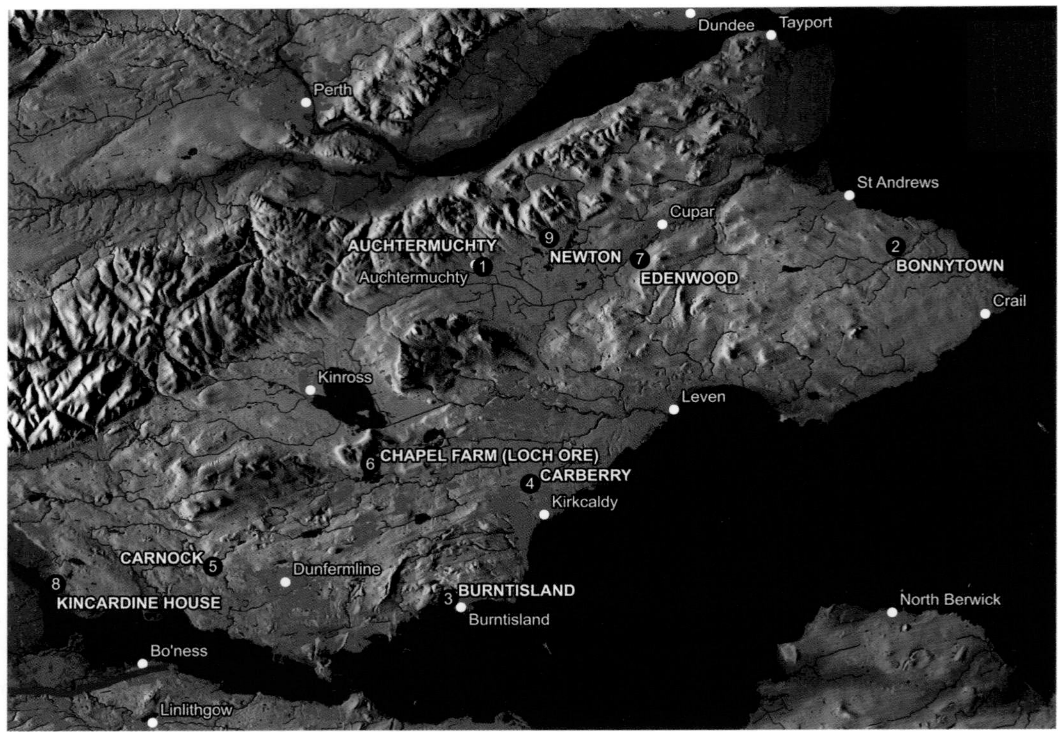

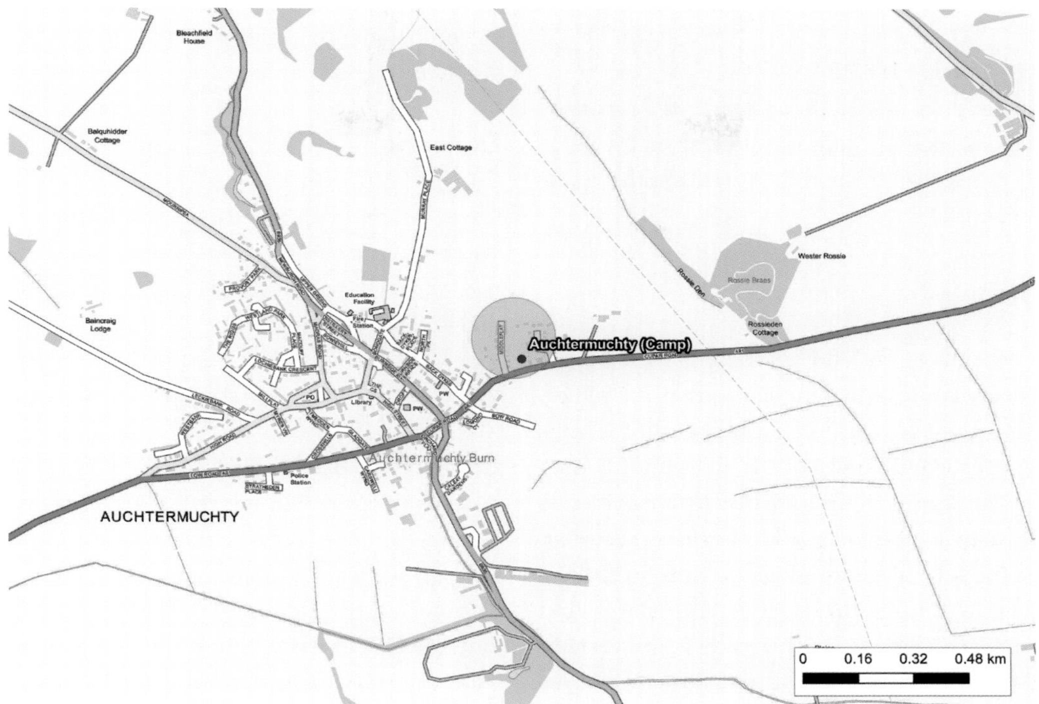

camps in Fife. Discovered through aerial photography by St Joseph in the 1960s, it covers an area of around 24 hectares. Excavation failed to find any artefacts. St Joseph originally speculated that it was Flavian and later changed this to Severan, but there was no strong evidence to support any dating. An annexe identified to the southwest in 1973 has yet to be excavated.

Exploring

The camp is at the eastern end of the village, on Cupar Road, with parts of the site underneath the modern housing at Middleflat Court, Mathieson Court and Mathieson Gardens.

Bonnytown

Camp (Possible) | NO 544 124

Only about a mile and a half from the Fife coast, the possible camp was identified from the air in 1962 by St Joseph, and is the only one in this area. The defences of the camp were partly excavated in 1966, although no datable artefacts were uncovered. Rebecca Jones has noted multiple linear cropmarks around the site, making it difficult to discern the site in aerial photographs. Without further excavation it is not possible to confirm whether or not it is Roman.

Exploring

The site is at Bonnytown Farm, to the southwest of the village of Boarhills. Heading towards St Andrew's on the A917 from Boarhills, turn left after Boarhills church and before you get to St Andrew's golf course.

Burntisland

Possible Fort | NT 22 85

According to *The Old Statistical Account of Scotland*, a nearby fort on Dunearn Hill was referred to locally as 'Agricola's Camp', implying Roman occupation. While this is not confirmation that the military were stationed here, the area around Burntisland does make a good, natural harbour. However, other than a coin found elsewhere in the village, there is no evidence to suggest the site was home to a Roman fort.

Carberry

Possible Camp | NT 284 947

The 1845 edition of *The New Statistical Account of Scotland* claims that there was a camp at Carberry but also notes that at the time of writing there was no trace of it left.

Carnock

Camp (Possible) | NT 045 885

It may or may not be a coincidence that the hill on which this supposed camp is located is called Camps Hill. With excellent views of the surrounding area from the summit, it is approached by a number of straight roads. A Roman site has been suspected in the area for several hundred years, with Sir Robert Sibbald in the 17th century opening a nearby mound and finding a coin hoard. Other early accounts note two military fortifications on the hill – the two farms on the site are known as East Camps and West Camps. While there are no traces on the ground, the circumstantial evidence indicates that Carnock would be a good candidate for further exploration.

Exploring

Camps Hill is on the very edge of the village of Carnock, and can be reached by turning into the village from the A908 on to Camps Road. Follow this road through the village, past the Community Centre and up on to Camps Hill.

Chapel Farm (Lochore)

Camp (Possible) | NT 167 962

As early as 1726, Gordon recorded the remains of a Roman camp at Lochore, noting that the ditch and rampart were still visible on one side, and that there was also a possible fortlet. When Maitland (1757) and Roy (1793) visited, they noted that some of the features could still be seen but by 1817 the construction of a farm at Lochore had destroyed any visible remains. Crawford, who visited in 1925, said there

was not enough evidence to confirm that the site was Roman and in 1949 excavations failed to find any artefacts to support the dating of the site, with the excavators concluding that it was not Roman. The site is not in a strong strategic position and has been prone to flooding, and some archaeologists argue that it may have been a medieval homestead. Without further work, it is not possible to confirm the site's origins one way or the other.

Exploring

The site is on the northern edge of Loch Ore, part of the Lochore Meadows Country Park, with the alleged site underneath Lochore Meadows Equestrian Centre. There is ample car parking in the area, and there is a path around the loch which passes the southern extremity of the site. Views are limited by the woodland at this point.

Edenwood

Camp | NO 357 115

Edenwood is the second confirmed Roman site in Fife, discovered from the air in 1978 by St Joseph and by Maxwell who were working separately. A limited excavation of the ditch took place in the late 1970s, which also recorded an annexe. The site is undated due to a lack of datable artefacts.

Exploring

The site is accessible, although only limited remains (a series of small, linear earthworks) are visible in woodland to the northeast and northwest (in Greening Wood, marked on the Ordnance Survey map of the site). The camp is near the National Trust property, Hill of Tarvit, and can be reached on the A914, to the south of Cupar. It is adjacent to Edenwood Farm.

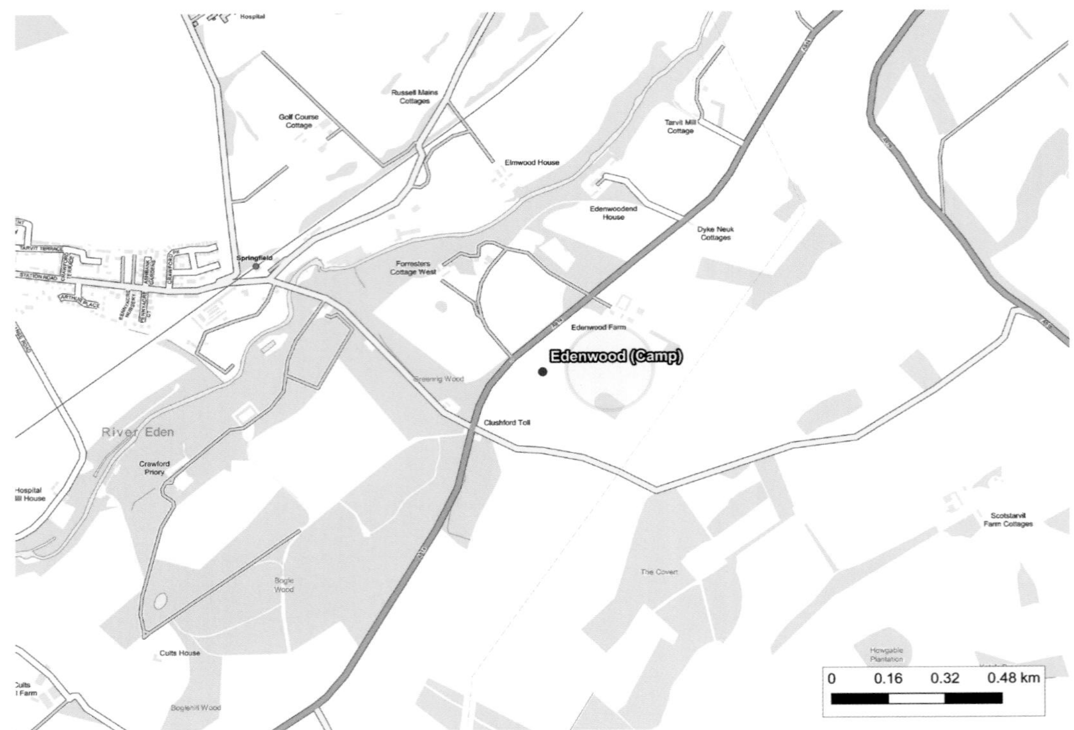

Kincardine House

Possible Fortlet | NS 930 872

A possible fortlet was first spotted in an aerial photograph of the area, which was taken in the 1970s by Welsh. It is still to be surveyed or explored further, although there has been some speculation that the area was developed for agriculture in the 19th century and it is this that may have caused the cropmark to form.

Newton

Possible Fort | NO 291 132

This site was identified from aerial photographs by the Roman Gask Project in 2003, showing up as a rectilinear cropmark with rounded corners covering an area of 1.4 hectares. This was followed up by the project with a geophysical survey of the site, which confirmed an enclosure, although it did not appear to be Roman.

Chapter 7

THE ANTONINE WALL

The Antonine Wall is one of the most impressive feats of Roman engineering in Britain, second only to its earlier counterpart, Hadrian's Wall. It is comprised of a series of forts and fortlets along a turf wall, which stretches from the Firth of Forth in the east to the Firth of Clyde in the west.

The story of the construction of the Antonine Wall begins with the ascent of Fulvius Aelius Hadrianus Antoninus Augustus Pius (AD 86–161) to the imperial throne in AD 138, shortly after the death of the Emperor Hadrian. Antoninus Pius had been named heir and successor to Hadrian and would go on to reign for 23 years, but in the beginning he needed to prove his credentials. Unlike most of his imperial predecessors, he had never taken part in military activity and Britain was to become the scene of his first military offensive. In AD 139, the Roman governor in Britain, Quintus Lollius Urbicus, was tasked with taming the Lowlands, and advancing the Empire's frontier north, beyond Hadrian's Wall (although the reality is that some of the forts in southern Scotland may have already been operating as outposts). Some time around AD 142, Urbicus seems to have secured the Forth–Clyde isthmus to such an extent that the construction of a new wall could begin in the name of the new Emperor. Inscriptions recovered from the wall give Antoninus Pius the credit of giving the order to build it.

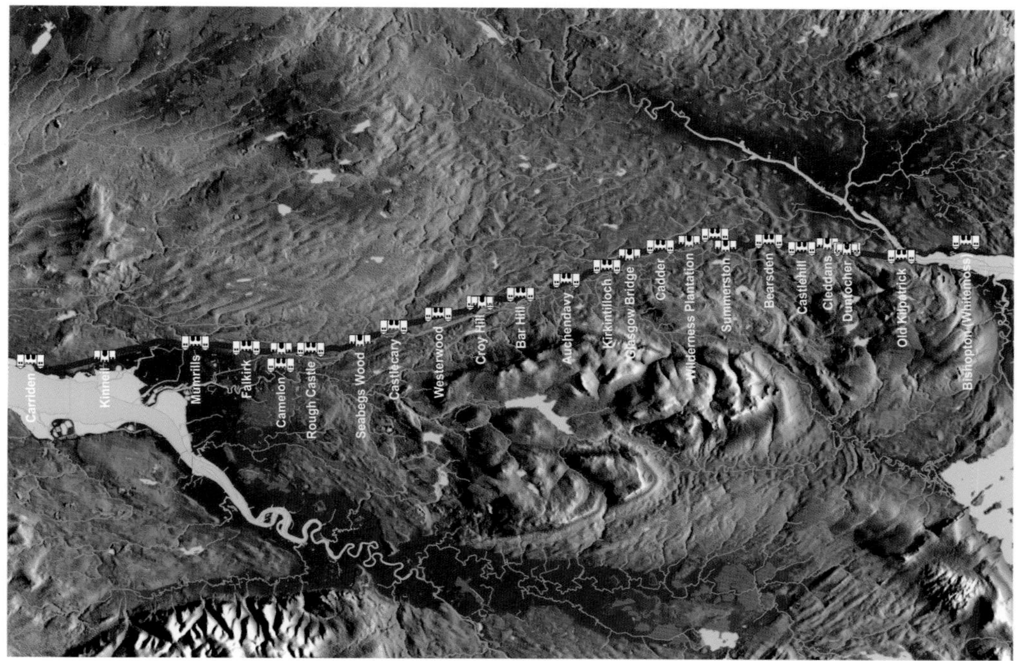

The Other Wall

At 37 miles long, the Antonine Wall stretches from Carriden on the Forth to Old Kilpatrick on the Clyde. Some old accounts claim that the eastern terminus was at Grahamsdyke (underneath modern Bo'ness) while, at the western end, the barrier continued towards Dumbarton. While the physical ends of the wall in the east and west have not been found, most archaeologists agree that the terminals are at the forts of Carriden and Old Kilpatrick.

Like its southern counterpart, the Antonine Wall is more than just a physical mound. It has several components, but mainly comprises a rampart (the wall itself), usually constructed from turf or clay, which was probably between 3 and 5 metres high, and around 4.3 metres wide. The turves were placed on a stone base and in front of the turf wall was a slight rise or berm. In some places, there is evidence of pits (known as *lilia*) having been cut into the berm and filled with thorns, as an additional obstacle to any attackers. In front of this was a typically Roman V-shaped ditch (between 6 and 12 metres wide and just under 4 metres deep), which probably ran for the full 37 miles, and beyond this an outer mound. Behind the wall was the Military Way, a road running parallel with the site. It is unknown whether or not there was a walkway on top of the wall itself.

There are seventeen known forts along the length of the wall: (from west to east) Old Kilpatrick, Duntocher, Castlehill, Bearsden, Balmuildy, Cadder, Kirkintilloch, Auchendavy, Bar Hill, Croy Hill, Westerwood, Castlecary, Rough Castle, Falkirk, Mumrills, Inveravon and Carriden. Archaeologists studying the Roman wall have noted that the forts are located every two and a quarter miles or so, with another two yet to be located in the vicinity of Kinneil and Seabegs. Between the forts were a series of fortlets, the first of which was identified and recorded in 1947 when Duntocher was being excavated. To date, nine fortlets have been confirmed along the wall; many more are anticipated, but a number may lie underneath post-Roman developments.

In 1984, William Hanson and Gordon Maxwell published their notable book *Rome's North-West Frontier: The Antonine Wall*, which summed up the thinking of the time on the wall. In it, they suggested that there should be forty-one fortlets (*see* below) on the Wall; while some, such as those at Watling Lodge Seabegs and Duntocher, have been confirmed, others have still not been located.

An exposed stretch of the foundations of the Antonine Wall at New Kilpatrick Cemetery (Dunbartonshire), showing how the turves were placed on a stone base.

Hanson and Maxwell's List of Probable Fortlet Locations (1984)

Dunbartonshire

Bogton (NS 62 72) | Cawder House (NS 60 72) | Hillhead (NS 66 74) | Manse Burn (NS 55 72) | Old Kilpatrick (NS 46 73) | Shirva (NS 69 75)

Falkirk

Allandale (NS 80 78) | Bantaskin (NS 87 79) | Callendar House & Park (NS 89 79) | Lauriston (Grahamsdyke) (NS 910 795) | Kinneil (NS 982 805) | Milnquarter (NS 82 79) | Nether Kinneil (NS 96 80) | Polmont School (NS 93 79) | Tentfield (NS 85 79)

Glasgow

Easter Balmuildy (NS 58 71)

Lanarkshire

Arniebog (NS 76 77) | Easter Dullatur (NS 740 770) | Garnhall (NS 78 78) | Girnal Hill (NS 720 761) | Tollpark (NS 77 77)

Key Sites

Although the wall itself does not survive to any great extent, traces of the various components can be seen across the length of the frontier. Some of the better examples are listed below. It is relatively easy to visit many of the sites on foot, following the John Muir Way, which runs across central Scotland and follows the line of the wall in many places (http://johnmuirway.org).

General

The best-preserved section of the wall and its components can be found at **Rough Castle**, where the ditch is well preserved, along with the wall as a slight rise, and the fort. It also has good interpretation panels and makes for a pleasant, gentle visit. For those inclined towards a more strenuous outing, **Bar Hill** commands excellent views of the wall to the east and west, along with a well-preserved section of the ditch, which can be seen snaking off towards **Croy Hill**. Although none of the distance slabs remain in their original locations, an impressive replica of the **Bridgeness** slab can be found to the east of Bo'ness, near the site of **Kinneil** fortlet.

The Wall

While the wall does not survive to anywhere near its original height, it can be seen as a low mound in a couple of places, including **Callander Park**, **Rough Castle** and between **Bar Hill** and **Croy Hill**. The excavated and exposed foundations of the wall can be seen at **New Kilpatrick Cemetery**.

The Ditch

The deepest and best-preserved section of the ditch can be found at **Watling Lodge**, where it survives to an impressive depth. Other sections are visible at **Rough Castle** and **Bar Hill**.

Forts and Fortlets

While none of the fortification remains on the Antonine Wall are as notable as those along Hadrian's Wall, there are still some to be seen. The most impressive turf fort is at **Rough Castle**, while the bath house at **Bearsden** remains one of the best examples of such a structure in the Roman world. The foundations of buildings can be seen at **Bar Hill**, while **Castlecary** is also worth a visit for the site interpretation. The fortlets at **Kinneil** and **Cadder** are marked out on the ground, giving a good indication of the size of the structures and, in the case of the latter, the view of the surrounding area and of the Clyde to the south.

Museums

There are a number of museums along the wall with exhibits and artefacts, including the major institutions in Glasgow (**the Hunterian**) and Edinburgh (**the National Museum of Scotland**). The museums at **Kinneil** and **Kirkintilloch** should also be visited.

Further Information

Much has been written about the Antonine Wall, from in-depth research papers on the construction methods and various sites, to a history of the antiquarians rediscovering the frontier. Particularly recommended is *The Antonine Wall: A Handbook to Scotland's Roman Frontier* by Anne Robertson and Lawrence Keppie (2015).

The wall also has an official app, which can be downloaded to help experience life on the Antonine frontier, along with a website giving visitor information and an interactive map (www.antoninewall.org).

PART THREE: MID-SCOTLAND

Chapter 8

STIRLING

STIRLING IS AN AREA OF CONTRASTS, BOTH geographically and archaeologically. The flood plains of the Forth formed marshlands and mosses that were in existence 2,000 years ago and for two millennia dictated the easiest routes across the region. To the north, the land rises dramatically, forming hills that turn into the mountains of the Scottish Highlands.

It is near Stirling that the River Forth becomes fordable, giving the area huge importance, not just for the Romans, but also for later generations as kings and armies fought to control the region. Controlling the crossings was the key to controlling the Highlands.

The Romans, being brilliant engineers, took advantage of the landscape to construct fortifications along the border between the Lowlands and the Highlands. From sites such as Malling, which sits on the shores of the Lake of Menteith, to Drumquhassle, which commands spectacular views of Loch Lomond, each site was positioned to take advantage of the natural landscape, and ultimately to help the Romans conquer Scotland.

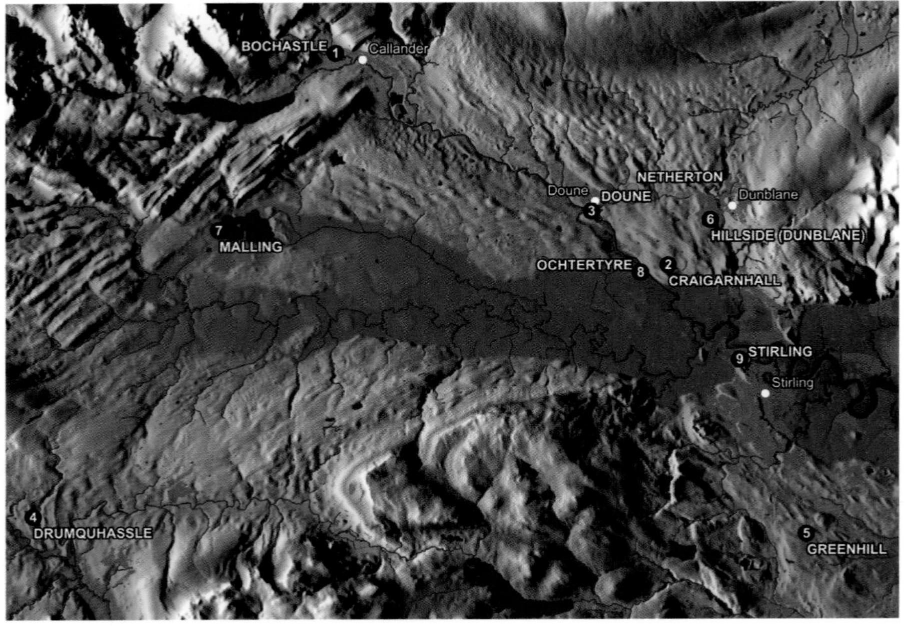

Bochastle

Fort | NN 614 079
Camp I | NN 611 077
Camp II | NN 611 077

Located between two rivers – the Garbh Uisge to the north, and the Gobhain to the south – Bochastle is home to a fort and two camps. Strategically positioned at the entrance to a glen that leads to the Highlands, the fort and camps were built to guard the route northwards, and to prevent any native incursions into the Roman military zone.

Roman activity near Callendar has been suspected since at least 1724, when Alexander Graham of Duchray referred to the land containing the site as Castle Field. He also noted that a gold coin of Nero had been found near by. The fort was excavated in 1949 by Anderson, with various features being recorded, including sections of the defences, although sections of the rampart and ditch were lost because of river erosion and construction of the railway line (now dismantled). Only the western defences are still visible, as a small mound, but from certain angles the fort platform is a bit more discernible. The excavations were not particularly well recorded, and subsequent geophysical survey work in the early part of the 21st century has contradicted the results of the original dig. In 2006, Woolliscroft and Hoffmann of the Roman Gask Project, who undertook the survey of the site, uncovered evidence for the foundations of a number of internal buildings, whereas the original excavators could not find these and had decided that they had been destroyed by flooding. There was an indication that the ditches of the camp and fort intersected, indicating that the former was built first, with the fort constructed on top at a later date.

Little datable evidence came to light during the excavations, although the last season produced coarse pottery from the 1st century. The geophysical survey detected the four gates of the fort, which were parrot-beak style, a design associated with the 1st century.

The fort at Bochastle, with the remains of the ramparts visible in front of the trees.

The existence of the camp was suspected in the late 1960s, when partial cropmarks were observed in aerial photographs. Identification on the ground in the 1970s confirmed a camp of 21 hectares, although subsequent work has shown that it may have been reduced in size after being built. The camps are dated to the 1st century because of the Stracathro-style gates on the north and south sides of the camp. During excavations in 1953 and 1956, Anderson speculated there were two phases of construction during the Flavian period, despite the lack of datable remains.

A small enclosure, which may or may not be Roman, has been identified on the eastern side of the camp. Further investigation is needed, but there is some speculation that it could either be an annexe or even another camp, although it is quite small at 0.53 hectares.

The site of the camps at Bochastle.

Key Dates

1724: Grant implies remains on the site of Castle Field
1945: St Joseph records the camp during aerial reconnaissance
1953–56: The fort is excavated
1969: St Joseph photographs the site from the air noting an adjacent enclosure, and goes on to excavate part of the camp
1988: A watching brief on the camp fails to find any Roman remains
2006: The Roman Gask Project undertakes a geophysical survey of the fort

Exploring

To reach the sites by car, follow the A84 west out of Callander, and after half a mile turn left on to the A821, just before Kilmahog. Immediately after crossing the river Garbh Uisge, take a left down the track. Follow the track until it turns right and heads under the former bridge. This is the best place to park, with the fort on this side of the railway.

The camp and fort are located along the Rob Roy Way, and are easily reached by heading westwards from Callander. Where the path leaves the embankment and slopes to ground level (at an old railway bridge which has since been removed), the camp is on your left, and the fort is visible by going 'under' the bridge and turning right.

The remains of the fort ramparts are the most visible part of the site, and can be seen from the track near the site. The field is frequently full of livestock, but the western defences can be approached with care. The site is quite often boggy and wet. The fort gate is clearly visible as a gap between the ramparts. Beyond this, to the northeast, is another section of the rampart. Heading underneath the railway line, the camp is in front of you, although no remains are visible.

Craigarnhall

Camp | NS 756 985

Craigarnhall is another Roman site identified by St Joseph in the latter half of the 20th century. Located on the northern side of the River Teith, it is opposite a similar camp on the southern side at Ochtertyre, and it is quite possible that the two sites are guarding a crossing over the Teith. This route would have been strategically important, protecting one of the routes north used by the army.

Excavations undertaken by St Joseph established the extent of the site by locating the defences,

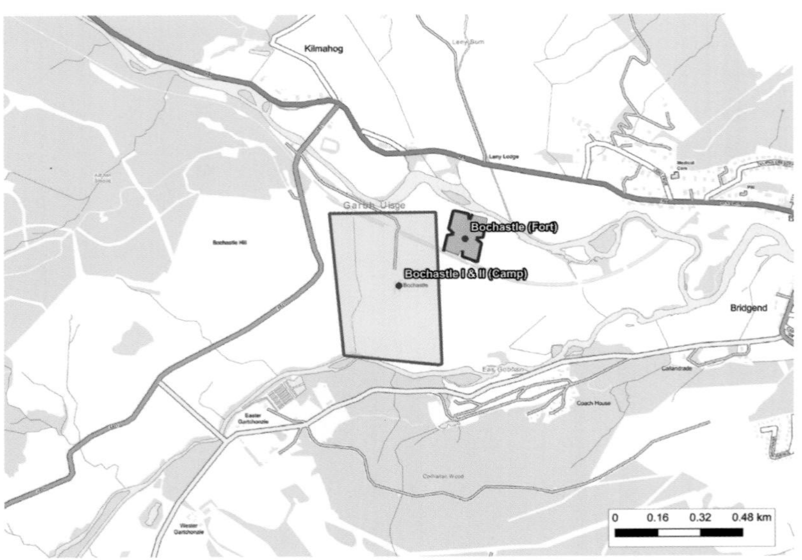

confirming *tituli* at the gates, and recording the area covered by the camp as being 25 hectares. The site has been extensively eroded by agricultural works, with one of the defensive ditches only being 0.4 metres in depth at one point, and 0.7 metres on the south-western side. In places, the ditch was rock cut, which is unusual because of the effort involved, although it has been recorded at a few other sites such as Raedykes. The site also had a small annexe on the southeast side.

Key Dates

1971: Sightings of cropmarks from the air are followed up by excavation of the defences by St Joseph
1979: Further aerial photography of the site

Exploring

The site, just a few miles from Bridge of Allan, is not particularly easy to access. From the roundabout at the end of the M9 (where it becomes the A9), take the first exit on to the B824 towards Doune. After about a mile, take the first minor road on the left, following this for about three-quarters of a mile, taking the left-hand track at Easter Row Farm. Carry on down this lane to Craigarnhall; the camp is in the fields to the left, by the plantation.

Doune

Fort | NN 727 013

The fort was discovered in 1983 by Maxwell flying over the site in search of a crossing point over the River Teith. Constructed on what is now known as Castle Hill, the fort does indeed guard a ford over the Teith. The site continued to be important long after the Romans had left and there is a medieval castle (of Monty Python fame) near by. As Maxwell, who originally identified the fort, went on to excavate the defences, he noted that Doune had a triple-ditch system on the eastern side, curving inwards at the gates. This style is otherwise known as 'parrot beak' and is unique to Flavian sites. Further aerial survey work a year later helped to identify the remaining defences, indicating that the fort was 2.25 hectares in size.

Aerial photography in 1985 identified more features, but it was not until 1999 that excavation took place in advance of building work at the school. Unfortunately, the excavations were never fully published, although Woolliscroft and Hoffmann subsequently analysed the preliminary results as part of their book *Rome's First Frontier: The Flavian Occupation of Northern Scotland.* The excavations revealed buildings, the *intervallum* road running around the inside of the

Playing cricket on the site of the fort at Doune.

ramparts, and pottery that confirmed a 1st-century date for the site. In 2010, a small excavation near the school uncovered evidence of ditches and postholes, which the excavators believed pre-dated the fort. Part of the northeastern defences, the rampart and three ditches were uncovered, and this included a timber building interpreted as a cavalry barrack block.

In 2010, the team from the Roman Gask Project undertook a geophysical survey of the site, revealing the southwest and northwest gates and concluding that the northeast gate was under the main entrance to the primary school. Their findings also showed that the fort was surrounded by a triple-ditch system on all sides, rather than just the one side, as Maxwell had identified.

Key Dates

1983: Maxwell looks for a crossing point over the Teith and locates the fort from cropmarks

1984: Further aerial photography reveals more details of the fort

1999: Watching brief fails to find any Roman artefacts or features

2010: Limited excavations in advance of development reveal parts of the Roman fort as well as a number of pre-Roman features

2010: Geophysical survey of the fort reveals the defences and some internal features

Exploring

From the east, heading into Doune from the east

on the A820, take the left immediately opposite the church on to Castlehill Court. At the crossroads, opposite the school, turn left and at the T-junction turn left again and park. There is a gate and an interpretation board ahead. Go through the gate and follow the footpath towards the cricket pitch, which is on top of the fort.

Drumquhassle

Fort | NS 484 874

Commanding panoramic views all round, but particularly of Loch Lomond to the west, Drumquhassle fort was strategically positioned at the western edge of the Highland fault line.

Following identification from the air in 1978, excavations in the same year confirmed both the Roman origin and the size of the site, at 3.2 hectares. Pottery fragments confirmed a Flavian date for occupation of the fort. By the 1990s, the adjacent quarry at Drumbeg had decided to expand gravel extraction, threatening the area around the site, although the fort itself is protected as a Scheduled Monument. This led to monitoring of the gravel works as they began to encroach on the northern annexe. No datable finds were uncovered, although there were a number of glass and pottery fragments.

From at least 1998, the site has been field walked on a regular basis, and a number of datable artefacts have been recovered, including 1st-century coins, a slingshot, pottery, and a harness mount. In 2004, the Roman Gask Project undertook a large-scale geophysical survey of the site, confirming that the fort had a double ditch, and the usual parrot-beak gates associated with Flavian fortifications. They also recorded evidence indicating there was a rectangular enclosure around a spring, which may be Roman in origin, although, without excavation, the team were unable to confirm this.

Key Dates

1978: Aerial photographs reveal the fort, which is subsequently confirmed through excavation
1997: The annexe is excavated in advance of quarrying
1998–2000: Field walking in the area around the fort reveals a number of Roman finds
2004: Extensive geophysical survey reveals several features including a double-ditch defence

The view from Drumquhassle overlooking Loch Lomond in the west.

Exploring

To reach the site from Drymen, head east on the B858, taking the first right onto the A811, heading south. Take the first left onto the minor road and carry on for just under a mile, passing the grassed over remains of the quarry on the right. Just beyond this is a tree-lined road to the right. The fort is immediately before this; on the right is a recessed gate which leads into the site. If you end up at Easter Drumquhassle Farm and campsite, you have gone too far.

The fort is located next to the main road, and is easily accessed through the gate. The fort is ahead. While there is nothing to be seen on the ground, the spring is in the next field on the edge of the Strathendrick Golf Course. From the road, go straight ahead through the field, past the small enclosure with some minor ruins on the right. The well is in a dip and is marked on the Ordnance Survey maps as a blue dot.

Greenhill

Possible Tower | NS 816 866

OGS Crawford, when looking for potential Roman sites, noted that Greenhill would have made a good location for a signal tower. However, the evidence on the ground was lacking, and it does not appear to have been a site occupied by the Roman army.

Key Dates

1949: Crawford suggests that Greenhill would make an ideal location for a Roman tower
1953: Site visit by RCAHMS fails to locate any evidence for a tower

Dunblane (Hillside)

Camps I & II | NN 775 005

Almost lost under modern development, the two camps at Dunblane are, as the name suggests, perched on the side of a hill. They enjoy good views in every direction except the north, which is obscured by the hill.

The site was discovered through aerial photography in 1945, but it was not until the mid-1960s that excavations took place, leading to the discovery of the second camp, which is located within the boundaries of the first one. Given the size of the larger camp, at 12.9 hectares, the smaller camp, which covers 5.9 hectares, fits easily within the ramparts. The two camps share part of the southwestern defences, and the entrance, which had a *titulus,* a 1st-century defensive feature. Sections of the ditches were cut

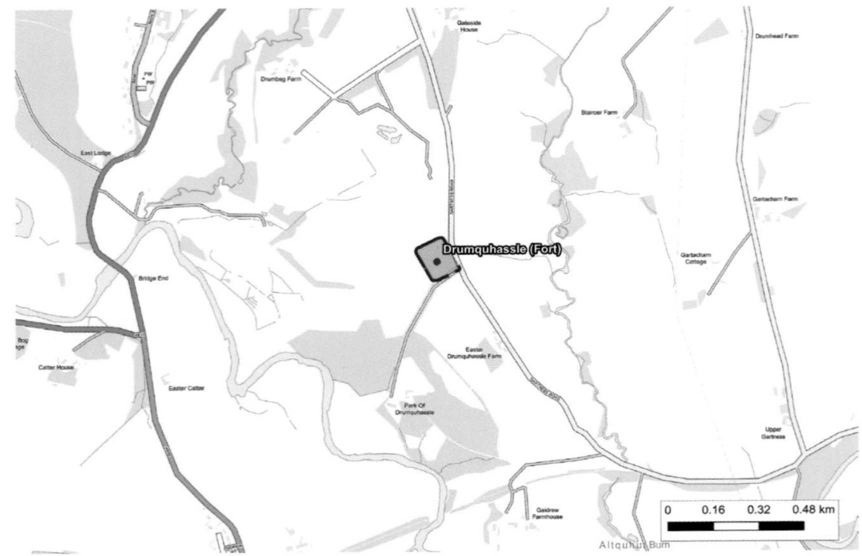

The remains of Dunblane (Hillside). Most of the rest of the site has been built over.

Large parts of the Dunblane camps have been lost to modern development.

through bedrock, something recorded on a few sites.

Robertson, who undertook the excavations, hypothesized that the camps were in occupation at the same time, although later excavations have disproved this. In the mid-1990s, Mackenzie excavated the southwestern gate, and noted two different styles where the ramparts ended on either side of the gate. As both camps shared this area of the site, Mackenzie argued that the smaller camp had been created when the larger site was reduced in size, reusing part of the southwestern gate.

Key Dates

1945: Both camps are identified by St Joseph during aerial reconnaissance
1966 and 1969: Excavations uncover the eastern and southern defences of Camp II and the south ditch/rampart of Camp I
1979: Aerial photographs of the camps indicate that Camp I was constructed first
1995: Excavations of the camps are undertaken in advance of development

Exploring

From the A9, head into Dunblane on either the B8033 or the A820. Where the two roads meet, by the railway line, take the sharp turn to the west and enter the housing estate at Sunnyside. Take the first

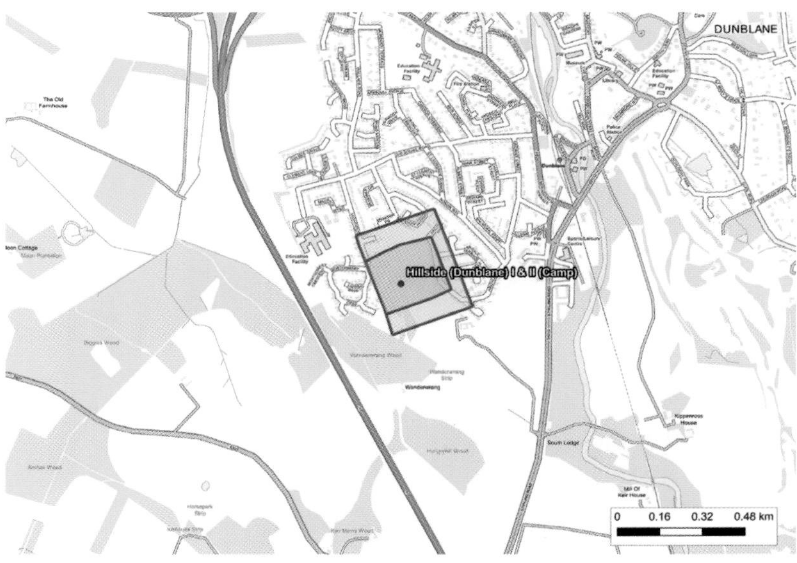

left, then continue up the hill on to Clarendon Place, taking the right-hand fork. At the T-junction, take the left on to Hillside Avenue and continue on, keeping left on Argyle Way until the top of the hill and park at the little cul de sac. Walk on to the parkland at the top end of the site.

To reach the other end of the site, head towards Douglas Place. The ground here is more overgrown, and there is little to see.

Malling

Fort | NN 564 000
Camp I | NN 560 000
Camp II | NS 565 998

Located on the western shore of the Lake of Menteith, the fort and the two camps are built on a gentle rise, around 20 metres above sea level. The immediate topography is not naturally defensive, although the lake itself would have acted as a barrier, but may have been prone to flooding. Even today, part of the fort has been submerged by the increased water levels.

The fort was discovered from the air by Wilson in 1968, with St Joseph following this up with excavation of the site, revealing double ditches as well as gates and an annexe. Subsequent work between 1969 and 1972 revealed the southeastern defences and more of the annexe.

In the early part of the 21st century, Woolliscroft and Hoffmann used their own aerial photographs to identify some of the internal structures of the site. The fort appeared to face northeast, towards the lake, and this was confirmed in 2011 after they undertook extensive resistivity and magnetometry surveys of the site. Their geophysical results clearly traced the defences and the 1st-century eagle-beak gates. They also noted the north and south defensive ditches, which continued in the direction of the water's edge without turning, indicating that the western ditch is covered over by the lake. This led Woolliscroft and Hoffmann to speculate that the ditch to the east, which had been considered by St Joseph to have been part of the annexe, may actually be the eastern defensive ditch and rampart of this fort. If this is true, it would indicate that the fort is actually much bigger than the current estimate of 3.6 hectares. Woolliscroft and Hoffmann's survey work also detected a number of roundhouses to the south of the fort, although it is not known whether these were occupied before or after the Romans were in the area, or during their stay.

Less is known about the camps, although Camp I was originally discovered in 1969 from aerial photographs, and lies to the southeast of the fort. The second camp was only identified from the air in 1981 by Maxwell. The southwest corner of Camp II is linked by a linear ditch, around 280 metres long, to the western corner of the other camp. It is broken by a possible entrance, which indicates that the two camps form an outer defensive work for the fort.

Camp I is presumed to be Flavian because of its Stracathro-type gates. Jones speculates that Camp II may also have had Stracathro-type gates because of an indication of a bank, at an angle, on the northwest entrance to the site.

In the distance is the fort site at Malling.

Key Dates

1968: During an aerial survey of the area, Wilson records cropmarks indicating a Roman fort
1969, 1972: Aerial photographs indicate sections of the fort defences, the presence of an annexe, as well as Camp I. Limited excavations confirm the findings
1981: Camp II is discovered during an aerial survey by Maxwell
2010: Extensive geophysical survey of the fort reveals the defences, internal layout and possible annexe as well as part of Camp I

Exploring

The sites at Malling are not easily accessible or visible. Viewing them involves crossing many fields, passing the edge of the lake, which can be particularly boggy. The camps and fort are clearly marked on the Ordnance Survey map, but these are not recommended to visit due to the difficulty in reaching the sites.

Ochtertyre

Camp | NS 745 982

Located on the south side of the River Teith, opposite the camp at Craigarnhall, this camp was probably guarding an important and strategic fording point over the Teith.

The camp was identified from the air by Maxwell in the early 1980s, although only parts of the defences were seen as cropmarks, including a large section of the southwestern side where the corner turns south-east. A gateway with *titulus* in the southwestern side was also identified. Jones has speculated that this site could be enclosing an area of 8.4 hectares, substantially smaller than the 25 hectares of Craigarnhall across the river. While it seems likely that the two may have been 'partnered', there is no archaeological evidence to date either side, or prove that they were occupied concurrently.

Exploring

Head west from Stirling on the A84, over the ancient crossing at Drip, and carry on for almost a mile. Take the first minor road on the right for about a quarter of a mile after the farm of Blackdub. The site is mainly on the left after passing the entrance to Ochtertyre and Kames Steading on the left (*see* overleaf).

Stirling

Gowan Hill – Possible Fort | NS 790 943

As is the case with Edinburgh, it is often assumed that the volcanic rock on which the castle sits would have been home to a Roman fort. However, the reality

is somewhat different, as the Romans preferred to build fortifications on hillsides or at strategically important locations such as river crossings. The archaeological evidence for a Roman fort or camp underneath Stirling Castle is lacking, although Maitland, in 1757, referred to a Roman station in the area. It may have been that Maitland was talking about the fort on the adjacent Motte Hill, which overlooks Stirling Bridge, although this site is undated, unexcavated and unlikely to be Roman.

The city of Stirling has a number of 'Roman' curiosities that may indicate Roman activity in the area. In 1707, Sir Robert Sibbald, the Astronomer Royal, described a stone on the brow of a hill that was like a garden bench and was inscribed *in excu agit leg II*, which translates as 'the day and night watch of the Second Legion'. The inscription has been debated by archaeologists, with most believing it to be a fake because the form of the letters was not Roman in style. The stone was defaced in the 18th century and has since disappeared into obscurity.

Patches of Roman road are known from the area, passing through St Ninians and Randolphfield, and into King's Park, after which its route is unknown. However, it is believed to run around the base of the Castle Rock, passing the King's Knott, which is unlikely to be Roman in origin. The route of the road passes through Raploch and crosses the Forth somewhere in the vicinity of Old Stirling Bridge, and a number of coins, dating to the Hadrianic and Trajanic periods, have been found along it.

Although a handful of finds from the area are not enough to prove a Roman connection, it seems likely that the army was active in the area, guarding a lost crossing point over the river.

The Other Sites

Netherton (Possible Camp | NN 743 020)

A 19th-century account notes that the field at Netherton is referred to locally as 'Roman Camp'. The account records that some finds, possibly Roman, came from the site and that the unevenness of the ground implies a possible manmade construction beneath the soil.

The site has since been used for gravel extraction and any possible Roman fortifications are likely to have been destroyed.

Chapter 9

FALKIRK

Falkirk is at the heart of Antonine Scotland, with its wall and the associated forts, fortlets and camps across the area. It also has some of the best-preserved Roman sites, such as the fort at Rough Castle with its defensive pits (*lilia*), and some incredible sections of the wall ditch. It also has one of the most enduring mysteries of archaeology, Arthur's O'on, a beehive-shaped structure, which was still standing until the 18th century.

The Falkirk area also plays host to the Big Roman Week, a regular programme of events and activities with a Roman theme taking place across the area in September. Follow @bigromanweek on Twitter for information.

Arthur's O'on (Stenhousemuir)

Building | NS 879 827

The original location of Arthur's O'on is unknown, but it gave its name to Stenhousemuir, a corruption of 'Stonehouse (or Arthur's O'on) Moor'. The beehive-shaped building was built from stone and is believed to have been constructed by the Romans. It existed up until 1743, when it was knocked down by the local landowner who wanted to use the stone to construct a dam on the River Caron. Ironically, the dam lasted only a couple of years before it was washed away in floods.

The building is referred to in a number of early accounts, including one from Nennius (*c.* 800),

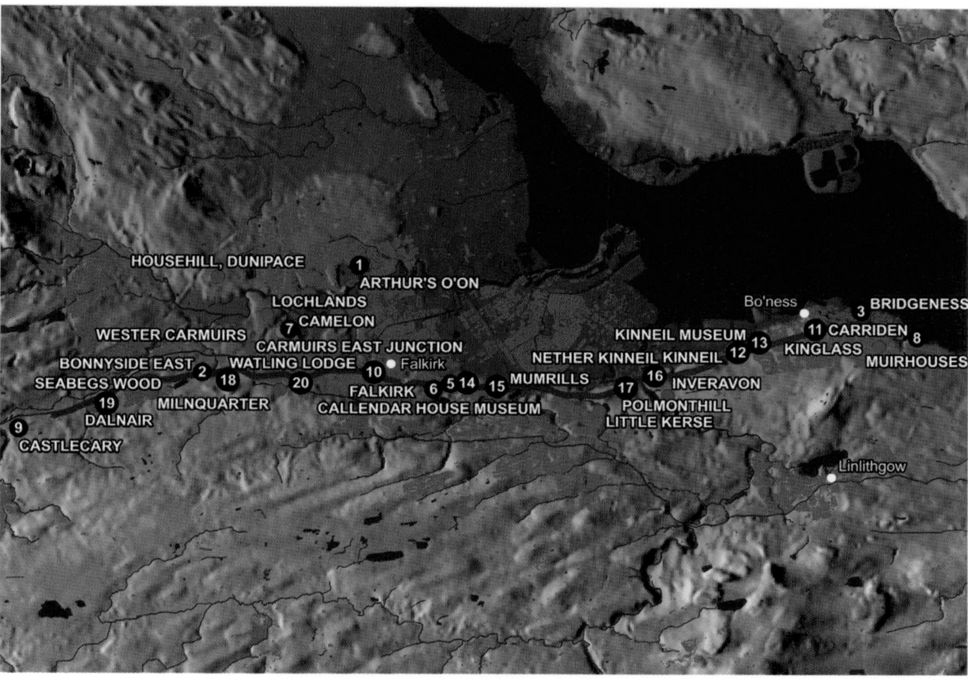

who wrote that, on the bank of the River Caron, the Emperor Carausius erected a 'round house of polished stone'. In 1384, John of Fordoun wrote about it in his *Chronicle of the Scottish Nation*:

> Caesar determined to sail across to Gaul, but being uncertain to his return, he hastily raised a small round chamber, like a pigeon-house, and of no use, apparently, but as a landmark to be built of large smooth stones, without mortar, not far from the mouth of the river Caron; and he wanted to build this little chamber as marking the extreme limit of the Roman possessions to the north-west, almost at the world's end, and as a lasting monument of his military renown.

Arthur's O'on was also recorded by the early antiquarians in some detail. Although there are some differences between the various accounts, they do give archaeologists a good idea of what the building was like. However, they do not explain its purpose, and this is something that has been debated for years. Was it a tomb for a soldier, a temple, or something else? In fact, there is little evidence to confirm that the building was built by the Romans, let alone what it was for. It is not built near a road and the forts at Camelon are around two kilometres away. It is not even known if it was built at the time when the forts were in use.

Attempts have been made to find the site, but these have not been successful. This may well be because the 18th-century landowner, Sir Michael Bruce, did such a thorough job of having it removed that no trace was left behind. Older maps do mark where the site is, but this is probably speculation by old map makers. If they were correct, the area would now be under modern housing.

Bonnyside East and West

Signal Platforms | NS 837 798

Two signal platforms from the Antonine Wall were excavated in the 1950s, but, despite their labelling, it is not clear if beacons were positioned on them. They could equally have been used as a platform to watch people moving back and forth.

Bridgeness

Possible Fort | NT 013 815

In 1709, Sir Robert Sibbald wrote that the remains of a Roman military site existed at Bridgeness but

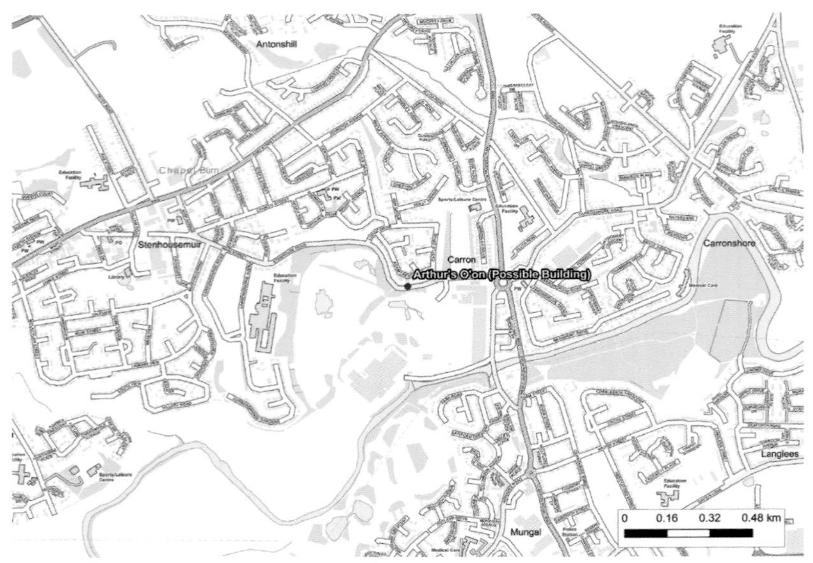

he gave no further details and there is nothing to be seen there today. However, it is where the Bridgeness Distance Slab was discovered, one of the best such examples and now on display in the National Museum of Scotland in Edinburgh. The slab records the construction efforts of soldiers building the wall, and how much that particular detachment had built. A replica of the slab can be seen today at Bridgeness.

In addition to the slab, a number of other pieces of possible Roman stone have been found near by so there could be a Roman fort somewhere out there waiting to be discovered.

Bridgeness, looking north towards the Forth. There may be a fort here somewhere.

Key Dates

1707: Sibbald records the presence of remains of a Roman site at Bridgeness
1868: The Bridgeness slab is found in three pieces
1937: Stones from a Roman arch are discovered in the ground underneath Harbour Road

A reproduction of the Bridgeness slab.

Exploring

Although there are no Roman remains at the site, a modern reproduction of the Bridgeness slab can be seen near the original find spot on Harbour Road, Bo'ness. The original is in the National Museum of Edinburgh.

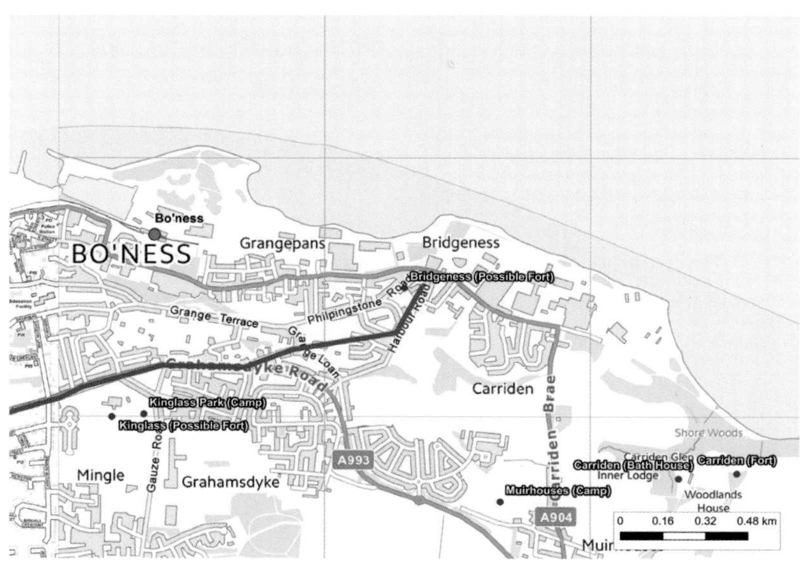

Burnshot

Possible Signal Tower | NT 046 798

Price discovered a mound that he thought may have been a signal tower next to a possible road running from Carriden to an unconfirmed site in the direction of Blackness. There is no trace of the mound today.

Key Dates

1977: Price records the mound with possible Roman origins
1978: Mound may have been destroyed during the laying of pipes in the area

Callendar Park

Possible Building | NS 905 795

Evidence of timber buildings has been found in various areas of the park, although there is some speculation that they may have been post-Roman. However, in 1989, excavation uncovered defensive pits (*lilia*, of which the best-preserved examples are at Rough Castle), which were placed in front of the wall. There was also evidence for a timber tower built into the rampart itself.

Callendar House Museum

Callendar Road, Falkirk, FK1 1YR | Free Entry
www.falkirkcommunitytrust.org/venues/callendar-house
Opening Times | Mon–Sun 10:00–17:00

One of the larger museums on the Antonine Wall, Callendar House has extensive displays on the local history of the wall and surrounding areas as well as the house (Callendar Park) itself. There are several well-preserved sections of the Antonine Wall within the grounds of the house.

Camelon

Forts | NS 863 809
Possible Harbour | NS 86 81

There are two forts at Camelon, apparently connected to one another, linked by a rampart and ditch. Both sites have been subject to industrial development over the years, but luckily there have also been excavations. The artefacts found have indicated occupation dates from the Flavian and Antonine periods, and there is also evidence of pre-Roman activity. The early excavations uncovered potential evidence of a bath house and a possible *mansio* (a Roman hotel). Camelon is a much more complicated site than it first appears, and there may even have been an earlier fort on the site and a settlement near by, although most of the evidence has been destroyed by industrial development.

Key Dates

1899–1900: Both forts are extensively excavated
1975–77, 1979: Excavations undertaken in the South Camp in advance of development
1998: Prior to construction, excavation to the south-east of the South Camp records artefacts and possible ditches belonging to an annexe
2011: Further excavations on the South Camp reveal a number of features and artefacts

Exploring

Although there is nothing to see on the ground, visiting the site can give a sense of its situation in the landscape. A supermarket now lies on the site of the southern fort and there is nothing visible. The northern fort now lies under the golf course, with no recognizable features on the surface.

Carriden

Fort | NT 025 807
Bath House | NT 023 807

Pottery found during excavations at the site in 1945 indicated occupation in the Antonine period. An area to the northeast of the fort is alleged to have been an aqueduct, which was first noted in the 1970s, but archaeologists have not been able to find it. Aerial photographs and geophysical surveying in 2006 have indicated a possible *vicus* to the east of the fort.

Parts of the bath house were uncovered in the

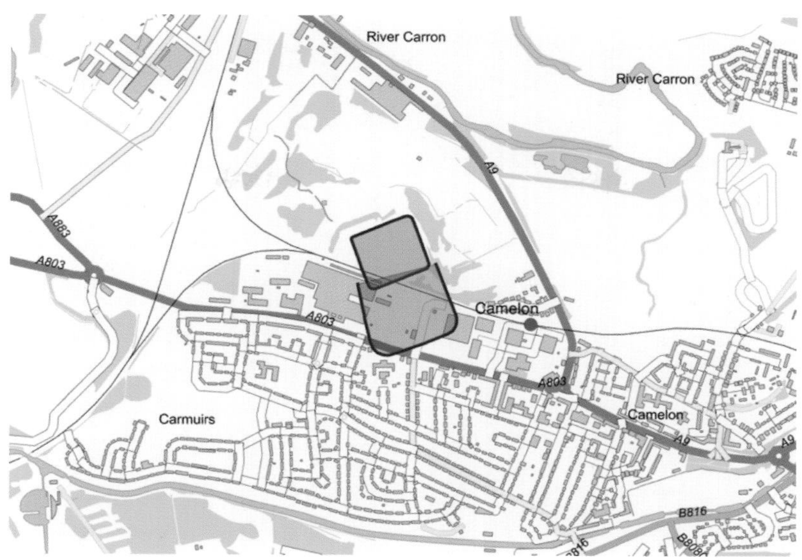

The site of the Roman fort at Carriden.

middle of the 19th century during building works, but it was not until 2006 that it was recorded by archaeologists. They noted that the foundations of the building were still standing and that at some point in its existence it was abandoned. It was then reused in the 2nd century for iron working before a large defensive ditch was put through the site.

Key Dates

1945: St Joseph notes the site from aerial photographs and excavates the eastern defences
1970s: Roman artefacts are uncovered during agricultural works
1977: Aerial photographs record the fort and an adjacent settlement
1994: Excavation outside the western side of the fort uncovers evidence of the annexe
2006: Geophysical survey outside the fort uncovers further evidence of an annexe and a possible building

Castlecary

Fort | NS 789 782

Originally recorded by William Roy in the 18th century, Castlecary was known about from at least the 15th century, but it was not excavated until 1902. The excavations showed that the fort was physically connected to the Antonine Wall and built from stone (one of only two forts to have stone ramparts), and the eastern annexe was also revealed. More recently, in advance of the expansion of the motorway, a geophysical survey of the site took place and showed that there may have been an adjacent *vicus*. Curiously, while most of the finds dated to the Antonine period, there were a handful of pieces that may have come from the Flavian period, although there is no evidence for an earlier fort.

Key Dates

15th century: Early accounts of the fort
1769: The bath house is discovered
1793: Roy records the upstanding remains

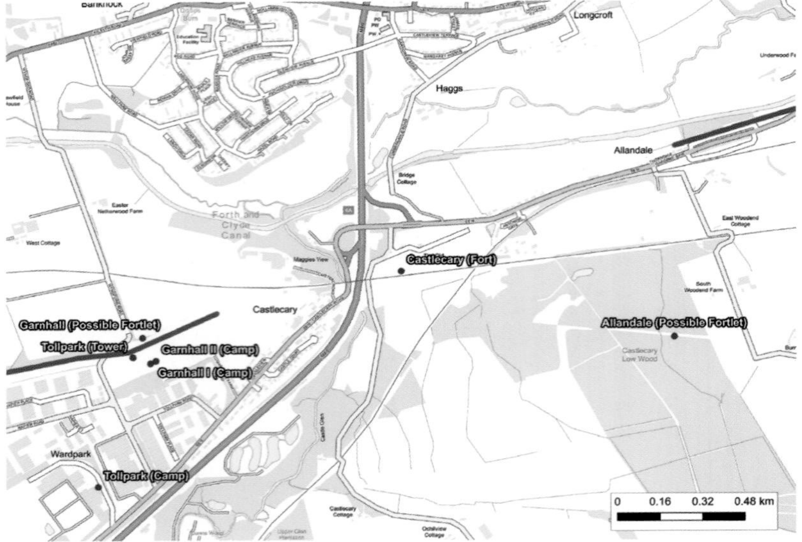

1841: Construction of the Edinburgh–Glasgow railway destroys part of the site
1902: Excavation of the fort and discovery of the annexe
1995: Geophysical survey of the fort and annexe undertaken in advance of potential motorway widening
2006: Further geophysical survey detects a number of features, some possibly associated with the adjacent settlement

Exploring

Located to the east of the village of Castlecary, the site is next to the M90. Take Junction 6A off the M90 (westbound exit) and on to the minor road almost opposite the junction with the B816. The minor road passes under the viaduct and the fort is on the left just before this. The fort is in the adjacent field, with the centre by the small group of trees.

Falkirk

Possible Fort | NS 886 798
Langton – Possible Camp or Fort | NS 89 79
Pleasance – Fort | NS 887 797
South Pleasance Avenue – Fort | NS 885 797

All of the Falkirk sites have been built over, so archaeologists only have occasional glimpses into the town's past. As the forts on the wall are built at fairly regular intervals, archaeologists know there is one lying under the town, and that there are also fortlets and camps, as well as the wall itself awaiting discovery. In 2008, on the site of a residential development, parts of the fort were discovered and it was found that the rampart and ditch of the fort were shared with the wall. Using other pockets of evidence, archaeologists now believe that the fort at Falkirk covered an area of around 0.8 hectares.

The alleged camp or fort at Langton was originally recorded by Sibbald around 1707, although it has not been found since.

Kinglass

Possible Fort | NT 002 810
Kinglass Park – Camp | NT 003 810

Partial cropmarks have indicated that there may be a Roman fort underneath the playing fields of the school, although subsequent re-analysis of the aerial photographs failed to find this. There are some cropmarks indicating the existence of a camp, so it is possible that there was some confusion when interpreting the images.

The fortlet at Kinneil, marked by the wooden posts.

Key Dates

1948: Some of the defences of the camp are seen in aerial photographs
1955: Probing locates the 'missing' sections of camp defences
1998: Watching brief fails to locate the defences originally found by probing

Kinneil

Possible Fort | NS 982 805
Fortlet (Roman) | NS 977 803

In view of the regular spacing between the fortifications on the Antonine Wall, there should be another fort in the vicinity of Kinneil House. However, recent geophysical survey and analysis of the site have drawn a blank. A fortlet was discovered near by in the late 1970s, after the local history group undertook field walking of the site and came across pottery fragments. A follow-up excavation revealed a fortlet with two timber buildings, which may have been barrack blocks. The fortlet site is now marked out by wooden posts showing its exact position.

Key Dates

1732: Horsley notes the remains of a fort at Kinneil
1929: Macdonald suggests there should be a fort in the area and suggests Dean House near by

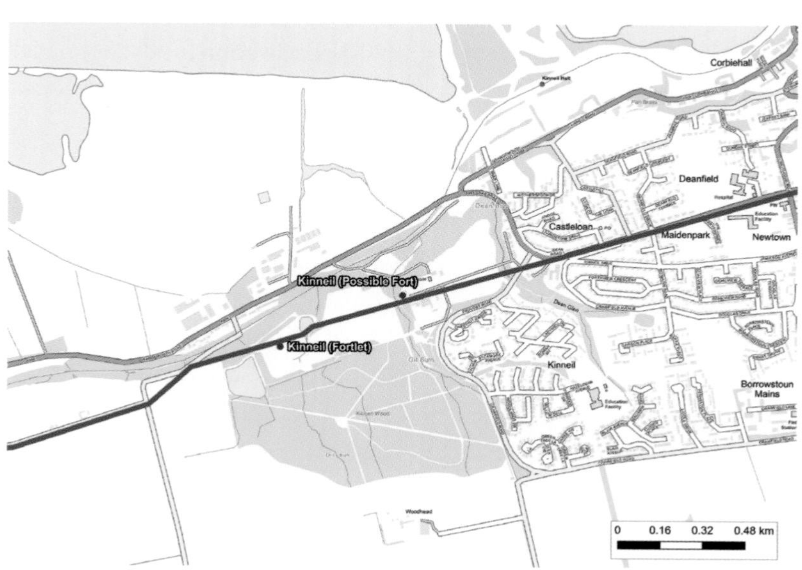

1973: Robertson argues that a fort should exist at Kinneil
1977: Field walking leads to the discovery of a number of Roman artefacts
1978–79: Excavations reveal the fortlet
1980–81: Trial trenching reveals fortlet defences, and then evidence of internal buildings
2008: Geophysical survey of the site

Kinneil Museum

Duchess Anne Cottages, Bo'ness, EH51 0PR | Free Entry
www.falkirkcommunitytrust.org/venues/kinneil-museum | @kinneil
Opening Times | Mon–Sun 12:30–16:00

The museum may be small, but it is deceptively big on the inside with a huge amount of information about the local history of the area as well as the story of the wall and the discovery of the fortlet. It also has a good section on the industrial heritage of the area.

Laurieston

Fortlet | NS 910 795

In 2004, during development work in the garden of a house, a well and a series of timber posts were excavated. These turned out to be part of the southern gate of a fortlet on the Antonine Wall.

Key Dates

2004: During construction works the features of a previously unknown fortlet are uncovered

Mumrills

Fort | NS 918 794

Mumrills is home to the largest fort on the Antonine Wall, and is one of the few sites to have two annexes – one on the eastern side and another adjoining the western defences (although this is now underneath modern housing). Given the size of the site, archaeologists have speculated that it may have been a fort that was occupied by both infantry and cavalry, the extra space being used to house horses. Artefacts have indicated an Antonine date for the site, although there has been speculation of Flavian activity at Mumrills. While no evidence for military structures of the Flavian period has been found within the fort area, excavations in 1996 did uncover Flavian pottery and traces of a timber-framed building.

Key Dates

1923–28: Excavations of the site establish the defences and some of the internal structures, as well as the annexe
1958, 1960: Further excavations of the site
1982: Watching brief on the annexe uncovers artefacts
1994–95: Excavations on the annexe
2004, 2011, 2016: Field walking of the area uncovers large numbers of artefacts, including pottery
2007: Magnetometry and resistivity surveys of the fort note that the fort shows up poorly in the results
2010: Excavation in advance of development locates the southern rampart and *intervallum* road

Exploring

Mumrills is to the east of Polmont and close to the M9. Large parts of the annexe have been developed, but the fort is relatively free from this. Although there are no upstanding remains, the walk around the site, and the field where the fortification was located, is a pleasant one.

The site of the large fort and annexe at Mumrills on the Antonine Wall.

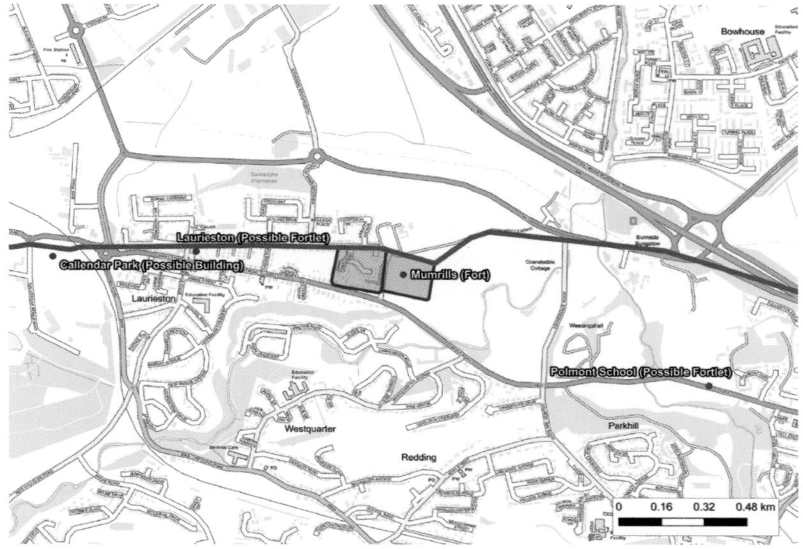

Nether Kinneil

Possible Fortlet | NS 96 80

In the 1980s, William Hanson and Gordon Maxwell analysed the positioning and spacing of all the fortifications along the Antonine Wall and theorized that there were a number of sites, particularly fortlets, still to be found. These included Nether Kinneil, where they predicted there would be another fortlet. However, there were no visible remains at the site and, to date, no excavations or geophysical surveys have taken place here to look for evidence of any structure beneath the soil. (*See* the section on the Antonine Wall.)

Polmonthill

Possible Fort | NS 948 794
Camp | NS 9471 7904

Anne Robertson suggested that there should be a fort in the vicinity of Polmonthill, arguing that it would have been needed to guard the crossing point of the River Avon, although there is a fortlet across the river at Inveravon. No trace of the fort has been found yet.

The camp, along with an annexe, was discovered in the 1940s. All the defences except those on the northeast side have been traced.

Key Dates

1951: The camp is photographed from the air
1964: Further aerial photographs of the site by St Joseph show the camp and an annexe
1974: Robertson suggests there should be a fort in the area, to guard a crossing over the River Avon

Rough Castle

Antonine Wall Remains, Fort and Defences | NS 843 798

Rough Castle is one of the most impressive Roman sites in Scotland. Not only are there impressive

The Antonine Wall at Rough Castle.

The only visible example of *lilia* in Britain.

> ## *Lilia*
>
> *Lilia* are a type of defensive pit used by the Romans to provide an extra layer of security against anyone attacking the wall from the north. The pits were filled with thorny plants, which were covered over with leaves. It was a pretty nasty form of defence; anyone running towards the wall who failed to notice them would fall in, severely injuring themselves. There are a handful of other examples of *lilia* elsewhere along the Antonine Wall and Hadrian's Wall, but they are unknown on sites before this period and have not been found elsewhere in Scotland.

stretches of wall and ditch, but it is also possible to see the remains of the fort and annexe, and the only example of *lilia* or defensive pits on display in Britain.

The fort itself is visible on the ground, with the early excavations revealing the granary, administrative buildings and barracks, while the bath house was uncovered in the annexe. At the eastern end of the fort annexe are three ditches. While one is certainly associated with the fort that is seen today, some archaeologists have speculated that their peculiar shape points to an earlier fort underneath. Excavations in the 1950s attempted to discover if there was a Flavian site, but failed to find any evidence to support this.

Exploring

The Rough Castle site is to the west of Bonnybridge and well signposted from the village. Follow the signs and you will come to the end of a small track where you can park. Go through the gate and follow the path. The fort itself is about half a mile from the car park, but there is lots to explore in the park, with plenty of interpretive signs around the area. Good footwear is a must, as the path can be uneven and muddy.

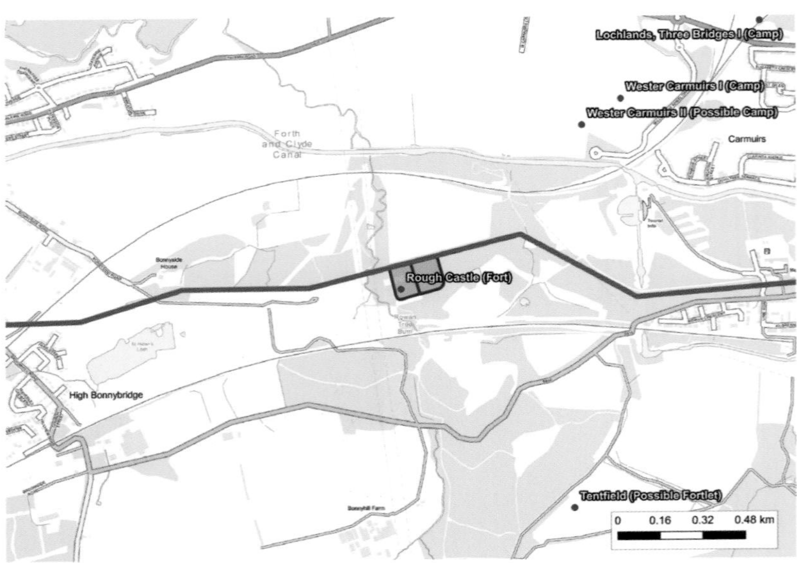

A small stretch of the Antonine Wall and its ditch are visible at Seabegs Wood.

Seabegs Wood

Fortlet | NS 8116 7920

Seabegs is another stretch of visible wall and ditch, along with a fortlet. While it may not be as impressive as Rough Castle, it still gives a good indication of the structure, with the remains of the wall being visible as a low mound. The fortlet was not located until 1977, and excavated shortly after. The archaeologists found that it was constructed at the same time as the Antonine Wall, along with postholes for the internal buildings.

Key Dates

Pre-1977: Pottery finds from fields indicate a possible Roman site near by

1977: Excavation of the area uncovers the fortlet, including two defensive ditches

2001, 2003: Watching brief fails to find any Roman artefacts

Exploring

Seabegs is owned by the National Trust for Scotland and entry is free. It lies to the west of Bonnybridge. Head westwards on Seabegs Road, and the site is on the left at the start of the wooded area. There is a tiny layby where you can park. The fortlet is to the west, beyond the wood.

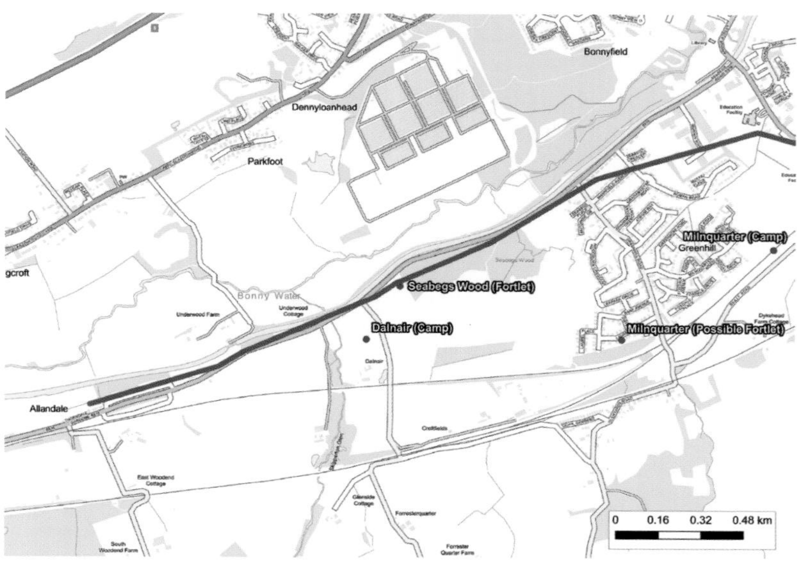

The impressively deep ditch at Watling Lodge.

Watling Lodge

Antonine Wall Ditch and Fortlet | NS 862 797

Watling Lodge is one of the better-preserved sections of the Antonine Wall, with the ditch clearly visible. The fortlet, along with a gateway through the wall, was discovered in 1894 when it was excavated. It was excavated again in the 1970s and 1986, confirming that it covered an area of 0.03 hectares and had stone foundations.

Key Dates

1894: The fortlet is discovered revealing the south and east ramparts

1972–74: Further excavations reveal the defences and layout of the fortlet

The Other Sites

Carmuirs East Junction (Possible Camp | NS 859 810)

A number of camps were built near Carmuirs. One camp, at the east junction, was recorded as a ditch with a corner. It was excavated but no Roman material was found, indicating that it may not actually be Roman.

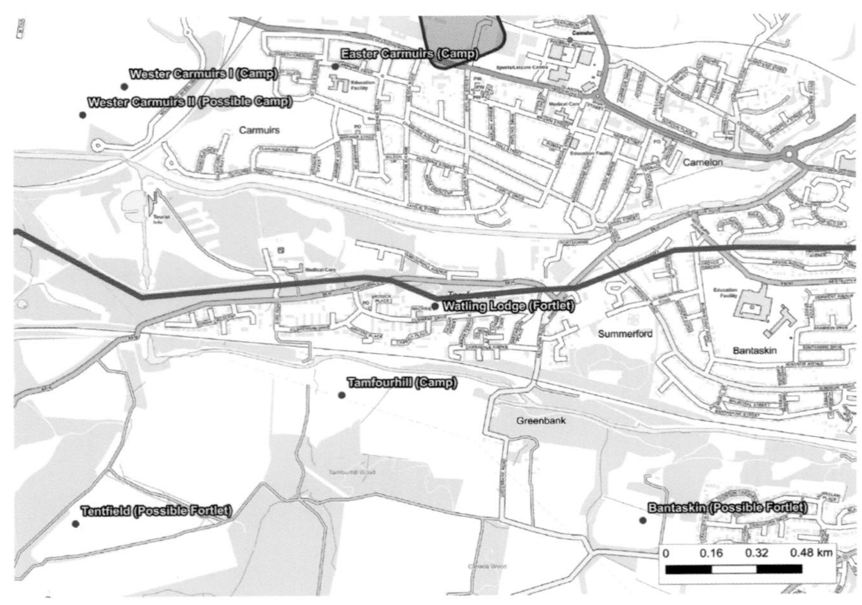

Dalnair (Camp | NS 810 790)

Recorded in 1957, this camp is close to the Antonine Wall. Parts of the defences have been noted, but not enough to give the approximate size of the site.

Househill (Dunipace) (Camp | NS 843 825)

Located near the numerous camps at Lochlands, Dunipace is one of the largest sites in Scotland, at 53 hectares. It is possible that, because of the size, it was built during the Severan campaigns, although no artefacts were found during excavation.

Inveravon (Camp I | NS 958 796, Camp II | NS 961 793, Camp III | NS 961 793)

Overlooking the River Avon, the camps were identified from the air by St Joseph. As the camps overlap each other, it is not clear which was built first.

Little Kerse (Camp | NS 943 789)

Identified from the air in the 1940s, the camp at Little Kerse is now partially underneath a golf course, while the M9 covers the southern side. An annexe is attached to the south end of the fort, and was excavated in the 1960s, giving an Antonine date.

Lochlands (Camp I | NS 854 819, Camp II | NS 853 816, Camp III | NS 856 816, Camp IV | NS 854 815, Camp V | NS 854 814, Camp VI | NS 853 812, Bogton Camp | NS 854 812) and Lochlands, Three Bridges (Camp I | NS 858 810, Camp II | NS 857 810, Camp III | NS 857 809, Camp IV | NS 858 809, Camp V | NS 857 808)

Lochlands appears to have been an important location for the Romans, with at least seven camps in the immediate vicinity, and more possible camps, which have not been confirmed through investigation yet, along with the forts at Camelon. Unsurprisingly, with so many camps in one place, dating them is not straightforward because they overlap in places and some of the defences are not clearly defined. However, there is evidence for Flavian and Antonine occupation and some indication of activity during the reign of Hadrian.

Milnquarter (Camp | NS 825 793)

Originally recorded from the air, this camp has not been surveyed or extensively excavated, so little is known about it.

Muirhouses (Camp | NT 016 806)

Muirhouses is the location for a 2.2-hectare camp that is located to the south of the presumed line of the Antonine Wall. The wall's precise route is unknown in this area.

Tamfourhill (Camp | NS 859 794)

Discovered from the air, it has been suggested that the camp was constructed to house soldiers while they were building the Antonine Wall.

Wester Carmuirs (Camp | NS 851 805 – Possible Camp | NS 850 804)

The camp at Wester Carmuirs is fairly close to the Lochlands complex of sites, and may have been part of that grouping. Initially discovered in the 1950s, it has not yet been excavated so it cannot be confirmed whether it is related to, or contemporary with, the Lochlands sites. Cropmarks have also indicated that there may be a further camp awaiting discovery.

Chapter 10

DUNBARTONSHIRE

On the northern side of the Clyde, Dunbartonshire has a range of Roman sites, including the western end of the Antonine Wall, which stretches across central Scotland. While many of the sites in the area date to the Antonine period, and are linked to the wall, there are tantalizing glimpses of earlier Roman sites underneath these. One thing is for sure: the Romans knew the strategic importance of being able to control the Forth–Clyde isthmus long before they built the wall.

Auchendavy

Fort | NG 677 749

One of the earliest recorded forts, Auchendavy was visited by early antiquarians such as John Horsley and William Roy. As a result, archaeologists have a good idea of what the site was like prior to the construction of the Forth–Clyde canal in the 18th century, which destroyed part of the southern defences of the site. For example, Horsley noted a triple ditch and rampart surrounding the site, while Roy noted the well-preserved defences and Roman road through the site, neither of which are visible today. Geophysical surveys of the site have indicated a possible annexe to the immediate northeast of the fort, although this has yet to be confirmed by excavation.

Key Dates

1732: Horsley visits the site and notes several features including a triple-ditch defensive system. This later proves to be inaccurate for some sections of the defences

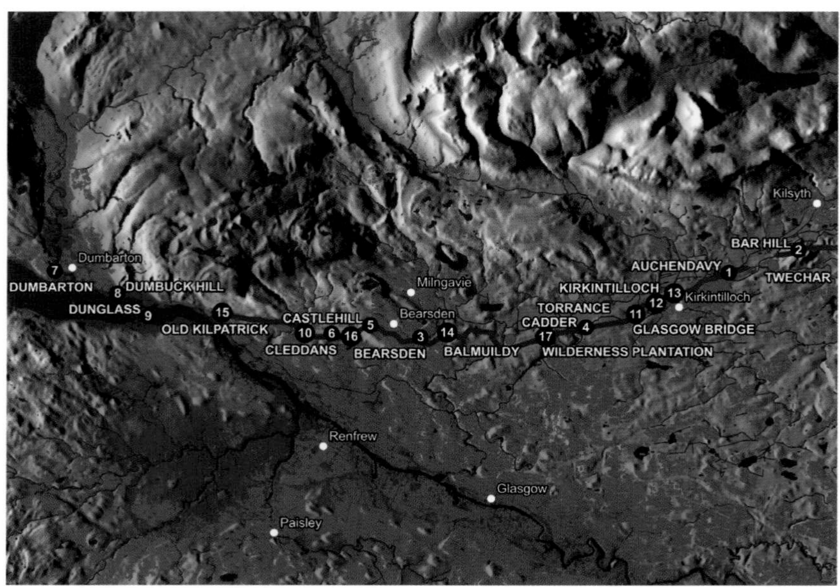

The northern half of the fort at Auchendavy.

1790: Roy records the site, including planning the visible remains
1793: Construction of the Forth–Clyde canal destroys part of the southern defences
1951: St Joseph flies over the site and records the eastern and southern defences
1984: A ground survey of the site is undertaken
1998: Geophysical survey of the fort plots the ditches
1999: Watching brief reveals ditches and pottery
2001: Further geophysical survey
2003: Watching brief reveals a single ditch on the western side of the fort, confirming earlier aerial photographs
2006, 2007: Geophysical surveys of the fort and immediate surrounds

Exploring

The farm buildings, which were in existence when Roy was on the site in 1793, still exist but have been converted into housing. Across the road, the edge of the fort platform is vaguely discernible in the field. The site has excellent views to the west and, to a lesser extent, to the east, giving a good idea of why it was chosen by the Romans.

The fort is to the north of Kirkintilloch, on the A803. As the road heads out of Kirkintilloch, take the right-hand fork on to the B8023, which follows the line of the Military Way. After about a third of a mile, the road goes through the fort, with the converted buildings on the right, and a farmhouse on the left.

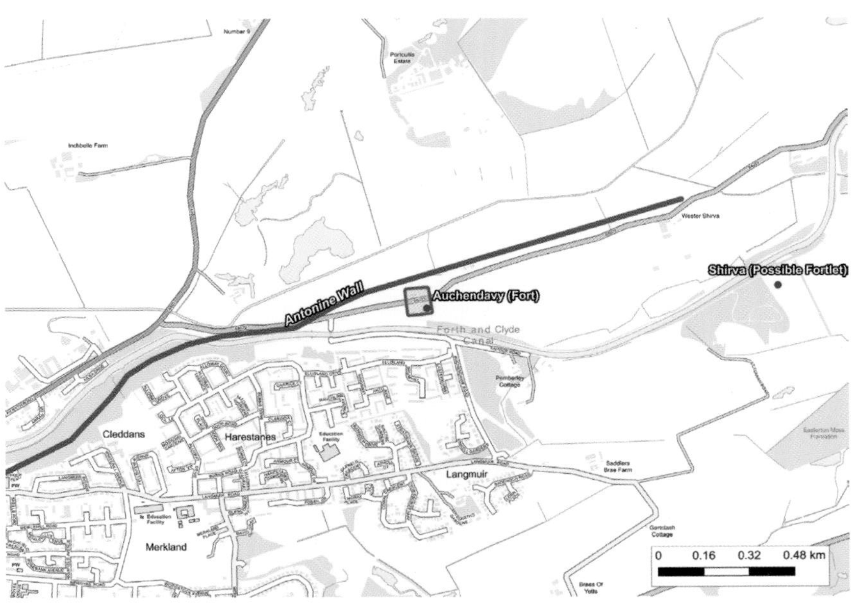

Bar Hill

Fort | NS 707 759
Camp | NS 707 757

Getting to the top of Bar Hill involves a steep walk, but it is worth it to see the magnificent views to the Clyde in the west and, on a good day, to the Forth in the east. A key part of the Antonine Wall, Bar Hill is the highest fort in Scotland, and was noted in the late 18th century.

The first excavations of the camp took place in 1903 by a Mr Whitelaw, and this was probably prompted by the discovery of an altar and parts of buildings that had been uncovered. Whitelaw speculated that within the larger camp was a smaller camp, and he uncovered evidence of postholes, pottery and ballista balls, as well as a number of coins. He also speculated that the smaller camp was constructed under Agricola, although coins of Commodus (AD 177–192) were recovered.

The fort was excavated by Macdonald and Park (1902–05), uncovering the remains of the *principia*, granaries, water tank and bath house (the foundations of which can still be seen today). The excavators also found evidence of a wooden barrack block, with the stumps of the original posts still in place.

Inscriptions from the site, along with evidence of arrowheads and bows, indicate that it was occupied by the First Cohort of Baetasians, and at another time by the First Cohort of Hamians (Syrian archers). Bar Hill does not have an annexe, although one ditch was located to the south of the site, and another to the west; neither were excavated and some archaeologists believe they may have been protective ditches for a settlement. There was also evidence of a ditch underneath the main site, pre-dating it. At the time, the archaeologists suggested that it may have belonged to the Flavian period, although subsequent excavation in the 1970s failed to find any datable artefacts.

Exploring

The site covers a wide area and, as it is on a hill, there are a few parts that are hidden away. The *principia* is at the highest point in the fort and in the centre. To the northeast of the *principia* is the bath house, just over the brow of the hill. To the east, just outside the fort, is the actual summit of Bar Hill – a bit of a steep climb. At the top is a trig point, which offers the best spot for views of the area. This hill was originally believed to have been a small hillfort, with a possible Roman tower or signal station on it (although there is no hard evidence for this). There is a steep, downhill path to the north of the summit, at the bottom of which is the ditch of the Antonine Wall. The ditch runs off to the east, snaking its way to Croy Hill in the distance. Follow the ditch to the west (the remains of the wall in the ditch are modern), and you will join the fort, which used the wall ditch as part of its northern defences.

To get to Bar Hill, head south on the B8023 from Kilsyth, turning left before the road crosses the

The interior of the fort at Bar Hill.

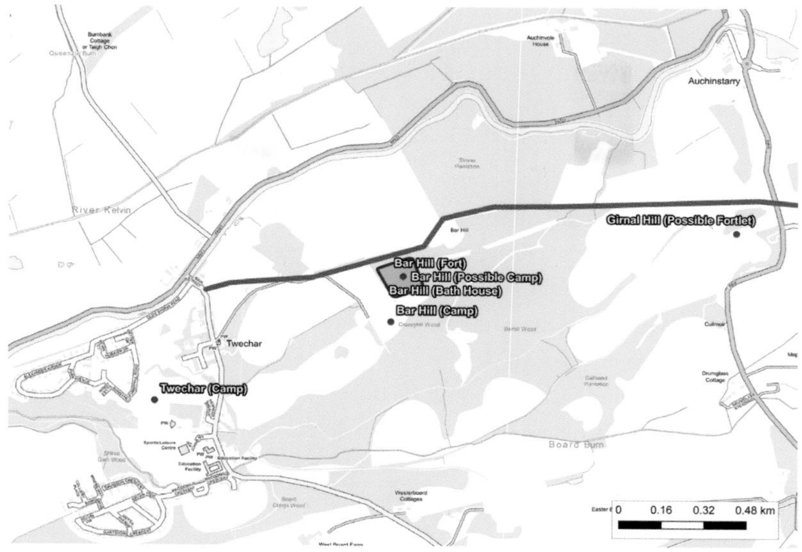

Forth–Clyde Canal (there is a small sign marked Bar Hill). Follow the road alongside the canal for a mile and take the first left over the water. At the top of the rise, there is a small industrial estate on the right (where you can park), and the path up Bar Hill on the left. The track is about a mile in length and very rugged and steep in places. After the first 30 metres, there is a pillbox on the left, dating to the Second World War which shows that the hill had remained of strategic importance. Once you are over the steepest part of the hill, the fort is to the east as a clump of trees. On the right-hand side of the track, opposite the signposted path to the fort, is a Second World War fuel supply tank.

The weather and terrain are unpredictable on Bar Hill, so stout footwear and waterproofs are recommended.

Bearsden

Fort & Bath House | NS 546 720

Although the fort is no longer visible at Bearsden, the bath house is worth seeing as the remains are amongst the finest examples of this building type in Britain. The site was noted as early as the 17th century, but when Roy came to record it in 1755, he noted that the fort had been significantly eroded by ploughing. It was not until the 1970s that Bearsden was extensively excavated. These excavations, by David Breeze, lasted eight years and provided a wealth of information about Bearsden, including two periods of Roman occupation.

The original plan for the site had included a large timber fort, and there is evidence that the *principia* and at least one granary had been constructed before the plan was changed. Making use of the defences, Bearsden was then divided into two parts, creating a smaller fort and an annexe. The reason for these alterations is a mystery, but there were inevitable consequences for the rest of the fort layout. The annexe was now located where the *praetorium* (the

The foundations of the bath house at Bearsden.

commander's house) itself had originally been located to the site of the original granary. This led to the dismantling of the bath house and its relocation to the position it is in today.

To date, no evidence has been uncovered of a settlement around the site, despite geophysical surveys and watching briefs on areas under development.

The bath house was both extended and developed while it was in use, including the installation of new floors and the inclusion of a hot dry room. It was constructed as a long, rectangular building with three wings off the main building. Most of it is now on display, with timber posts marking where the internal walls would have been. The Antonine Wall would have been to the north of the site and now lies underneath the flats that are visible in the images. The fort would have been on the other side of the road, but there is nothing to be seen today.

Exploring

The bath house at Bearsden is very easy to find, located on Roman Road. Heading east from the town on Roman Road, the site is on the left surrounded by flats. Parking is restricted in the area, so it is easier to park in one of the town car parks and head to the bath house on foot.

Cadder

Fort | NS 616 725

The fort at Cadder would have been physically linked to the Antonine Wall, using the structure as its own northern defences (as at Bar Hill). The site was recorded by Horsley in 1732, but not excavated until the early 20th century. Archaeologists originally thought that the style of the gates indicated that a Flavian-era date, but in light of more recent work on other sites, this seems unlikely and it probably dates to the Antonine period. Excavation of the 1.4-hectare site revealed evidence of timber internal buildings, and the possibility of reconstruction on at least two occasions.

The site was destroyed by quarrying in the 1940s.

Key Dates

1732: First mention of the site at Cadder
1913: An initial excavation takes place confirming the Roman origin of the site
1929–1932: Extensive excavations take place revealing the defences and many internal features
1957: Archaeologists visit the site to confirm the fort has been destroyed by quarrying
2008: Excavations searching for the bath house and prompted by aerial photographs fail to find any evidence of Roman activity

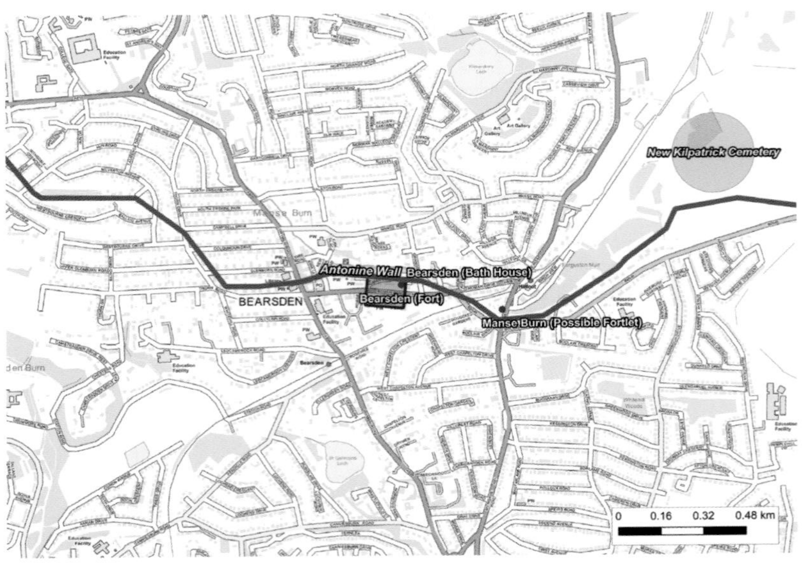

Castlehill

Fort & Possible Fortlet | NS 524 726

First discovered when stone remains were dug up on the site, the location of this fort was confirmed using subsequent aerial photography and fieldwork. Pottery finds have indicated an Antonine date for Castlehill.

There is an indication from early accounts of a smaller structure adjacent to the fort, attached to the Antonine Wall, but outside of the fort defences. This is yet to be explored further on the ground to confirm whether or not it is a fortlet.

Key Dates

1826: An altar is found on the hill
1847: Part of a column is discovered at Castlehill
1934: Based on these finds, Macdonald speculates that there may be a Roman fort here
1951: St Joseph, flying over the site, confirms a series of defensive features
1970s: Various Roman pottery fragments are discovered on the site
1980: Using early accounts of the area, Keppie suggests that there may have been an Antonine Wall fortlet outside of the area covered by the fort
2008: Geophysical survey of the fort

Cleddans

Fortlet | NS 508 722

Partially excavated in 1979, the fortlet was found to have been constructed before the Antonine Wall builders had reached Cleddans. Once they had, it was joined on to the wall.

Key Dates

1979: Limited excavations at Cleddans locate the fortlet

Dumbarton

Possible Site | NS 39 75
Possible Harbour | NS 39 75

Irvine, writing in 1686, tells of the remains of several Roman fortifications on the north side of the Clyde. At Dumbarton there was said to be a great Roman fort by the town, as well as other remains near Dumbarton Castle. More recently, there is a suggestion that the Military Way, the road running alongside the Antonine Wall, extends as far as Dumbarton. The River Clyde would have been fordable in the area (*see* 'Dumbuck Hill') and such a crossing would have needed guarding. Given the strategic advantage of the site, commanding good views both up and down the Clyde, there may well have been a Roman fort somewhere near Dumbarton.

Dumbuck Hill

Possible Site | NS 42 74

Irvine's 1686 account claims that there was a fort at Dumbuck Hill as well as at Dumbarton. If there was one here, it would have been perfectly positioned to oversee the fort over the Clyde.

Dunglass

Possible Site | NS 43 73

Irvine's account of 1686, which mentions Dumbarton and Dumbuck Hill, also suggests that there was a site at Dunglass, which was connected to the Antonine Wall defences. Writing in 1893, Bruce goes even further, claiming that there is a traditional local belief that the Antonine Wall actually terminated at Dunglass rather than Old Kilpatrick. There has never been any evidence uncovered on the ground to support this assertion.

Duntocher

Fort & Fortlet | NS 495 726
Bath House | NS 494 727

Although the fort was recorded by early antiquarians, including Horsley and Roy, their plans differed, and the origins and layout of the site were confirmed only by excavations in the 20th century. Robertson's work revealed that the fort was actually smaller than

Looking into the fortlet at Duntocher. The grass on the fortlet is kept cut short to mark the outline.

expected, but next to a large annexe on the western side, which may have explained the discrepancies in the early accounts.

In the 1970s, excavations revealed the stone foundations of the fortlet (believed to be the earliest structure at Duntocher), with the fort adjacent. Work on the latter failed to find the southern gate, indicating that it may not have had one. This would have been unusual for a fort on the Antonine Wall. The bath house was located in 1775, to the west of the fort and next to the Duntocher Burn. It was excavated in the 1970s and found to be well preserved, before being back-filled to protect it.

Key Dates

1775: Workers uncover the remains of the bath house
1933: Clarke undertakes limited excavations of the fort site
1948–51: Extensive excavations of the fort
1977–78: Excavations locate the foundations of the fortlet
1978: A possible section of the bath house and pottery are recovered
2004: Exploratory excavations take place but fail to locate Roman remains
2016: Geophysical survey of the fort, annexe and fortlet shows a number of features including a triple ditch for the former

Exploring

Duntocher is easily visited, and worth it for the commanding views from the site. Both the fort and fortlet are within Golden Hill Park, with the outline of the fortlet traceable in the grass.

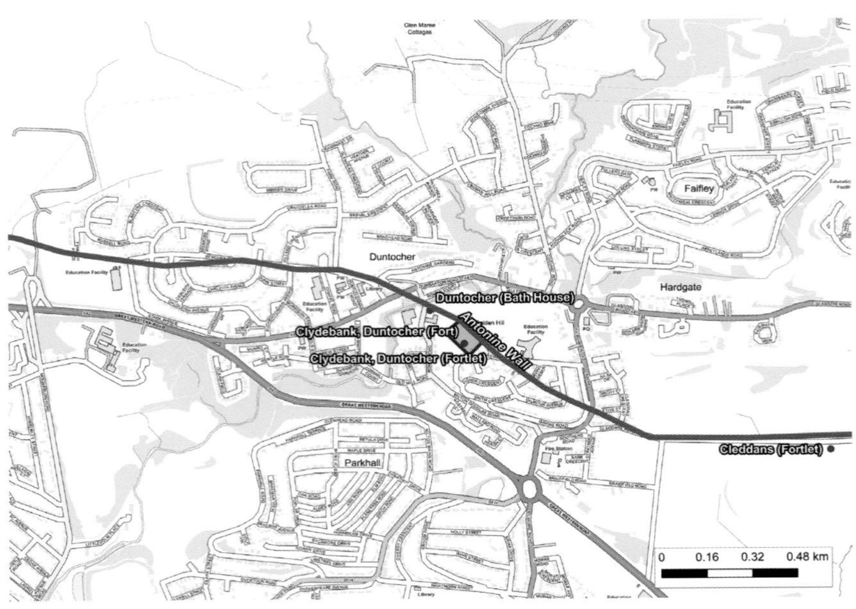

Glasgow Bridge

Fortlet | NS 63662 73097

Identified from the air, the fortlet appears to have been physically joined to the Antonine Wall, and is similar in design to the fortlet at Wilderness Plantation. It was excavated in the 1970s.

Key Dates

1955: The fortlet is first recorded in aerial photographs
2008: Extensive geophysical surveys of the site record the defences

Kirkintilloch

Fort & Fortlet | NS 651 739
Hillhead Fortlet | NS 66 74

In the middle of the 20th century, construction around the site uncovered remains of buildings and roads, indicating the presence of the fort, which had been partly destroyed by the building of a medieval peel. Further work in the 1970s and 1980s uncovered additional ditches (which may have belonged to an annexe), as well as evidence for occupation during the Antonine period.

Key Dates

1914: Macdonald excavates in parkland and discovers a number of Roman artefacts
Early 20th century: Further finds from the area lead Macdonald to conclude there is an undiscovered Roman site in the vicinity
1953–61: Excavations reveal internal structures indicating a fort nearby
1975: Parts of the ditch are located during development work
1978–79: Further excavations confirm more details of the defences but raise the question of whether the site is a fort or annexe
2006: Geophysical survey fails to confirm the existence of a Roman fortification

Kirkintilloch – Auld Kirk Museum

Auld Kirk Museum, Cowgate, Kirkintilloch, G66 1HN | Free Entry
www.edlc.co.uk/heritage-arts/auld-kirk-museum
Opening Times | Tues–Sat 10:00–13:00 & 14:00–17:00

A small museum housing artefacts and information on the Antonine Wall, in particular the fort and fortlet at Kirkintilloch.

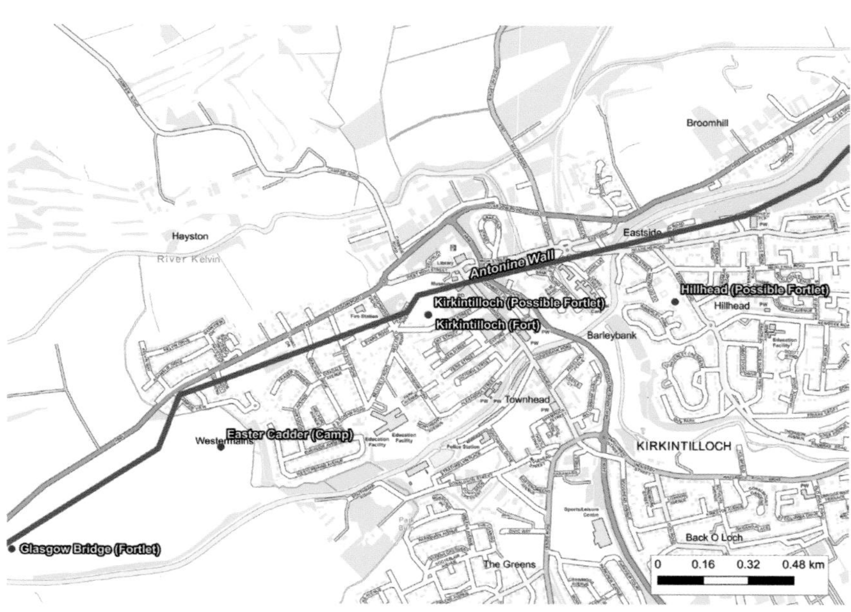

Foundations of the Antonine Wall visible in New Kilpatrick Cemetery.

New Kilpatrick Cemetery

Antonine Wall Remains | NS 556 723

New Kilpatrick Cemetery is the surprising location for two well-preserved sections of the Antonine Wall. Uncovered in 1902 and 1922, the exposed stretches show the stone foundations of the wall, on top of which would have been placed rectangular blocks of turf, probably to a height of at least three metres.

The ingenuity of Roman engineering is visible in the construction. The foundations are edged with rectangular-cut yellow sandstone (now grey due to weathering), while in one section a drainage channel or culvert is visible, letting water flow from one side of the wall to the other without affecting the turf on top.

Exploring

New Kilpatrick Cemetery is located on Boclair Road, to the east of Bearsden (a ten-minute drive from Bearsden bath house). There is limited parking on the main road. On-street parking can be found in the streets opposite the cemetery.

Both sites are easy to locate within the cemetery. At the entrance, take the right-hand fork and follow the path, then take the first left. The first section is towards the top of the hill. Next, continue on the path, keeping right and continuing around the upper part of the cemetery. The second set of foundations are on the left as you head uphill on the path, near where the routes meet.

Old Kilpatrick

Fort | NS 460 731
Mount Pleasant – Possible Fortlet | NS 46 73

The fort at Old Kilpatrick marks the end of the Antonine Wall (*see* 'Dunglass'), although any evidence for this, and for the fort, has long since disappeared. The end of the wall was destroyed in the late 18th century during the construction of the Forth–Clyde canal, while at the same time, the bath house was uncovered. It was not until 1913 that Macdonald confirmed the existence of the fort during excavations, while further work was undertaken by Miller (1923–24) in advance of housing being built on the site. Miller confirmed the existence of the six gates of the fort (1.8 hectares) and the original location of the bath house, within a southern annexe. Excavations also took place in the early 1990s and again in 1999 in advance of further development.

While neither end of the Antonine Wall has ever been located, archaeologists agree that the western end would have been at the fort at Old Kilpatrick.

More foundations of the Antonine Wall. A culvert, constructed to let water run through the wall, can be seen towards the back of the visible remains.

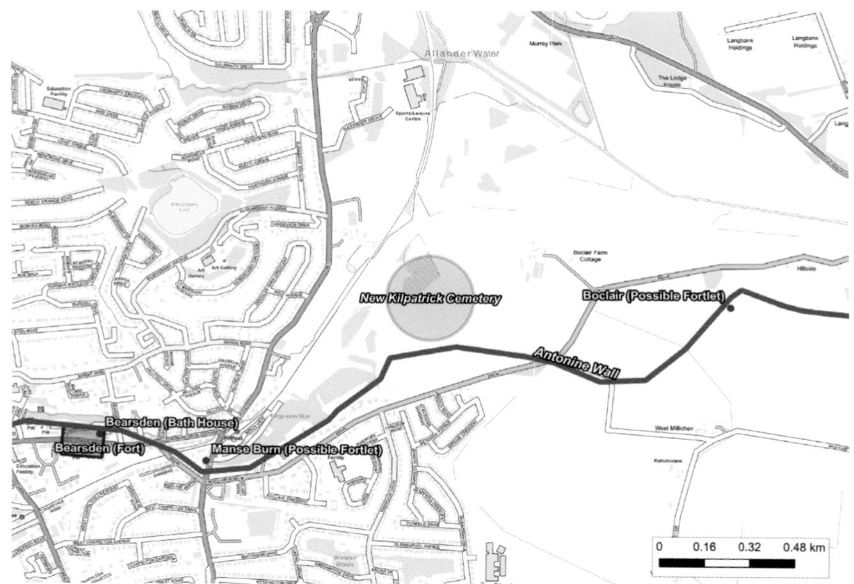

Canal construction has destroyed any remains, but it seems unlikely that the fort would have been the only structure at the end of the wall. Perhaps the remains of a harbour are lying in the River Clyde awaiting future discovery.

Exploring

Follow the signs for Old Kilpatrick, turning off the A82 by the Erskine Bridge. Head west, through the town, and look for the bus depot is on the left. The Antonine Wall and Old Kilpatrick fort are underneath the depot and the housing estate to the east of the site. After the depot, take the first left, and left again when facing the canal. Park by the bus depot and take the footbridge over the canal, which is on top of the suspected line of the wall.

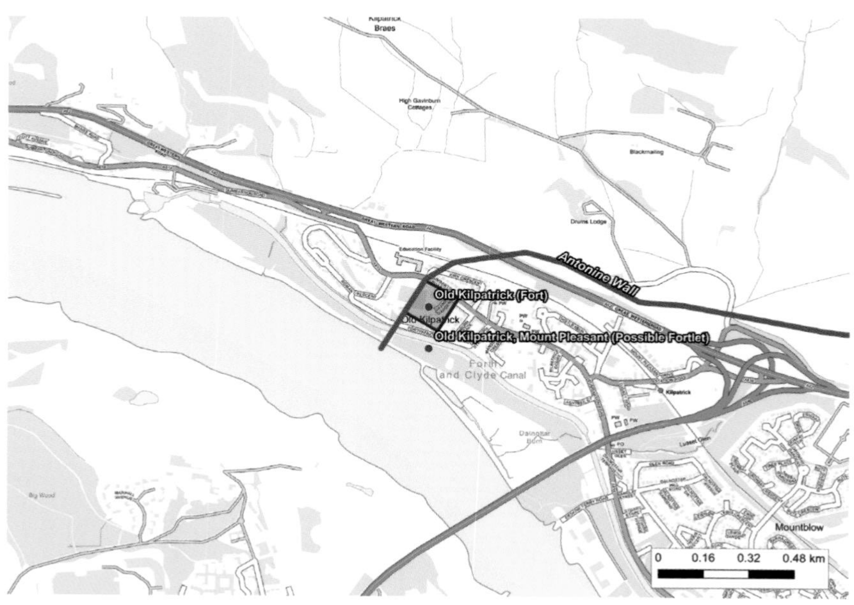

Peel Glen

Possible Fortlet | NS 521 725
Possible Bridge | NS 522 724

Horsley, who visited Peel Glen in the 18th century, recorded the visible remains of a fortlet. However, Roy, who was writing 60 years later, said there was little to be seen. It is likely that, if there was a fortlet at Peel Glen, it would have been part of the Antonine Wall.

The remains of a bridge, not far from the fortlet, were recorded by both Gordon and Horsley, while Roy speculated that the visible stones were part of a paved causeway or ford.

Wilderness Plantation

Fortlet | NS 598 721
Wilderness East Possible Enclosure | NS 600 721

Identified from aerial photographs, the fortlet seems to have been constructed at the same time as the Antonine Wall. It was extensively excavated in the 1970s, with evidence for a timber barrack block being uncovered. There was further evidence that the timber structures were removed and the floor was cobbled at a later date. While the fortlet was dated to the Antonine period, there was also evidence of later occupation of the site, during the 15th and 16th centuries.

The enclosure was identified from aerial photography, but it was destroyed by quarrying in the 1960s, so it is not clear to archaeologists whether this was an annexe or another camp.

The Other Sites

Balmuildy (Camp | NS 586 722)

Covering an area of 4.7 hectares, the camp at Balmuildy is located just to the north of the Antonine Wall. It has a confirmed annexe on the northeastern side, with the possibility of another on the south-eastern extremity.

Easter Cadder (Camp | NS 64400 73470)

At 1.4 hectares, Easter Cadder camp is smaller than most similar structures. Archaeologists have speculated that this is because it was used to house soldiers constructing the Antonine Wall.

Torrance (Possible Camp | NS 613 741)

Torrance was originally recorded by Gordon in 1726 as a large, square 20-hectare camp surrounded by a single ditch. Rebecca Jones has suggested a Flavian date for the site, given the location of the camp to the north of the Antonine Wall.

Twechar (Camp | NS 698 754)

Twechar was identified from the air in 1976. While parts of the camp have been recorded, indicating a size of 2.1 hectares, most of it is likely to be underneath modern housing.

PART FOUR: THE WEST OF SCOTLAND

Chapter 11

GLASGOW

GLASGOW, LIKE EDINBURGH, IS A CITY THAT has generally failed to give up its Roman secrets. While the Antonine Wall passes through its northern suburbs, there is very little evidence of physical remains closer to the city. Some finds have cropped up, though. In 1876, workmen digging a trench through Glasgow Green uncovered a complete Samian bowl dating to the Antonine period, while over fifty coins have been found from across the city. Given that the Romans were active in the surrounding areas, it seems likely that they would have taken advantage of a place that was to prove important in later years because of its location next to the River Clyde. Whether or not there are remains under Glasgow is a question to which the answer may never really be known.

Balmuildy

Fort | NS 581 716
Bridge | NS 580 718

The fort at Balmuildy has been known about since at least the 18th century, when Gordon visited the site and noted the visible defences, which were then recorded by Roy in 1793. However, by 1853 one antiquarian had written that the site had been radically

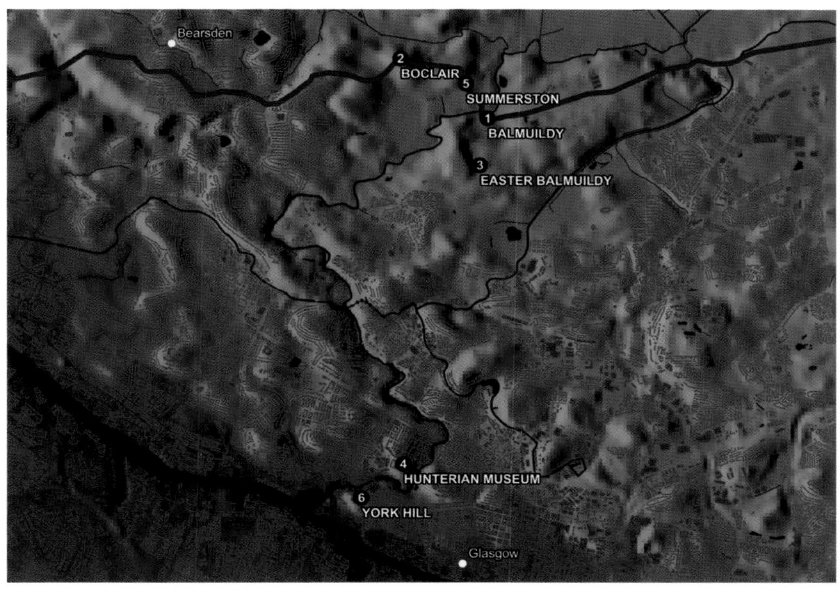

developed by Charles Stirling, who had ploughed through the last vestiges of the defences.

In the early part of the 20th century, S.N. Miller excavated the site, confirming that it was defended by a stone wall and was around 1.6 hectares in size. He confirmed that the southern corners of the fort were rounded, while the northern ones were squared, to join it to the Antonine Wall. Stone buildings were found during the excavations, including the HQ and commanding officer's house, while the barracks were likely to have been built from timber. There was also a bath house inside the fort, against the northeastern rampart, and an annexe to the east of the site (underneath Easter Balmuildy Farm). Within the annexe was another bath house, which was built on top of the east ditch of the fort, and which may have existed only briefly. There were signs that it was deliberately destroyed at some point. There was also some evidence that there may have been a temple within the annexe, something which has not been seen elsewhere on the wall.

The road leaves the front gate of the fort, heading towards the River Kelvin to the northwest. In the 1940s, when the river was being dredged to deepen the channel, stone blocks and wooden beams were recovered at the point where the road would probably have crossed the Kelvin. The wood was dated to the medieval period, but the blocks were confirmed as being Roman, indicating that the bridge had been in use for centuries after the Romans had departed.

Exploring

The site is located between Bishopbriggs and Bearsden, at the point where the A879 (Balmore Road) crosses the Kelvin. The A879 bisects the southwestern corner of the site. The fort is in a field between Wester and Easter Balmuildy farms.

Boclair

Possible Fortlet | NS 568 725

Fortifications on the Antonine Wall were generally regularly spaced, allowing archaeologists to predict their location. Boclair is one such predicted site. Anne Robertson excavated it in the 1970s and failed to

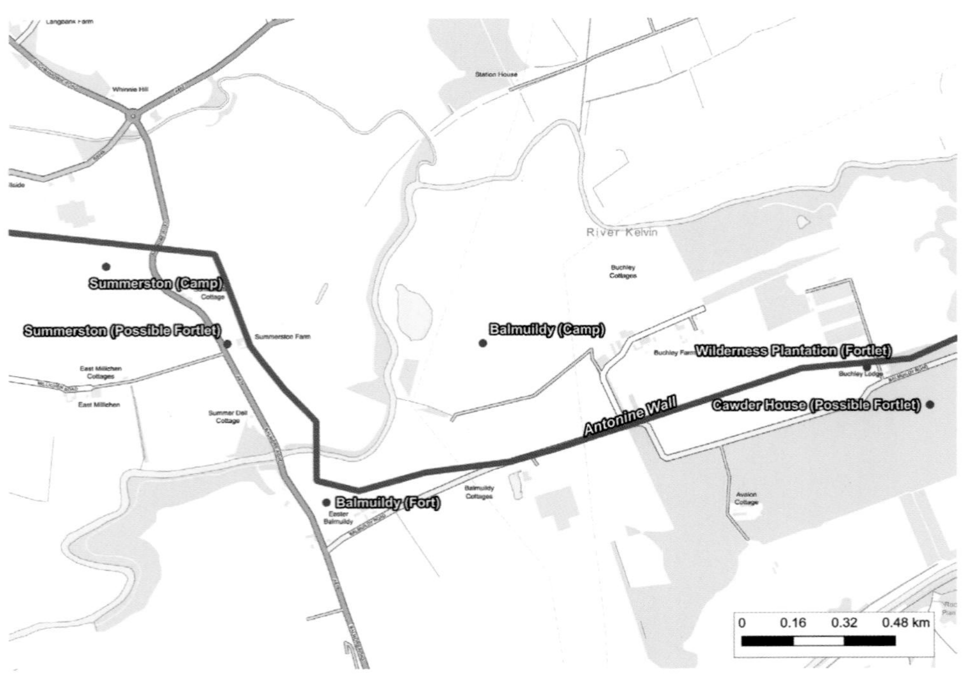

find any traces of a fortlet, but, in the 1980s, excavation of the nearby site at Summerston revealed a fortlet that was built after the camp had been abandoned. It seems likely that this is the fortification that Robertson expected to find.

Easter Balmuildy

Possible Fortlet | NS 58 71

Easter Balmuildy was predicted by Hanson and Maxwell to be the site of a fortlet, although evidence of this is yet to come to light. (*See* 'The Antonine Wall' for more details.)

Hunterian Museum

University of Glasgow, University Avenue, Glasgow G12 8QQ | Free Entry
www.gla.ac.uk/hunterian | @hunterian
Opening Times | Tues–Sat 10:00–17:00 | Sun 11:00–16:00

The oldest public museum in Scotland also has one of the finest collections of Roman artefacts. The focus of the museum is the Antonine Wall, through the 'Rome's Final Frontier' exhibition. It has four themes: the construction of the wall, the Roman army on the edge of the Empire, cultural interactions between Rome and those living around the frontier, and the antiquarian rediscovery of the monument over the past 350 years.

Although not on the same scale as the National Museum of Scotland in Edinburgh, the Hunterian provides an insightful introduction to life on the Antonine Wall, and its impact on Scotland.

Summerston

Camp & Fortlet | NS 574 724
Possible Fortlet | NS 578 722

The 2.3-hectare camp at Summerston was identified from the air in 1977, and excavated the following year. The evidence indicated that the camp was only in use during the Antonine period.

The excavators uncovered evidence of a fortlet to the north of the camp, which also seemed to date to the same period, although they failed to find any internal features other than a single possible posthole.

Key Dates

17th century: Sibbald notes a Roman site at Summerston
1974: Robertson suggests that there should be a fortlet in the immediate area
1980: The camp is located during aerial reconnaissance. This is followed up by excavation

Yorkhill

Earthworks & Artefacts | NS 563 661

Another possible glimpse of Roman Glasgow was seen in 1867 when an earthwork on the summit of Yorkhill was excavated in advance of development. A number of Antonine artefacts were discovered, including pottery, rings, glass and coins (including one dating to the Trajanic period). Early antiquarians speculated that the site was home to a Roman fort, however later archaeologists have argued that the earthworks probably belonged to a native fort or settlement. As the site has long since been covered over by the hospital, what really occupied Yorkhill in the Roman period will probably remain a mystery.

Chapter 12

RENFREWSHIRE

Like Inverclyde to the west, Renfrewshire is not renowned for copious amounts of Roman fortifications. In fact, the county only has two confirmed Roman sites: the early fortification at Barochan Hill and the later Antonine fort at Whitemoss (Bishopton). The former has good views across the Clyde from the hill, while the latter sits on the banks of the Clyde, guarding routes up- and downriver. Unusually for an early site, the fort at Barochan Hill is located on its own, with the nearest Flavian fortification more than a day's march away, at Drumquhassle by Loch Lomond, while Bishopton is an extension of the Antonine Wall defences. Perhaps there are other Flavian sites waiting to be discovered, or maybe Barochan Hill really was a remote outpost watching over the River Clyde.

Barochan Hill

Fort | NS 414 690

The views over the River Clyde, and to the Argyle peninsula and beyond, would have been strategically important for the Romans who built and occupied the fort at Barochan Hill. The fort was constructed on Barochan Hill, around 60 metres above sea level, with a gentle rise of about 5 metres between the highest and lowest parts of the site. There is little natural topography to improve the defences of the site, with the northern slope gently falling away to a glen, while the northeast side of the hill has been quarried away.

In 1886, a bronze Roman *patera* (a type of shallow bowl) was discovered a quarter of a mile from the fort, giving the first indication of Roman activity in the area. However, it was not until 1953 that the

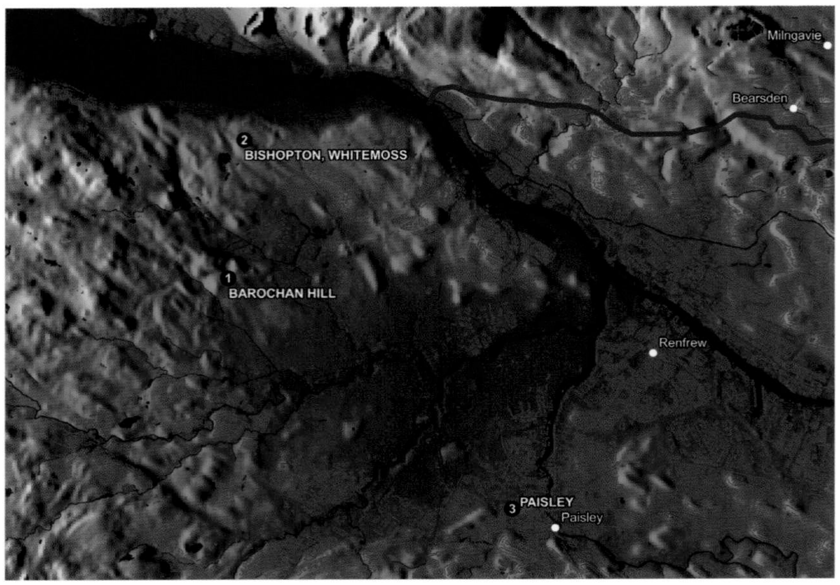

The fort at Barochan Hill is underneath the plantation in the background.

fort was first identified, from the air, and it was then excavated in 1972, 1975 and 1984–86. Despite the early excavations focusing on the defences, some of the internal buildings were also revealed. The first datable artefacts were revealed by Newall in 1974, and consisted of a number of 1st-century potsherds, and a coin from AD 86. Newall speculated that there may have been two phases of occupation, with the site being reoccupied around AD 86, when archaeologists argue the legionary fortress at Inchtuthil was abandoned. Other than field walking in the early 1990s, the site has not been subsequently investigated.

Despite the advantages of the site, when the Romans returned to the area under the Emperor Antoninus Pius, they opted to build a fort at Whitemoss rather than reoccupy Barochan Hill.

Exploring

Take the B790 east from Bridge of Weir. In Houston, take the second left on to the B789. After about a mile, at Barochancross, turn right along Corsliehill Road and Barochan Hill is ahead. The fort site is on the opposite side of the hill and obscured by the plantation. The lane which skirts around the side of the fort is overgrown, so it is worth parking near by and heading to the site on foot.

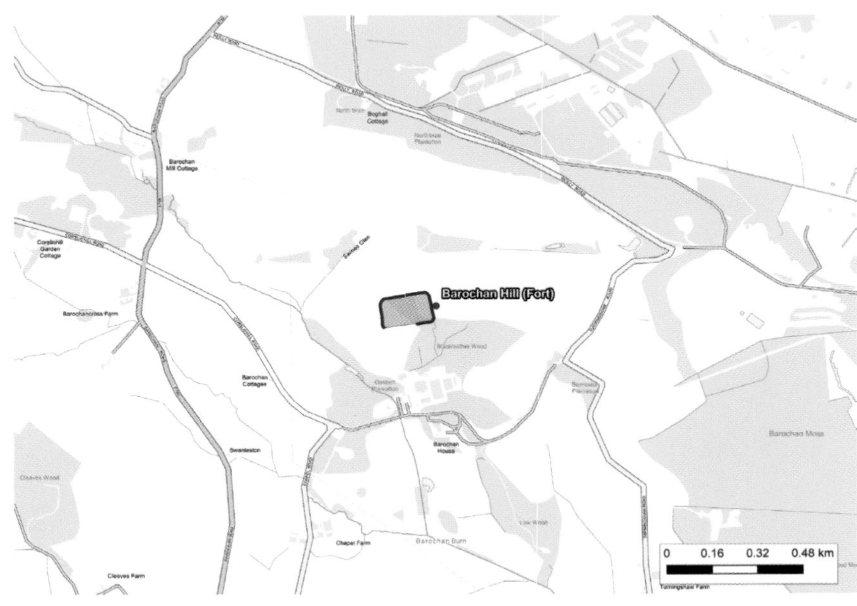

Bishopton (Whitemoss)

Fort | NS 418 720

Whitemoss is located on the southern bank of the River Clyde, around the point where it begins to widen out, making it the perfect location for receiving supplies from the sea. The site has excellent views up and down the Clyde, as well as to the opposite shore, although some of the views are slightly restricted today by modern construction.

The fort was originally recorded in 1949 by Kenneth Steer who had been analysing war-time aerial photographs for archaeological features. Subsequently, a series of excavations took place in the 1950s, with traces of buildings uncovered, including the defences, barracks and the headquarter building in the centre of the fort. Pottery evidence recovered from the site indicated an Antonine date, implying that the fort protected the western flank of the Antonine Wall, preventing enemies using the Clyde to circumvent the barrier. This was particularly important given that the wall itself terminates just across the Clyde at Old Kilpatrick.

Excavation indicated four phases of occupation, all dating to the Antonine period. There were also signs of additional defensive structures to the northwest of the fort, which seemed to be independent of the main site. At the time of the excavations, Steer argued that these belonged to another fort, pre-dating the one being excavated. However, it may equally be plausible that this is an annexe to the fort. After the third period of occupation, the fort was burned down, probably by the Romans themselves, to prevent the enemy from occupying the site.

Key Dates

1949: Steer notes cropmarks resembling the outline of a fort

1950–54: Excavations are limited to confirming the Roman origins of the fort by locating the ditches. Further excavations locate the *principia* and other internal features

2002 and 2016: Watching briefs fail to locate any Roman features

Exploring

The site is easily accessed from the M8, heading westbound past Bishopton. Take the first left at the Junction 31 roundabout, following the signs for Bishopton.

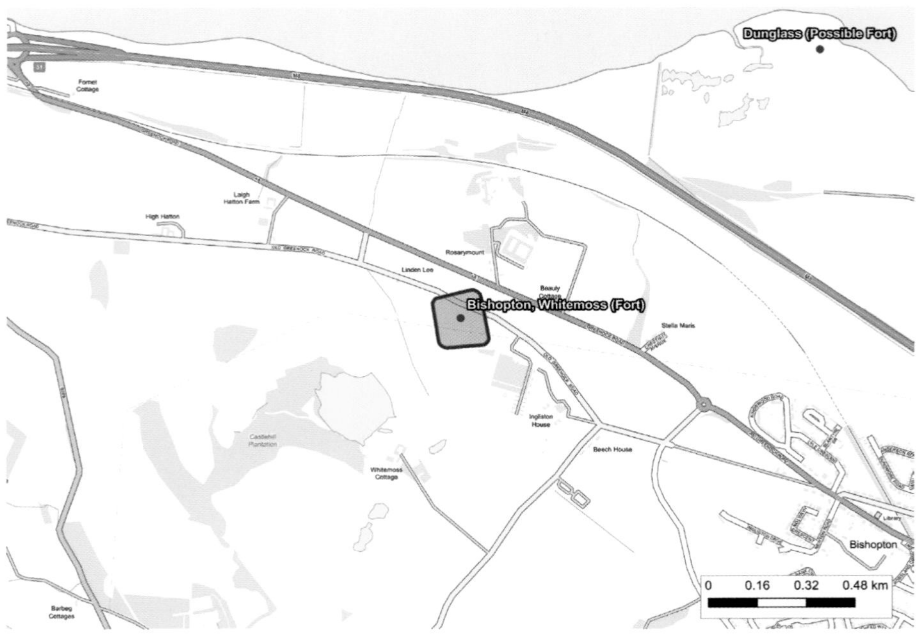

There is a car park at the roundabout, which overlooks the Clyde, giving similar views to those at the fort site. To get to the fort itself, follow the Greenock Road towards Bishopton, taking the first right, then left on to the Old Greenock Road. The fort is next to the Ingliston Country Club.

Paisley

Possible Fort | NS 477 640

There are two early written accounts, one dating to the 17th century and another to the early 18th, both of which describe a Roman camp at Paisley. The earlier account was written by Principal Dunlop of the Glasgow University:

> At Paisley there is a large Roman camp to be seen. The praetorium [the HQ building], or innermost part of the camp is on the west end of a rising ground, or little hill called Cap Shaw-head, on the southeast descent of which hill standeth the town of Paisley. The praetorium is not very large, but hath been well fortified with three foussees and dikes of earth, which must have been large when to this day their vestiges are not so great that men on horseback will not see over them. The camp itself hath been great and large, it comprehending the whole hill. There are vestiges in the north side of the foussees and dike, whereby it appears that the camp reached to the river of Cart. (*The New Statistical Account of Scotland*)

John Horsley, who extensively recorded Roman antiquities in 18th-century Scotland, noted that Paisley was well known for the remains of a fortification. The antiquarian George Chalmers, writing in the 19th century, suggested that the *praetorium* or *principia* was underneath the bowling green, next to the John Neilson Institution. However, Ordnance Survey noted at the time that an observer overseeing the construction of the institution did not record any signs of Roman activity or objects.

The story of Roman activity in Paisley is unclear. The early accounts are certainly convincing, but there is a lack of hard evidence. If there had been a Roman site centred on the John Neilson Institution, stretching as far as the river in the east, it would have been huge. Roman sites as large as this are usually camps – temporary structures with minimal foundations – which may explain why nothing was found during the construction of the institution. It remains to be seen whether or not there was Roman activity at Paisley, but the old saying of no smoke without fire comes to mind.

Chapter 13

INVERCLYDE

Inverclyde is one of the poor relations when it comes to Roman remains, with only one confirmed Roman site in the area. Through the years there have been a handful of other possible sites, but only the fortlet at Lurg Moor has been confirmed through excavation. There must surely be more sites still to be discovered, as Lurg Moor fortlet is unlikely to have existed on its own.

Devol Moor

Tower (Possible) | NS 328 729

Overlooking the River Clyde and Port Glasgow, the mound at Devol Moor is about 17 metres across with a rampart 2.3 metres wide. Given the views from the site, and its shape, it was believed to be Roman when Frank Newall and Bill Lonie undertook an initial survey in 1991. Newall followed this up in 1995 with excavation. The results, including a stone tool found on the surface, led to the conclusion that the site was prehistoric.

Exploring

The mound is located in a field (next to Port Glasgow Golf Club) by the trig point at Auchenleck.

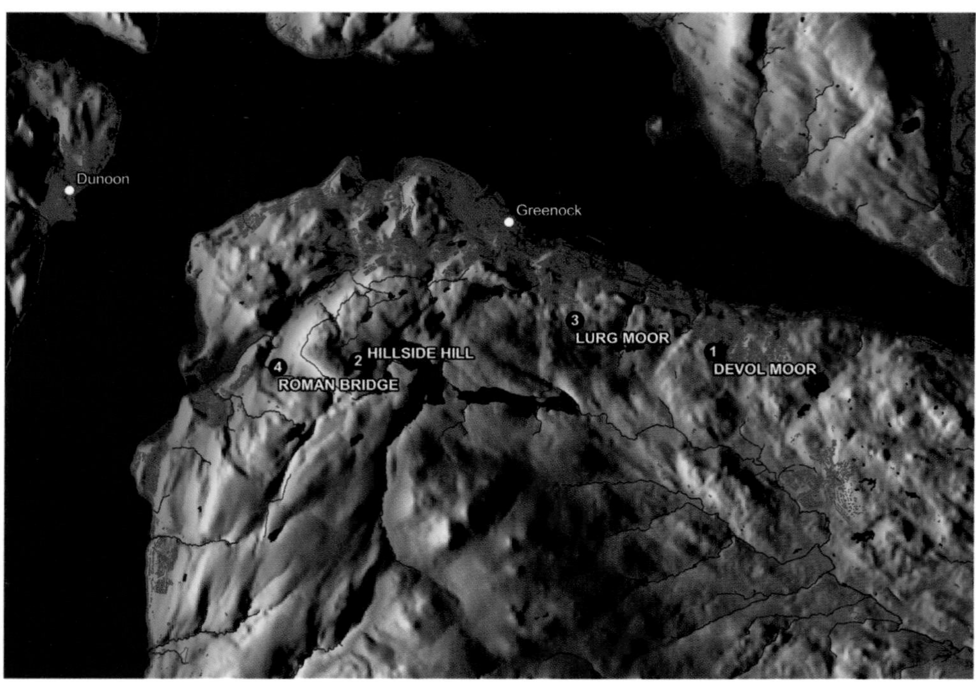

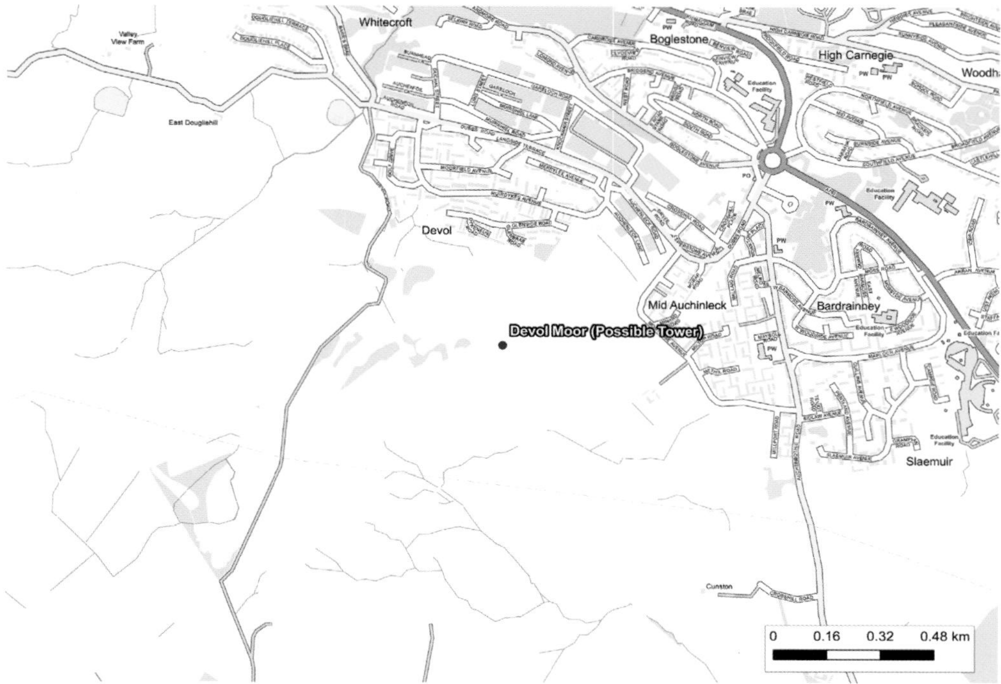

Hillside Hill

Tower (Possible) | NS 244 727

Newall speculated that the mound at Hillside Hill could have been the site of a Roman signal tower, given its size – 13.5 metres across. There was some evidence on the ground for a ditch around the site, along with a possible entrance. Archaeologists subsequently analysing the site have concluded however that, because of the limited views from the site, it is unlikely to have been a Roman tower.

Exploring

Hillside Hill is located above Inverkip and next to Loch Thom and can be reached via a path from Shielhill Farm. Parking is available at Greenock Cut Visitor Centre.

Lurg Moor

Fortlet | NS 295 737

The fortlet at Lurg Moor was strategically positioned to take advantage of excellent views of the surrounding moorland as far as the Clyde, one and a half miles to the north. It also provided a viewpoint from which to watch over the Roman road from Largs, which passes in front of the site.

Discovered by R.W. Feacham in the 1950s, the fortlet consisted of a timber tower and barrack block to accommodate the soldiers and was surrounded by a turf rampart and ditch. Kenneth Steer, excavating the nearby Antonine fort at Bishopton (Whitemoss) at around the same time, predicted that there would be a series of Roman installations running west, all dating to the Antonine period. Incidentally, the next known fortlet in the chain is at Outerwards, which is around six miles to the southwest of Lurg Moor, and still on the line of the Roman road. An Antonine date for Lurg Moor was confirmed in 1959 when pottery was found to the southwest of the site. A new extensive survey undertaken by Historic Environment Scotland has recorded a counterscarp bank.

Exploring

The remains of the fortlet can be seen as a

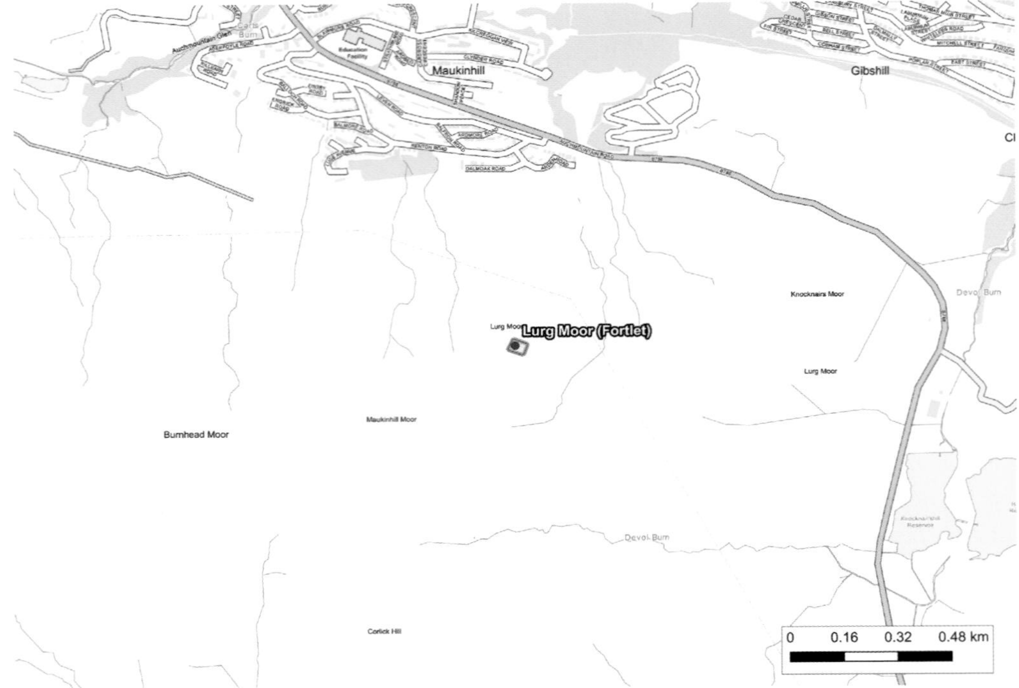

well-preserved grassy earthwork in the moorland. One unusual feature of the fortlet that is still visible is the eastern ditch, which is cut through rock and is around 6 metres wide and the same deep. The road into the fortlet can be seen as it approaches the causeway and enters the interior of the site. The Roman road from Largs passes just outside the fortlet and is visible as a long, 4-metre wide humped mound.

Roman Bridge

Bridge | NS 223 725

Despite the name, it is unlikely that the bridge is actually Roman. It was probably constructed in the 16th century, making it medieval. However, that is not to say that it is not built on the site of another bridge, which may have helped to give it its name.

Looking northwards, over the River Clyde and towards Argyle and Bute.

Chapter 14

ARGYLL AND BUTE

Despite Argyll and Bute's relatively close proximity to the numerous Roman sites across the water on the Clyde peninsula, there is virtually no evidence of Roman activity in the area, beyond a handful of finds and a possible site at Dunoon. Perhaps this is because this is where the 'enemy' was located, and the Romans preferred to keep watch on the natives from a distance.

Dunoon Golf Course

Possible Fort | NS 17 78

Writing in 1970, Paterson wrote about the local folklore of a Roman military installation located on the edge of Dunoon, but she goes on to write that this appears to be a misinterpretation of another site detailed in *The New Statistical Account of Scotland*. The location would have been perfect for a fort, with great views all round, and would have allowed the Romans to control access to and from the River Clyde, but to date there is no evidence for Roman activity in the area.

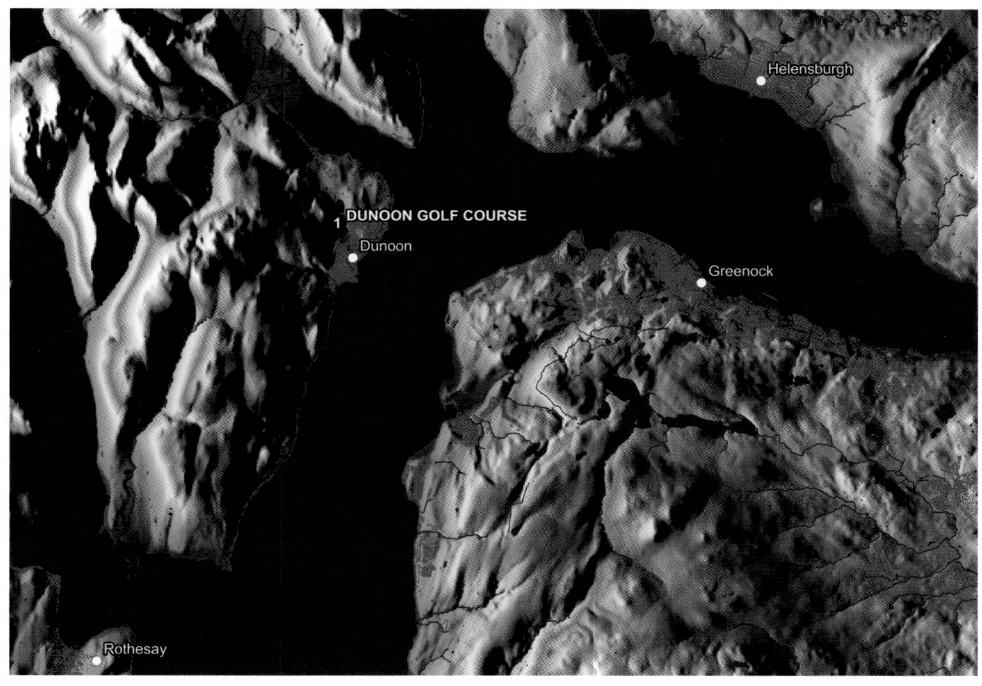

Chapter 15

AYRSHIRE

The west of Scotland is a bit of a Roman mystery! Archaeologists have found very little evidence for Roman activity in the area, although that does not mean that there are not more sites waiting to be found. There are some tantalizing hints of Romans, with a possible bath house at Ardrossan, tiled floors under Largs and two camps at Girvan, with no other confirmed Roman sites for 30 miles. Roman Ayrshire surely still has many more secrets to give up.

Ardrossan

Bath House | NS 23 42

John Smith's 1895 book *Prehistoric Man in Ayrshire* offers a tantalizing glimpse into a possible building here, noting that 'Roman baths are said to have been at one time unearthed in the neighbourhood of Ardrossan'. This is the only record archaeologists have for potential activity in the area, although coins of Maximian (AD 286–305) and Constantine I (AD 306–337) have been found in and around the town. While Roman forts and camps were normally constructed at the mouth of a river, something which Ardrossan does not have, the North and South Bays would have made good natural harbours for ships passing by; indeed, Ardrossan is today the main ferry port for Arran.

Key Dates

Pre-19th century: Unspecified evidence of Roman baths are uncovered somewhere within Ardrossan

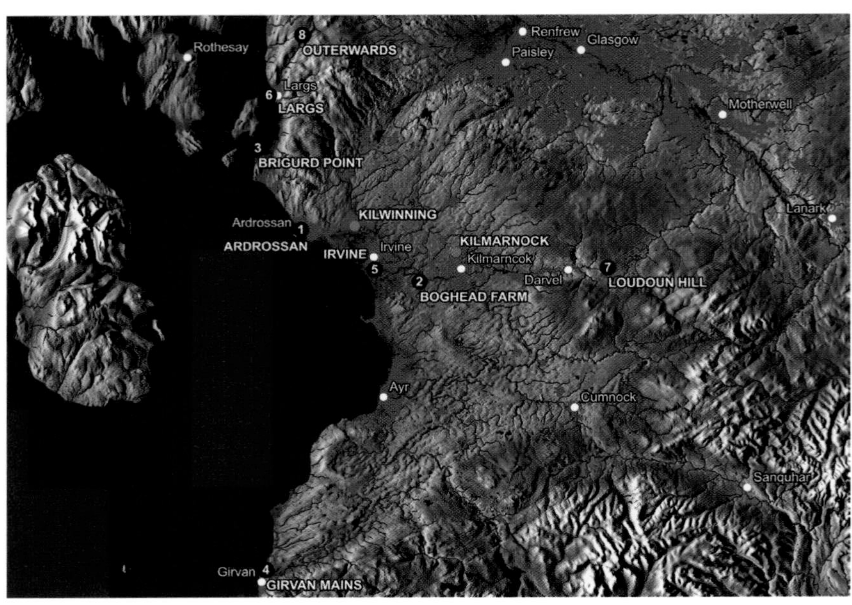

1940: A coin of Maximian is found on the North Shore
1961: A coin of Constantine I is found in a garden at Kirkhall Drive

Boghead Farm

Possible Building | NS 375 353

The remains of a bath house or reservoir here are recorded in the 19th-century *New Statistical Account of Scotland*, along with a warning that the site is only accessible when the weather is dry as it is frequently prone to flooding. The site was excavated in 1893, revealing a circular area surrounded by stones, with a possible opening on one side. George Macdonald, who excavated the site, concluded that it most probably was not Roman, and local opinion speculated that it was in fact a horse pond.

Key Dates

1845: The *New Statistical Account of Scotland* records the site as being Roman
1893: Macdonald excavates the site but finds nothing to confirm it is Roman

Brigurd Point

Harbour | NS 177 523

Brigurd could quite possibly be the only known Roman harbour in Scotland. Located just to the north of West Kilbride, and facing a gap between the islands of Little Cumbrae and Great Cumbrae, the harbour was identified in the 1960s by Frank Newall, who argued that it was the terminus for the Roman road from Kilwinning. In fact, there is no firm evidence to confirm that it is Roman. Only the foundations of the harbour are visible at low tide, showing as a slight rise of rocks that is around 46 metres wide and 55 metres long.

Key Dates

1966: Newall first records the remains of what appears to be an old harbour wall, although there is no evidence to confirm a Roman date for the site
2013: Archaeologists visit the site, confirming Newall's findings

The quiet west-coast town of Ardrossan.

The view from Brigurd Point.

Exploring

Heading north from West Kilbride on the A78 for about two and a half miles, take a left at the roundabout signposted for Hunterston Power Station. Go on for about half a mile and Brigurd Point is on the right. It is advisable to check the tide times if you want to see the harbour. The remains of the harbour are visible at low tide, although they are not always easy to spot. Large boulders stand two courses high for a long stretch, giving the appearance of a slight rise.

Girvan Mains

East Camp | NX 190 991
West Camp | NX 187 990
Possible Camp | NX 185 988

Girvan is home to two Roman camps overlooking the estuary of the Water of Girvan, which is just beyond the southern extremity of the River Clyde. The two camps are partially overlapping, with the East Camp being the larger of the two at 22 hectares. The East Camp was discovered in 1976 and subsequently excavated, revealing a fragment of 1st-century glass. While the camp has since proven to be much bigger than originally thought, it is also closer to the sea. The northern and eastern defences of the West Camp are yet to be discovered, but it seems unlikely that it would have been bigger than its eastern counterpart.

In 1995, a trench was dug to put a sewage pipe through the site, but the rampart and ditch remained elusive.

Key Dates

1976: St Joseph detects the East Camp while undertaking aerial reconnaissance
1977: Sections of ditch are excavated
1981: Identified from aerial photographs, the West Camp is confirmed when the V-shaped ditch is excavated
1982: St Joseph and Maxwell oversee excavations in advance of road widening
1983: The southern ditch of the East Camp is excavated
1989: Aerial photographs detect further elements of the defences of both camps
1993: Geophysical survey of part of the camps indicates that both are larger than previously thought
1995: Excavation in advance of development fails to locate camp defences
2009: No finds are recovered during several watching briefs

The site of the camps at Girvan.

Exploring

Both camps can be visited, although there is little to be seen on the ground. Heading north from Girvan, on the A77, the sites are about a quarter of a mile after the roundabout with the B741, and just after the bridge of the Water of Girvan. Both camps are marked on the Ordnance Survey maps.

Irvine

Possible Fort & Harbour | NS 32 38

Given its prominent position on the River Irvine, which itself is connected to forts and camps further inland, experts have speculated that there are likely to be a harbour and fort somewhere around Irvine. Although there is no evidence for buildings, several coins have been found in and around the town.

Key Dates

1930: Coin of Constantine I is found on the beach
1950s: Coin of Faustina I and another of Gallienus found in a garden
1959: Coin of Antoninus Pius found on a housing estate
1989: Maxwell speculates that an undiscovered Roman site may lie under Irvine

Largs

Possible Building | NS 20 59

Largs hints at a Roman past that has long been forgotten about. In 1879, the *Guide to Wemyss Bay, Skelmorlie, Inverkip, Largs and Surrounding Districts* recorded that a 'pavement formed of square tiles of red fireclay' had been found (in 1820) in the garden of the postmistress. She probably lived in the post office, located on what is now Tron Place. The guide went on to say that 'many authorities' had declared the tiles Roman. A number of Roman coins were found along with the tiles, and another source claims that this was a regular occurrence all over Largs.

Tron Place, Largs: Location of the first post office in the town and possibly the location where some Roman tiles were discovered in 1820.

Site of the indigenous hillfort that was located on the top of Loudon Hill.

Key Dates

1799: The first post office in Largs is opened on Tron Place
1820: Roman tiles are uncovered in the garden of the post office

Loudon Hill

Fort | NS 605 371

In 1837, *The New Statistical Account of Scotland* for Ayrshire described the Roman fort near Loudon Hill as extremely well preserved, but, by the following year, another account was noting that the site was slowly being destroyed by erosion and gravel extraction.

The threat from the latter increased over the years, and in 1938, St Joseph felt compelled to undertake extensive excavations of the fort before it was lost for ever. Not only did he find an annexe, but he also uncovered evidence of four phases of Flavian occupation, as well as one from the Antonine period.

Key Dates

1837: *The New Statistical Account of Scotland* records that the fort is in a good state of preservation
1938: Gravel extraction threatens the site, so St Joseph undertakes limited excavations before continuing to reveal as much of the fort as possible before it disappears
1955: The majority of the site is lost to quarrying
1978: All traces of the fort have been destroyed

Exploring

Today, the site has been completely destroyed by quarrying, which has itself now been abandoned. Across the road from the fort are two further historical sites, but again there is nothing to see on the

The site of the fort at Loudon Hill, destroyed by quarrying.

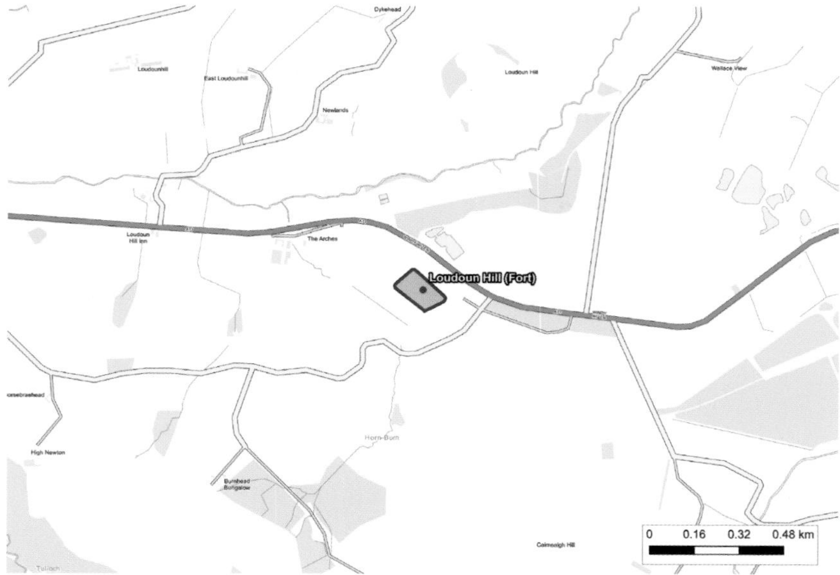

ground. Wallace's Cairn, where William Wallace lay hidden in 1297 before an attack on an English convoy, is marked by a modern sculpture known as *The Spirit of Scotland*. The other is the site of the Battle of Loudon Hill (1307), where Robert the Bruce forced the English Army under Aymer de Valence, the 2nd Earl of Pembroke, into a retreat, giving him one of his first major victories.

Travelling east from Kilmarnock on the A71, the site is around three miles past Darvel. Pass the Loudon Hill Inn Café and after 500m look for a small lane on the right. You can park at the quarry entrance, which is immediately on the right.

Outerwards

Fortlet | NS 231 666

Dramatically placed high in the hills above Skelmorlie, this fortlet has excellent views of the entrance into the Firth of Clyde. It was probably the last part of the system that supported the Antonine Wall. While the wall itself came nowhere near this far west, it was supported by a chain of forts, fortlets and towers, which would have acted as an early warning system for any hostile force that decided to sail up the Clyde.

The fortlet is similar to other buildings of the period, having a circular bank and ditch with space for two internal buildings, which were made of timber. Newall, who excavated the site, concluded that the fortlet was occupied on two occasions during the Antonine period. During the first period of occupation, the buildings were burned down, although it is not clear whether this was deliberate or accidental. Excavations found the entire site was covered in a layer of burnt debris and the gate had been pulled down, with one gatepost having been snapped in half. A few years later the site was reoccupied, but enough time had passed in the interim period to allow vegetation to grow inside the fortlet.

Key Dates

1970: Newall identifies the fortlet while undertaking a survey of the Roman road between Largs and Lurg Moor. Newall excavates the site
1976: Newall publishes the results of the extensive excavation

Exploring

The site is clearly identifiable when being approached on foot, with the rampart still existing as a slight rise, and the entrances visible on the causeway. The site is worth a visit for the views of the surrounding area alone.

From Largs, head northwards on the minor road towards Greenock. After three miles, there is a parking area at Outerwards Reservoir. From there,

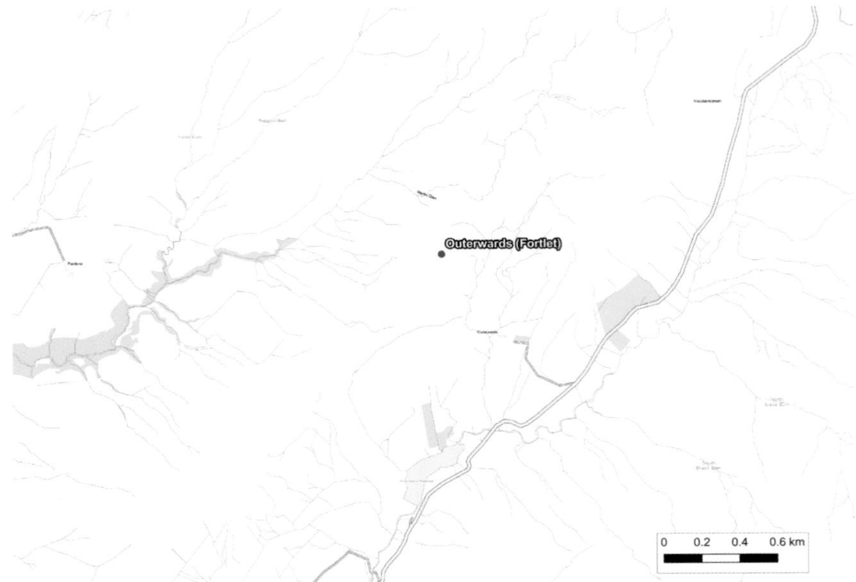

continue on foot on the road for about half a mile and then turn left and head up the track to Outerwards Farm. Pass through the farmyard and head up on to the ridge, then turn right and continue for about 100 metres along the track, until you come to the fortlet. The site is marked on the Ordnance Survey map.

The Other Sites

Ayr (Craigie House) (Camp | NS 3509 2156)

In 2016, a camp was located at a probable crossing point over the River Ayr. Unusually, no ditches or ramparts were discovered in the areas that were excavated, but instead the site was identified by a series of 30 ovens, which were positioned on rectilinear alignments. The fact that its boundaries were defined by ovens rather than traditional defences would seem to indicate a different type of camp, which may not have needed to defend itself from any local threats. Dating indicates the site belongs to the Flavian period. (Note: the site is not shown on the map.)

Kilmarnock (Possible Camp | NS 424 396)

Patterson's *History of the County of Ayr* (1847) recalls a local story of a camp near Kilmarnock, near a site known as Roman Well. The site was probably destroyed when the adjacent farm was demolished. An attempt was made to examine the site in the 1950s, but any remaining evidence appears to have been eliminated by the construction of a housing estate there.

Kilwinning (Possible Camp | NS 30 43)

Writing in the 18th century, Pococke recounted a journey he took from Kilwinning to Irvine. When crossing the River Irvine, he passed some mounds and earthworks that appeared to him to be Roman in origin. The site has not been seen since and awaits rediscovery.

PART FIVE: THE SOUTHWEST OF SCOTLAND

Chapter 16

DUMFRIES AND GALLOWAY

Dumfries and Galloway was a crossroads in Roman Britain, with one of the main roads north running through the area, from Carlisle towards Glasgow. To the west are a number of fortifications spread out on the southern shores, hinting at a possible Roman passage heading towards Stranraer, and then possibly north towards Girvan. Undoubtedly, there are more fortifications to be discovered, indicating that the area was much more important to the Roman military than archaeologists have previously thought.

Bankhead

Fortlet & Possible Camp | NS 747 120

The camp was discovered from the air as a series of cropmarks, but is still to be confirmed through excavation. The fortlet, excavated from 1952 until 1963, is similar in size and plan to the sites at Milton and Durisdeer, which indicates that it probably dates to the Antonine period. Interestingly, artefacts found during excavations have been dated to the 15th century, implying that the site may have been reused later.

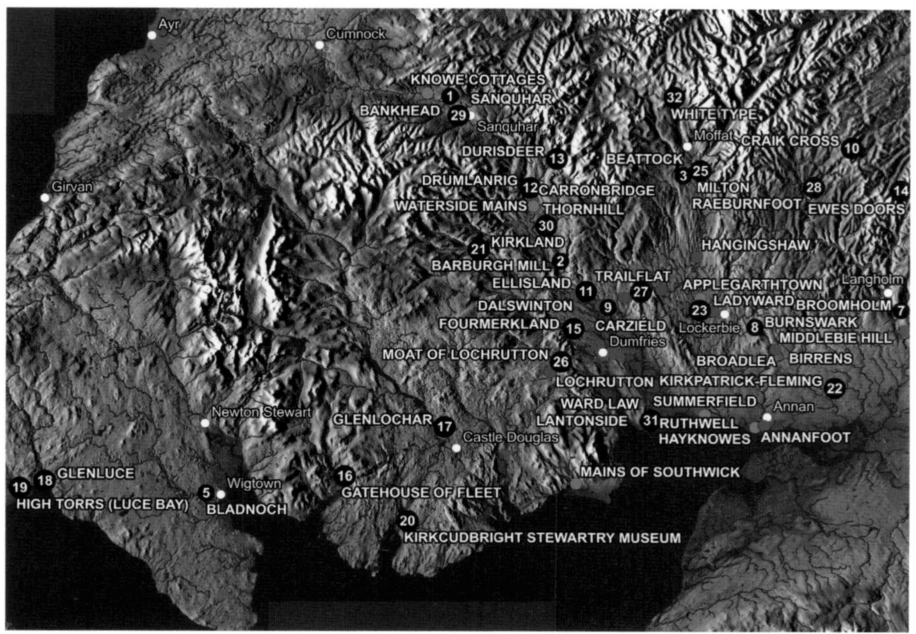

Key Dates
1950s: St Joseph identifies the fortlet and possibly a camp from aerial photographs
Late 1950s: Clarke and Wilson excavate the fortlet

Barburgh Mill

Fortlet | NX 902 884

Discovered in 1945, briefly excavated the following year, and then more thoroughly examined in the 1970s in advance of quarrying, the fortlet at Barburgh Mill was typical of this type of fortification. David Breeze, who undertook the later excavations, argued that the fortlet was constructed during the Antonine period.

It was the usual practice of the Romans to fill in ditches when a site was abandoned, but this was not the case with the fortlet at Barburgh Mill. Evidence yielded by the ditch indicated that it was not filled in until the 14th century.

Key Dates
1945: The fortlet is spotted from the air by St Joseph
1946: St Joseph undertakes limited excavation of the site
1971: Breeze leads a complete excavation of the site in advance of quarrying
2013: Watching brief does not locate any Roman features

Beattock

Bankend Camp | NT 084 020
Barnhill Possible Fortlet | NT 085 028
Barnhill Camps | NT 089 027 & NT 084 026

A number of camps exist at Beattock, located around the Evan Water, indicating that the area was at an important crossroads. The Bankend camp was identified through aerial photographs of cropmarks and has Stracathro-type gates, indicating a 1st-century date for the site. During partial excavations in advance of road expansion, the ditches were located, along with ovens, but there were no datable finds.

There is evidence of at least four Barnhill camps, of differing sizes. They over-lie each other, indicating that the site was adapted and a suitable camp built each time a new force took over. Based on environmental analysis, the camp at Bankend pre-dates those at Barnhill.

Underneath one of the camps lies a fortlet, which was excavated in 1984. Archaeologists have speculated that the fortlet underneath Camp I at Barnhill is Flavian, indicating that the camp,

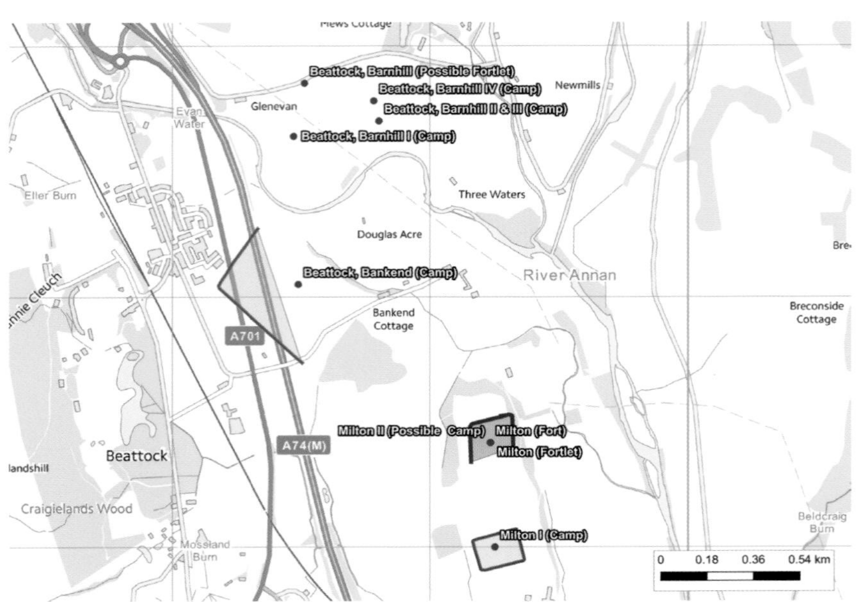

The fort at Birrens, with ditches in the foreground and the fort platform behind.

which was constructed later, probably dates to the Antonine invasions, in common with the remaining Barnhill camps.

Key Dates

1945: A number of camps are spotted by St Joseph when flying over the area
1957: Camp I at Barnhill is identified by St Joseph
1977: The fortlet and Bankend camp are identified during aerial reconnaissance
1984: Trial trenching on the fortlet indicates that it was likely to be Roman but does not find any artefacts
1992: Excavations of the Barnhill camps takes place
1994: The Bankend camp is partly excavated

Exploring

The camps are just to the east and southeast of the village of Beattock.

Birrens

Fort | NY 219 751
Camp | NY 224 750

Birrens, which is close to the siege camps at Burnswark, is an impressive site. The original defences of the fort are still visible, giving a good indication of how they would have appeared, although the southern side of the site has been eroded by the Mein Water. The fort and camp are located on the main route north in the west of Scotland.

The fort site has been excavated a number of times, first in 1895, when it was the first site in Scotland to be extensively explored, and then in 1936–37 and again in 1962–67. The site appears to have been occupied first by a small fort dating to the Flavian period. This was superseded by the construction of a larger Hadrianic fort on top of its predecessor, probably an outpost of Hadrian's Wall. Outside of the fort site, aerial photography has indicated that there are other buildings, including one with a courtyard, which may be a *mansio,* effectively a Roman 'hotel' for official travellers.

There are a number of camps in the area, including the two siege-work camps at Burnswark. Underneath the fort, Robertson uncovered evidence of a ditched enclosure, which was filled in before the construction of the later fort and may have been an early camp. There are three other possible camps in the area, although it is possible Camp III could also be an annexe for the fort as identified during a geophysical survey of the site in 2012.

Exploring

The fort at Birrens is very well preserved and well worth exploring. It can be accessed from a stile by Birrens Lodge, which leads into the northern end of the fort. The ditches are clearly visible, and you can pass through the northern gate, into the heart of the site. The field itself can be muddy and there may be livestock grazing in it.

Bladnoch (Kirwaugh)

Fortlet | NX 407 549

Although Bladnoch was first photographed in 1984, it was only recently identified as a fortlet. A geophysical survey of the interior revealed a rectilinear building, probably barracks. Although there were no datable finds, the surveyors speculated that it dated to the Flavian period.

Key Dates

1984: The fortlet is seen in aerial photographs. Geophysical surveying is undertaken

Broadlea

Fortlet | NY 224 744
Camp I | NY 217 748
Camp II | NY 219 746

Covering an area of 0.16 hectares, the fortlet shows up clearly as a cropmark in the aerial photographs, but has yet to be explored in any further depth.

Two camps have been spotted by the fortlet, with the first recorded by St Joseph from the air in the 1940s. At around 4.8 hectares, it is the larger of the two. The second camp was also discovered as a cropmark and is speculated to have been around 1.8 hectares in size, although not all of the defences have been identified. The camp was built on top of a Neolithic henge; instead of knocking it down, the Romans incorporated it into their defences, with one end of the henge being used as the camp corner and the other used for the entrance.

Key Dates

1943: Camp I is identified by St Joseph from the air
1945: Further aerial reconnaissance identifies Camp II
1947: The fortlet is identified during aerial reconnaissance

Broomholm

Fort | NY 378 814

Excavated shortly after its discovery in 1950, the fort at Broomholm saw multiple phases of occupation, starting with a small fort (and annexe) of about 1.8 hectares from the early Flavian period, which was then extended to create a slightly bigger site of 2 hectares. The excavators also found evidence for a third phase of occupation, which they thought dated to the Hadrianic period and would have been around 0.8 hectares.

The excavations also found some possible evidence of a posthole under the earliest Flavian rampart, which had been levelled during the construction of the defences. This indicates that there may have been an earlier structure on the site, pre-dating the Roman occupation.

Key Dates

19th century: Macdonald reports a number of coins found in the area near the fort
1950: Feacham identifies the fort
1955: The fort is excavated, revealing the occupation phases and the internal layout

Burnswark Hill.

Burnswark

Fortlet I | NY 186 787
Fortlet II | NY 189 786
Camp | NY 186 786
Camp (Siege Works) | NY 185 790

Burnswark, which was important long before and after the Romans arrived, is one of the most impressive and interesting sites in Scotland. As well as a series of Roman encampments, Burnswark Hill is also home to a Bronze Age cairn, an Iron Age hillfort, medieval enclosures, a Civil War battery and even an Ordnance Survey trig point. The hill itself is a major feature in the landscape, with excellent views across the region from the summit, which is relatively flat, making it a naturally defensive site for the settlements and fortifications on the top. It has even been suggested as the location of the main settlement of the local tribe, the Novantae, who appear on Ptolemy's map in this part of Britain.

With Roman camps on either side of the hill, it was suggested in 1785 that this place was the site of a Roman siege. This became the accepted theory until the mid-1960s, when an alternative idea (that it was actually a training ground) was put forward. As the native hillfort on the summit was abandoned several hundred years before the Romans arrived in Britain, it seems unlikely that Burnswark was a 'live' target.

Burnswark Hill was first recorded in 1720, and surveyed extensively by William Roy in the 1750s, but it was not until 1898 that the first excavation took place, under Christison, Barbour and Anderson. A second extensive series of excavations was undertaken by Jobey in the 1960s and 1970s, while more recently the hill has been subjected to geophysical and metal-detecting surveys, with some interesting results, including extensive finds of Roman weaponry, particularly slingshots.

The Roman camp on the north side is an unusual shape, not quite the normal playing-card figure that is typical of other camps in Scotland. The northern side of the camp is more rectilinear while the southern section is much thinner. Rebecca Jones suggests this is because there were originally two camps that were then joined together. R.G. Collingwood felt it was incomplete because he believed that there must be a missing section, and that boggy ground on the northwestern side had not been drained. St Joseph suggested that the eastern end was a small camp that had been extended, although excavations did not produce evidence of any defences that the Romans had subsequently removed when extending or joining the two areas. It does appear that one of the entrances

The northern camp at Burnswark, which is less visible on the ground than its southern counterpart. Part of the ditch and rampart defences are visible in the centre of the image.

The southern camp at Burnswark, with the three circular *tituli* in the middle and a section of rampart in the foreground.

on the southeastern side is almost *claviculae* in style, a type of gate that was prevalent in the Flavian period.

Like its counterpart on the other side of the hill, the southern camp is just as complex in its design. At three of the entrances to the camp are the usual *tituli*, but on the northeastern side are a series of three circular platforms rather than the usual rectangular mounds seen on the other entrances. The mounds are around 15 metres across and 3.5 metres high and interpreted as platforms for siege weapons such as ballista. Recently, this has been challenged with the suggestion that they were enlarged *tituli*, to protect the camp from large objects being rolled inside.

The 19th-century excavations recorded a stone building in the centre of the camp (which could not be found when the site was re-excavated in the 1960s and 1970s), which is unusual. Buildings are not normally associated with camps, as the army would have lived out of tents. Due to the temporary nature of the fortifications, any building would probably have been constructed from timber. The presence of a stone building within the camp suggests a more permanent arrangement.

In the northeastern corner of the camp is the second fortlet (although some archaeologists argue it is an Iron Age enclosure), part of which appears to lie underneath the defences of the camp, implying that the fortlet was constructed first. Incidentally, some time after the Romans had abandoned the fortlet, timber roundhouses were constructed on the same location. There is also some indication of an early Christian burial site on top of the fortlet.

No datable evidence has been recovered from the camps, but the fortlet is generally believed to have been built in the Antonine period. However, various archaeologists have put forward a range of convincing arguments with different dates, from the 1st-century (Flavian) to the 3rd-century (Severan) campaigns, while part of the northern camp was seemingly constructed in the early period.

An additional curious feature exists at the base of the western side of the hill, where a series of shallow ditches mark a circular feature that has never been fully explored. Given the shape and size of the feature, in particular the ditches, it seems likely that it dates to the Roman period, but the site needs to be investigated further to confirm its origins.

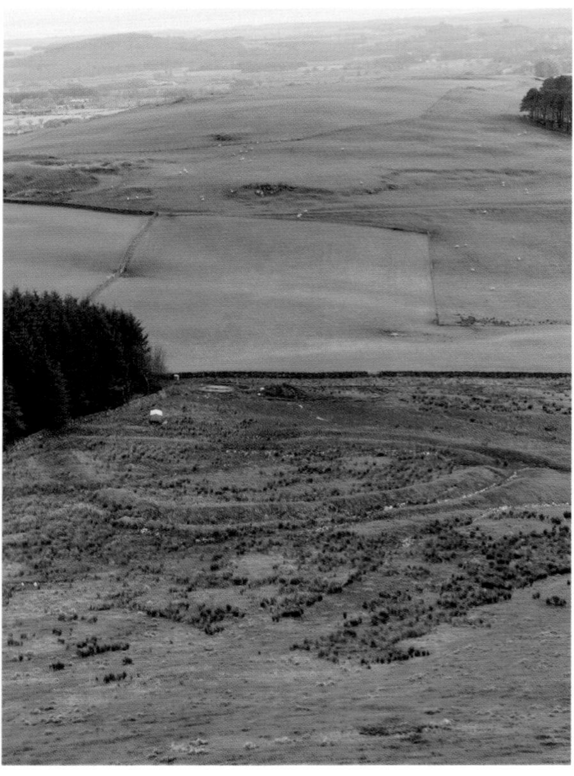

The circular feature on the western side of Burnswark Hill.

Exploring

The site is easily reached from the A74(M) at Ecclefechan. From either direction, take the turn off for the village, but keep on the road on the north side of the motorway following the B725 over the railway and carry straight on rather than following the B725. Follow this minor road for a couple of miles until the end of the road by the forest. The southern camp is about a 200-metre walk through the woods and through the gate, with the rounded *tituli* clearly visible, along with the defences. Burnswark Hill can easily be climbed, although the track marked on the Ordnance Survey map is less visible on the ground. The northern camp is on the opposite side of the hill, and again the defences are very clear, as is the *claviculae*, which is the entrance nearest the hill. The northern camp is best approached by walking around Burnswark Hill rather than by descending from the top.

As the ground around the base of the site can be wet and boggy, good boots and waterproofs are recommended.

Carzield

Fort | NX 968 817

Downriver from the complex of sites at Dalswinton is the fort at Carzield. During initial excavations in 1939, Richmond and Birley uncovered evidence that the fort originally housed a cavalry unit, dating to around AD 139–143 in the Antonine period. The fort had an annexe on the east and faced northwards, which was probably the direction of marching for the army at the time. In the 21st century, several watching briefs took place when service utilities were installed on the site. These revealed a number of features, including the cobbled floor of the barrack block, the various roads, parts of the central range of buildings and some artefacts such as a javelin with a section of the wooden shaft still attached. Unlike many forts in Scotland, Carzield has a bath house that has been located. This was excavated in the mid-1950s by Truckell.

Key Dates

1939: Excavation is undertaken by Birley and Richmond
1952: The adjacent settlement is discovered
1956: The bath house is located and planned
1967–68: Further excavations on the fort
2011: Watching brief on the fort reveals Roman layers and a small number of artefacts

Exploring

The fort platform can still be seen, along with part

of the rampart on the southeastern side.

From Dumfries, head northeast on the A701, cross over the roundabout with the A75, and straight over at the next one. Take the first left, signposted to Kirkton. Heading through the village, stick to the left and go past the church, then, after about quarter of a mile, take the first left to Carzield. The fort is in the field to the left, opposite Carzield Lodge, with the field boundary on top of the defences.

Craik Cross

Possible Tower | NT 303 047

First seen from the air in 1945, and excavated the following year, the site is next to a Roman road and commands excellent views of a number of local geographical features, including the Eildon Hills, Rubers Law and Burnswark Hill. The site is similar to other Roman towers in that a central area is surrounded by a ring ditch. In the middle was a mound, constructed from sods. No evidence of postholes, which would have supported a tower, has been found, although the small-scale excavation may not have uncovered them. No datable evidence was uncovered.

Key Dates

1945: The site is discovered during aerial reconnaissance by St Joseph
1946: The site is excavated although the results do not confirm its Roman origins

Dalswinton

Bankfoot Fort | NX 933 841
Bankfoot Camp I | NX 934 840
Bankfoot Camp II | NX 936 838
Bankfoot Possible Camp | NX 937 838
Bankhead Fort | NX 933 848

The area around Dalswinton is home to a complex of camps and forts, indicating that the area was of strategic importance during Roman times. With fortifications in at least three distinct areas (with a possible camp also identified at Portrack House), all of the sites were discovered from the air, with the first found by St Joseph in 1949. Further details were revealed during flying seasons in 1960 and 1965.

On the western bank of the River Nith, at Ellisland, are two camps, one on top of the other. On the opposite side are three possible camps and a fort at Bankfoot, which was discovered from the air in 1972, with another possible site further north at Bankhead. This was excavated by Richmond and St Joseph revealing Flavian occupation. In 2009, a magnetometry survey of the Bankfoot sites revealed detail of the internal structures in the camps, although there was little to be found in the northern annexe of the camp other than an oven or fireplace. Curiously, when the Bankfoot fort was surveyed, no features were recorded. This is unusual as there were always some buildings constructed in a fort; even if they were only wooden structures, they should be detectable in any geophysical survey. This suggests that the fort may have been temporary and occupied only for a very brief period, or that it was never completed. Only further exploration of the site is likely to reveal the answer.

Exploring

Dalswinton is easily reached from Dumfries, around six miles north on the A76. Where the A76 crosses the River Nith at Auldgirth, take the right-hand turn and head towards the village of Dalswinton. Immediately before the village, take a right towards Bankhead Farm, where the sites can be reached on foot. Go through the farmyard and follow the track past the railway line, and then take the underpass into Bankfoot Camp I. The forts and camps are marked on the Ordnance Survey maps.

There are a number of military installations at Dalswinton, including the fort (seen here) at Bankhead.

Drumlanrig

Fort | NX 854 989
Camp | NX 857 988
Possible Camp | NX 857 986
Islafoot Camp | NX 859 991

Drumlanrig is home to a series of camps and the fort, all of which were discovered from the air in the mid-1980s. The fort is around 1.2 hectares, with annexes on the eastern and southern sides, and is assumed to date to the Flavian period because of the style of gate. Parts of the fort were excavated for an episode of the television series *Time Team*, but in advance of this the site had already been surveyed, helping to identify the layout of the site and confirming the existence of the annexe to the east.

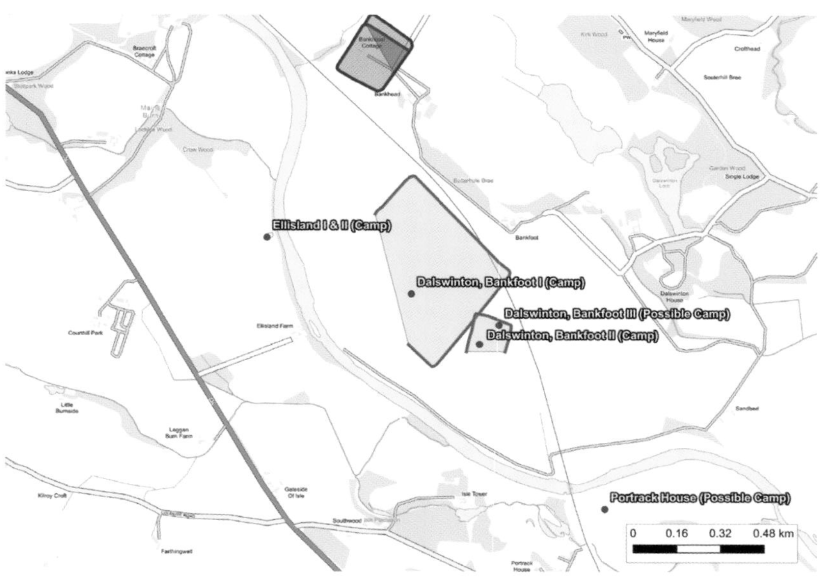

The fort site at Drumlanrig.

Time Team uncovered a range of pottery from across the Empire, including Spain, France and southern Britain, showing the diversity of the soldiers based in the furthermost reaches of the Empire. However, the excavations failed to find any material evidence of 1st-century occupation of the site, although there were signs of activity during the Antonine period. When the fort was abandoned, the ramparts were pushed into the ditches and the timber buildings were burned down.

There are three camps to the south of the fort, with the one at Islafoot being on the opposite side of the Nith. The camps vary in size with I being 1 hectare, and II being 3.5 hectares, while Islafoot is around 4.5 hectares. As Camps I and II are overlapping, neither their chronology nor their date is clear.

Exploring

Situated within the gardens of Drumlanrig Castle (which is itself open to the public), several of the defensive ditches and parts of the rampart can be seen as a low mound running across the edge of the parkland. The camps are more difficult to access as the fields are farmed.

Durisdeer

Fortlet | NS 902 048
Camps | NS 891 030

There are two camps at Durisdeer, discovered through aerial photography in the 1940s, neither of which has been fully investigated. Instead, it is the fortlet that is a must-see. Perched on a hillside, guarding the Roman road that heads northeast through the glen, the fortlet is one of the best-preserved sites in Scotland. Approaching the fortlet, the modern-day visitor is given a good idea of how intimidating such a structure would have been, and how it enabled the Romans to control the movement of people in the area.

The fortlet was excavated in the late 1930s, when two timber buildings, probably barracks, were revealed, along with evidence for two phases of occupation in the Antonine period. The fortlet is similar

The fortlet at Durisdeer is one of the best-preserved fortlets in Britain, with a bank surrounding the interior while a ditch surrounds the exterior.

in style to other such sites, with a ring ditch and an outer mound and an interior area surrounded by a rampart with a single entrance. Today, the rampart stands at between 1.2 metres and 4 metres high.

Exploring

The main road to the village of Durisdeer cuts through the camps (probably on the line of the old Roman road), and little can be seen on the ground. However, the real treat is the Antonine fortlet, well preserved because of its remote location.

Park in the village, outside the church (which is worth a quick visit), and follow the track on foot northwards. Go through the gate and carry on the main path in front of you for about half a mile. The fortlet is signposted and indicates when you should deviate from the main track. Wear stout footwear and be aware that there is a little burn at the foot of the hill. The field you enter once you have crossed the wall off the main track can be wet and very boggy. The climb to the fortlet is steep and the path uneven in places, but the views are worth the effort, as are the preserved remains of the fortlet.

Ewes Door

Tower | NY 372 986

Ewes Door has yet to be excavated, so archaeologists are not 100 per cent certain that the site is Roman. However, it does appear to be the right shape and it is only 30 metres from an old road that might also be Roman.

The site itself consists of a mound, around half a metre high and surrounded by a one-metre wide ditch, with an entrance way. When the site was surveyed in 2015, the surveyors thought they could make out the remains of two postholes, which would have held the base of the wooden tower. Given its similarities to other tower sites in the southeast, it is assumed to date to the 1st century, although no datable artefacts have been found.

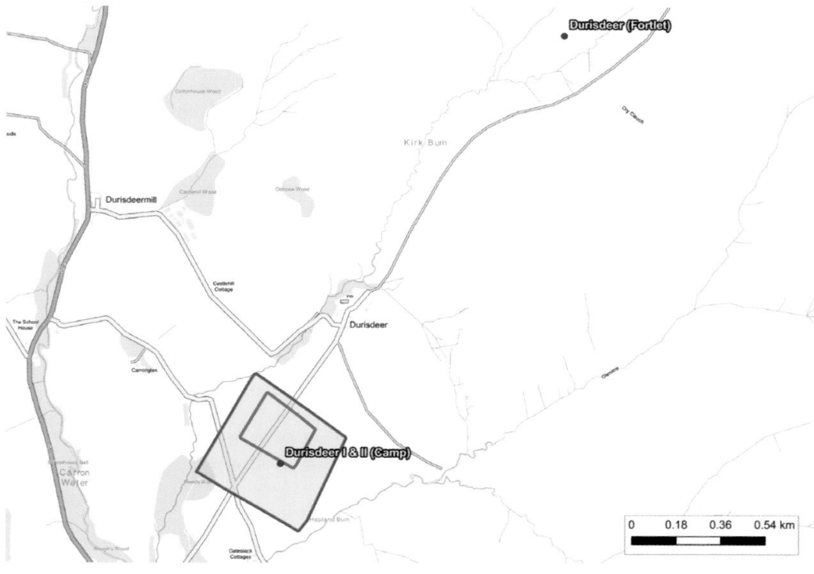

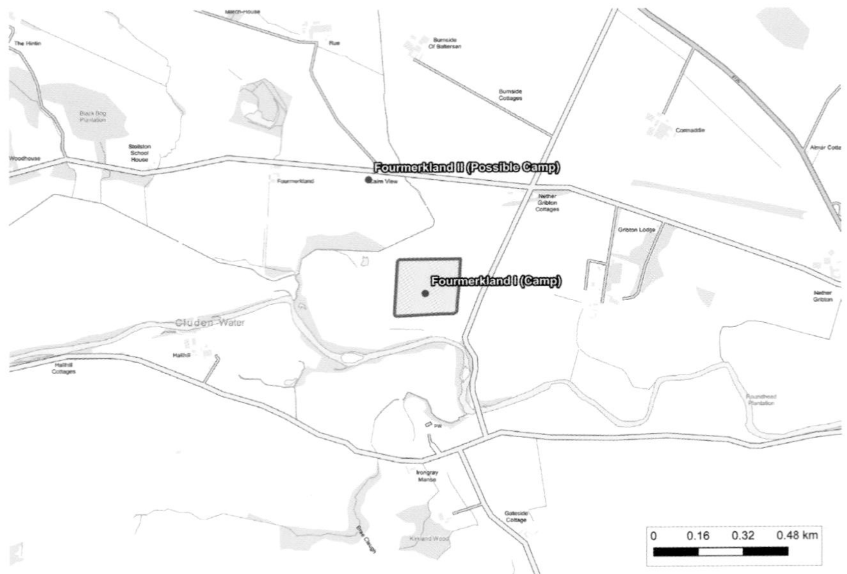

Fourmerkland

Camp | NX 913 804
Possible Camp | NY 372 986

The camp at Fourmerkland was discovered from the air by St Joseph in 1949, and confirmed through brief excavation. St Joseph also noted a second possible smaller camp, close to the first one, although it has not yet been confirmed as a Roman site.

Key Dates

1949: The site is discovered by aerial survey

Exploring

The camp is located to the northwest of Dumfries. Heading north on the A76, take a left on to the B729 at Newbridge just after passing over the Cluden Water. After a mile, carry straight on when the road turns right, and then at the crossroads take a left. The camp is on the right.

Gatehouse of Fleet

Fortlet | NX 595 573

Located next to the Water of Fleet, the 0.3-hectare fortlet at Gatehouse of Fleet was first identified by St Joseph during aerial reconnaissance. St Joseph excavated the site in 1960 and 1961, confirming that the defences enclosed a rectangular area with rounded corners, which had a single entrance in the northeastern side of the defences. His excavations failed to find any evidence of internal structures, although these would have been wooden and traces of posts and foundations can be elusive when excavated.

The second year of excavations did uncover postholes at the entrance, which would have supported a watch tower with a gateway below. These excavations also found a wooden building in the interior, likely to have been a barracks as there was evidence that it was subdivided into rooms. Behind this was a small store or granary where traces of burnt wheat were found. Opposite the barracks was another building, its purpose unknown. Fragments of pottery were dated to the 1st century, giving a Flavian date for the site.

When he discovered the site, St Joseph was puzzled that there was a fortlet too far upstream to be guarding a harbour. Instead, he argued that there must be additional fortifications further to the west into Galloway, and that the role of the fortlet was to guard the road heading towards those. Within a few years, archaeologists would be able to confirm the existence of some of those fortifications.

The site of the Gatehouse of Fleet fortlet.

Exploring

The site is to the north of Gatehouse of Fleet and can be reached by heading west on the B727, into the town and taking the second road (Church Street) on the right, just after the church. Continue on this road past the cemetery to the car park. Continue on foot for about a quarter of a mile until you see a clump of trees in the field in front of you. Turn left and follow the boundary towards the river (and under the pylons). The fortlet is at the edge of the field with the trees in front of you.

Glenlochar

Fort | NX 735 645
Camp I | NX 737 651
Camp II | NX 735 650
Camp III | NX 739 642
Camp IV | NX 738 647
Camp V | NX 738 647
Camp VI | NX 738 647

The concentration of camps, along with a fort, in this small area of Galloway shows how strategically important this part of the country was to the Romans.

Discovered by St Joseph in 1949 while he was undertaking aerial reconnaissance, the fort is constructed on a natural plateau next to the River Dee and probably guarded a river crossing. Limited excavations took place in 1952 to establish that the site was Roman, however, rather than confirming the existence of one fort, excavators St Joseph and Richmond uncovered evidence of three fortifications built on top of each other. The earliest fort was Flavian and appeared to have been burned down. The second fort

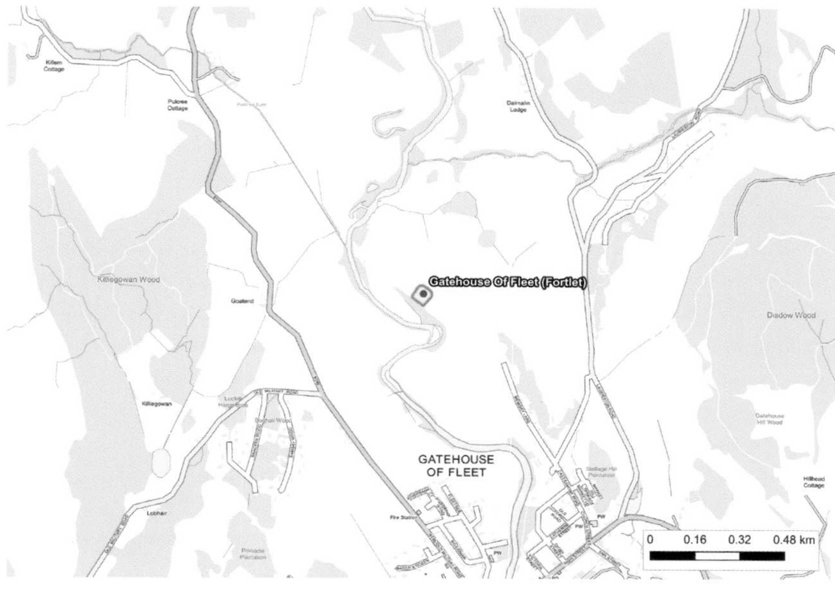

There are a significant number of camps, as well as at least one fort, in the area around Glenlochar.

was from the Antonine period, while the third one was from later in that period. There is some speculation that there is an even earlier fort on this site, as the aerial photographs show a ditch at the northern end of the plateau that may have belonged to an early fortification, although it could be part of an annexe.

The Roman road through Dumfriesshire approaches the plateau from the east and seems to be heading towards the earlier, ditched enclosure rather than the established fort. Surrounding the forts are at least six camps, all of which are still undated. Clearly, Galloway was very important to the Romans and they kept coming back.

Exploring

Heading northwards on the A713 from Castle Douglas, turn left towards Glenlochar. The fort site is on the left just before the bridge across the Dee, while the camps are on both sides of the road.

Glenluce

Camp | NX 198 566

At 17.9 hectares, Glenluce may not be the biggest camp, but it is the most westerly known site in Dumfries and Galloway and in Scotland. If it is the last camp, then it seems to be located randomly, but it is possible there are other sites around Stranraer or the Rhins of Galloway, just waiting to be found.

Located on the eastern bank of the River Luce, the camp defences and a *titulus* showed up clearly when the site was discovered in 1992. Aerial photography has also identified the Roman road, approaching from Glenlochar then heading northwards towards Loch Ryan. Given that the nearest known Roman sites to

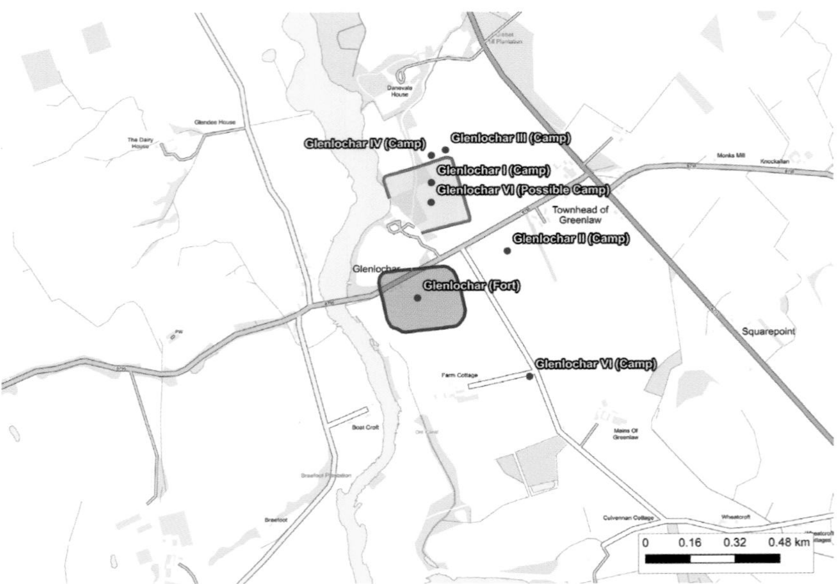

Glenluce are the camps at Girvan Mains, 25 miles to the north, or the complex of fortifications at Glenlochar, about 33 miles to the east, there must surely be more fortifications much closer, just waiting to be discovered.

Exploring

The camp is to the south of the A75 at Glenluce. Take the minor road on the left after the turn-off to Glenluce; the road is just after the hill with the transmitter on it and the camp is immediately on your right.

The muddy view from the camp at Glenluce, which overlooks the Solway Firth.

High Torrs (Luce Bay)

Cairn | NX 141 556

Excavated in the 1930s, High Torrs was the site of a cairn made up of large stones. Within the cairn were a number of objects, including Roman pottery from the 2nd or 3rd century and cremated animal bones, which may have had human remains mixed in with them, although the excavators were not sure.

Archaeologists have interpreted the cairn as the grave of a Roman merchant or traveller, although it is possible that the grave goods belonged to a wealthy member of a local tribe.

Kirkcudbright – Stewartry Museum

Stewartry Museum, St Mary St, Kirkcudbright DG6 4AQ | Free Entry
www.dumgal.gov.uk/article/15735/The-Stewartry-Museum-Kirkcudbright
Opening Times | Mon–Sat 11:00–16:00

The museum contains a wealth of information on the local area and has a good exhibition on the Roman activity at Burnswark.

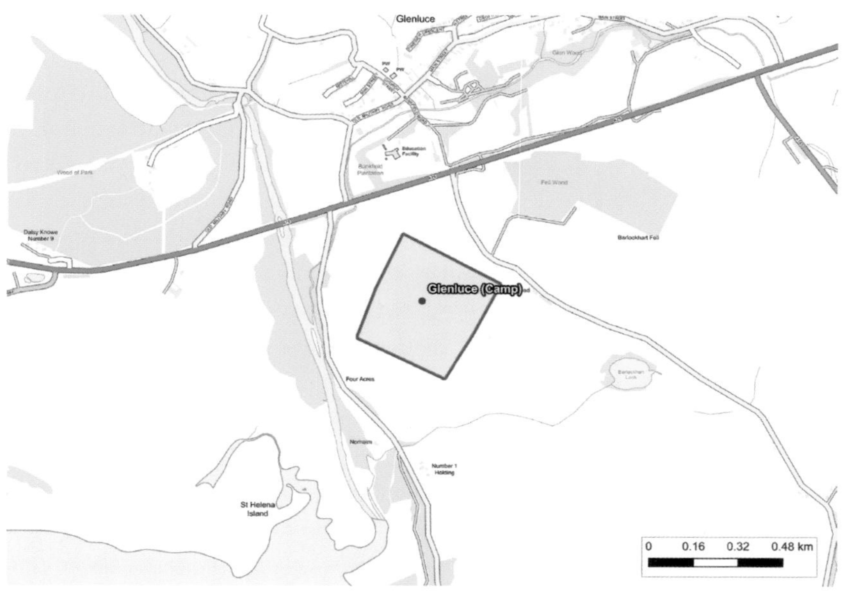

Kirkland

Fortlet | NX 804 901

Found in 1909, this 0.3-hectare fortlet was surrounded by a single ditch. Excavated in the 1990s, it was only occupied once, in the Flavian period. Curiously, there are no known Roman roads near by, which suggests that it is a very early site that was built and abandoned before the road network was established. When RCAHMS visited the site in 2008, they noted a broad ditch to the east of the fortlet. Although it is not clear whether this was in use when the fortlet was occupied or whether it is even Roman, but it does hint at more to be discovered about the site.

Kirkpatrick-Fleming

Possible Fortlet | NX 804 901
Camps | NY 280 702

There are two camps (and there may be a third) at Kirkland. One camp has been built inside the other, although it seems unlikely they were built and occupied during the same period. At 24.5 hectares, the outer camp is one of the largest in southern Scotland.

Over the years, the camps have been extensively excavated and surveyed, particularly in advance of the upgrading of the A74, which runs through the northeastern end of the camps. While there is not a confirmed date for the site, some 1st-century pottery was found in a ditch, although this could have been part of an annexe or another camp.

Key Dates

1949: St Joseph identifies Camp I during an aerial survey
1958: St Joseph discovers Camp II from the air
1968: Part of the site is geophysically surveyed and then excavated in advance of road construction
1995: Watching brief reveals the ditch on the north-east side of the camp

Ladyward

Fort | NY 113 820

The fort overlooks the place where the Dryfe Water meets the River Annan. It has a typical defensive structure of ditches and ramparts, although in this instance there are five ditches, which may indicate two periods of occupation, with the fort being shrunk or expanded during the second period. Such redevelopment of the fort is not unique and other examples have been recorded at the forts at Ardoch and Birrens.

Key Dates

1989: The fort is discovered during an aerial survey
2015: Magnetometry of the fort indicates that it was extensively damaged by fire

Lantonside

Fortlet | NY 010 661

Located at the mouth of the River Nith, the fortlet is similar to the one at Barburgh Mill and has yet to be surveyed or excavated. Aerial photographs have indicated that a large annexe may be located next to the fortlet.

Milton

Fort, Fortlet, Possible Camps | NT 092 014

Milton is another area that seems to have been a centre of Roman activity, with a fort, fortlet, camp, enclosures and possibly even a parade ground. Extensive excavation of the complex took place in the middle of the 20th century, with the excavator, J. Clarke, suggesting that the fort was abandoned before the Agricolan advance in the latter half of the 1st century. Clarke goes on to theorize that it was Agricola's predecessor, Cerialis, who invaded this part of Scotland. This is something on which archaeologists are undecided – Tacitus claims that it was Agricola who first invaded and conquered Scotland, although the archaeological evidence seems to suggest otherwise.

Moat of Lochrutton

Possible Fortlet | NX 897 739

An old account speaks of a large earthwork, now

virtually gone, which was next to Lochrutton Loch. It was broadly similar to fortlets elsewhere in the southeast and, with a Roman road within half a mile, it seems like a potential candidate for a small fortification.

Murder Loch

Fortlet & Possible Camp | NY 031 854

Identified from the air, and followed up by a small excavation, the site shares similar characteristics with other such fortifications. It is located between the fortlet at Fairholm and the fort at Carzield, giving weight to the theory that it is Roman, although there is no known road in the vicinity.

Key Dates

1974: The fortlet is seen as a cropmark in aerial photographs

1984: Further aerial photographs show a rectangular enclosure (possibly a camp) surrounding the fortlet

Raeburnfoot

Fort | NY 251 990
Camp | NY 250 995

The fort at Raeburnfoot has been known about since at least 1810, when the defences were still visible, although the remains were gradually being eroded by ploughing.

The earliest accounts suggested that there were two fortifications, one inside the other. However, excavations in 1897, 1946 and 1959 clarified that this was the site of a single small fort covering an area of around 0.5 hectares. The excavations revealed evidence of wooden buildings, including potential barracks.

The camp was discovered in 2004 during a re-analysis of old aerial photographs, and confirmed from the air the following year. Covering an area of around 13.2 hectares, it sits on high ground, overlooking the fort.

Exploring

The fort is difficult to access, but partial remains of the defences can be seen on the ground. A track follows the line of the Roman road to the east of the sites, running alongside the Rae Burn (*see* overleaf).

Sanquhar

Fortlet | NS 775 105

Located next to the confluence of the Crawick Water and the River Nith, the small fortlet covers an area of around 0.2 hectares and has not yet been explored.

Thornhill

Tower | NX 876 948

St Joseph recorded a mound with a flat top, along

Looking across the White Esk river towards the fort site at Raeburnfoot.

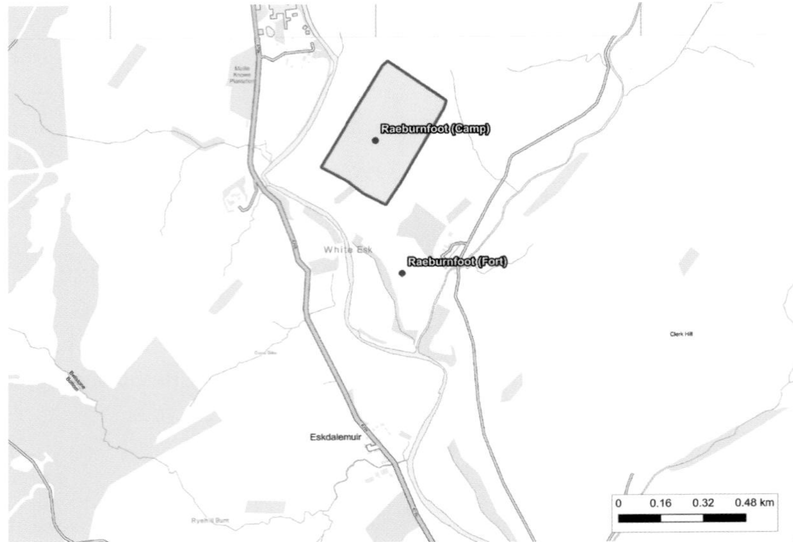

with an entrance, at Thornhill. He suggested it was a signal tower, an argument strengthened by its proximity to a Roman road.

The site has yet to be excavated, but there is some speculation that it is not a Roman tower, but a homestead dating from after the Roman period.

Key Dates

1949: St Joseph records the mound from aerial photographs

1995: RCAHMS reinterpret the site, suggesting it is a homestead

Ward Law

Camp | NY 024 668

First recorded in 1772, the camp was excavated in the middle of the 20th century. During excavation of the ditches, it was found that in places they were cut through rock, a feature that is rare in Scotland, although not unheard of. The best-known example of the technique is found at Raedykes in Aberdeenshire.

Within the ditch network is a native hillfort. Some archaeologists have speculated that the Romans used this to help them defend Ward Law, although it is not clear whether this site was in use at the same time as the camp. Maxwell and Wilson have proposed an alternative theory: that Ward Law was actually a military training site, with the hillfort used for practice.

In the 1940s there was some suggestion that a signal tower was added on to the native fort next to the Roman site. This idea has not been explored further and there are no traces of it on the ground.

Key Dates

1772: Pennant records the site, giving it Roman origins

1939, 1949–50: The camp is excavated, revealing the defences and some entrances

2009: Magnetometry survey of the defences

Exploring

The camp and indigenous fort are next to the B725 and, although there are almost no traces of the camp, the native fort can be seen and explored. Some care is needed, as it is densely wooded.

White Type

Tower | NT 055 119

White Type is a typical Roman tower site: a ditch surrounding a rampart that protects a secure area within. Discovered in 1930 and excavated the following year, the tower commands good views along the Roman road, and is similar in size to other sites dating from the Antonine period.

The Other Sites

Amisfield Tower (Camp | NX 996 839)

An 11.5-hectare site that was originally identified from the air. It is located next to the Roman road from Nithsdale, which heads south towards Annandale.

Annanfoot (Camp | NY 180 652)

The camp at Annanfoot was constructed at the point where the River Annan flows into the Solway Firth. It was excavated in the late 1970s and, although this was never published, archaeologists have speculated that it may have played a part in the earliest Roman invasions into Scotland. Part of the site has since been covered by housing.

Applegarthtown (Possible Camp | NY 103 838)

Aerial photographs taken towards the end of the 20th century recorded a number of cropmarks that indicated the presence of a camp, but further work or excavations are needed to confirm whether this is a Roman site.

Carronbridge (Camp | NX 868 977)

Identified in the 1950s, the site was subsequently excavated along with an adjacent enclosure. There was a lack of evidence to suggest that the latter was Roman, but the excavations did uncover parts of the rampart and ditch, along with some postholes and pottery. The enclosure was more extensively excavated in 1989 and 1990. Again, there were no datable finds, although evidence of roundhouses and an oven was found. Recent radiocarbon dating of the enclosure has given a date range of 145 BC to AD 415 for activity on the site.

Ellisland (Camps | NX 928 842)

There are at least two camps at Ellisland, both spotted from the air in the middle part of the 20th century. The first camp seems to share part of the defences with the second camp, which is the smaller of the two.

Gallaberry (Camp | NX 963 827)

First recorded in 1939, the site was later excavated in 1952 with the size being confirmed as just under 0.7 hectares. The excavations confirmed that the camp may have been constructed on top of a Neolithic cursus, a pre-Roman monument.

Gilnockie (Camp | NY 389 792)

Recorded in 1912, this camp covers an area of about 11.3 hectares. Parts of the rampart and ditch are visible on the northeastern and southeastern sides.

Hangingshaw (Possible Camp | NY 098 898)

A number of cropmarks spotted in the late 1960s indicated the presence of a camp at Hangingshaw, fairly close to a Roman road. The site has not yet been confirmed through excavation or geophysical survey.

Hayknowes (Possible Camp | NY 180 652)

Cropmarks seen at Hayknowes by Barri Jones led to an extensive aerial survey of Dumfries and Galloway in the late 1970s. Jones interpreted these as belonging to a camp, however this has not been confirmed on the ground.

Hillside, Annan Hill (Camp | NY 192 654)

The camp was identified from the air in 1958 and subsequently excavated in the 1960s and again in the 1980s, with some further work taking place at the beginning of the 21st century. The site was probably chosen because it is next to the point where the River Annan flows into the Solway Firth. The excavations failed to provide any datable artefacts so the occupation period of the site is still not known.

Knowe Cottages (Possible Camp | NS 721 131)

Discovered from aerial photographs, the camp defences were excavated in the 1950s. While the archaeologists found some elements of a camp, such as the defences, they did not find any artefacts or the gates, implying that the site may not be Roman after all.

Lochmaben (Camp | NY 091 822)

Although only part of the defences of this camp have been found, St Joseph speculated that it would probably be around 25 hectares, which would make it one of the largest sites in southern Scotland. The camp encloses a small hill, which is curious, although there is a similar layout at the camp at Raedykes in Aberdeenshire.

Lochrutton (Camp | NX 893 731)

One of the most recent discoveries, the Lochrutton camp was found when archaeologists looked again at old aerial photographs. Only parts of the defences were visible, but the camp seems to have been around 14 hectares. As well as the camp, a number of other features were seen in the photographs, including a rectangular enclosure, which could be an annexe or maybe even an early fort.

Mains of Southwick (Possible Camp | NX 93 57)

The story of Roman activity at Mains of Southwick comes from a letter written in 1779, claiming that a camp could be found on land near by. There is no trace of it today.

Middlebie Hill (Camps | NY 207 764)

There are two camps at Middlebie Hill. Both are next to the road, and fairly close to the fort and camp at Birrens. The first camp was noted in the 1940s, and the second camp, which lies within the first, was not located until the mid-1960s.

Portrack House (Possible Camp | NX 941 831)

Cropmarks suggest a length of ditch with a possible corner, which might indicate a camp. Within the site there appear to be traces of a rectilinear feature that could be another camp.

Ruthwell (Camp | NY 101 677)

Discovered in 1978, this 2.5-hectare camp is next to the Lochar Water, at the point where it flows into the Solway Firth.

Summerfield (Possible Camp | NY 11 67)

During his 1970s aerial survey, Barri Jones noted a series of cropmarks that indicated a possible camp at Summerfield. To date, the site has not been explored or confirmed.

Torwood (Camp | NY 121 819)

First recorded by Roy in the 18th century, Torwood is another camp located at the point where two rivers meet – here, the Dryfe Water and the River Annan. Covering an area of about 15 hectares, it has not been surveyed or dated. Only part of the defences can be still seen, as a low mound, with faint traces of the ditches running on the southern part of the site.

Trailflat (Camp | NY 048 850)

This small camp was located in 1983, and is by the Water of Ae. Covering an area of around 1.4 hectares, only parts of the defensive ditches have been located. The camp is probably guarding an as yet undiscovered Roman road.

Waterside Mains (Possible Camp | NX 869 969)

Cropmarks noted in the 1970s suggest the presence of a camp, but it has not been fully surveyed and some parts of it have not been recorded. Further work is needed to confirm whether or not this is a Roman site.

Chapter 17

LANARKSHIRE

Together, North and South Lanarkshire cover a considerable part of the central Lowlands. This area has a full range of Roman sites, which is unsurprising, given the main western route into Scotland at that time followed the corridor now serviced by the M74. From the fortlet at Redshaw Burn and the numerous camps dotted alongside the motorway, to the forts of the Antonine Wall, Lanarkshire has some of the most significant concentrations of Roman activity in Scotland.

Beattock Summit

Tower | NS 999 153

Originally photographed by the RAF, the Beattock Summit site was excavated in 1966 and proved to be similar to other tower sites, in particular those on the Gask frontier - an enclosed central area with a tower, surrounded by a rampart and ditch. No datable finds were uncovered but archaeologists think the tower was linked to the Antonine fortlet at Redshaw Burn, less than two and a half miles away. However, as suggested by the comparison with the sites, the tower is very similar to the 1st-century Flavian towers in Perthshire.

Key Dates

1940s: The site is photographed but only identified as a possible tower later
1966: The site is excavated, confirming its Roman origins

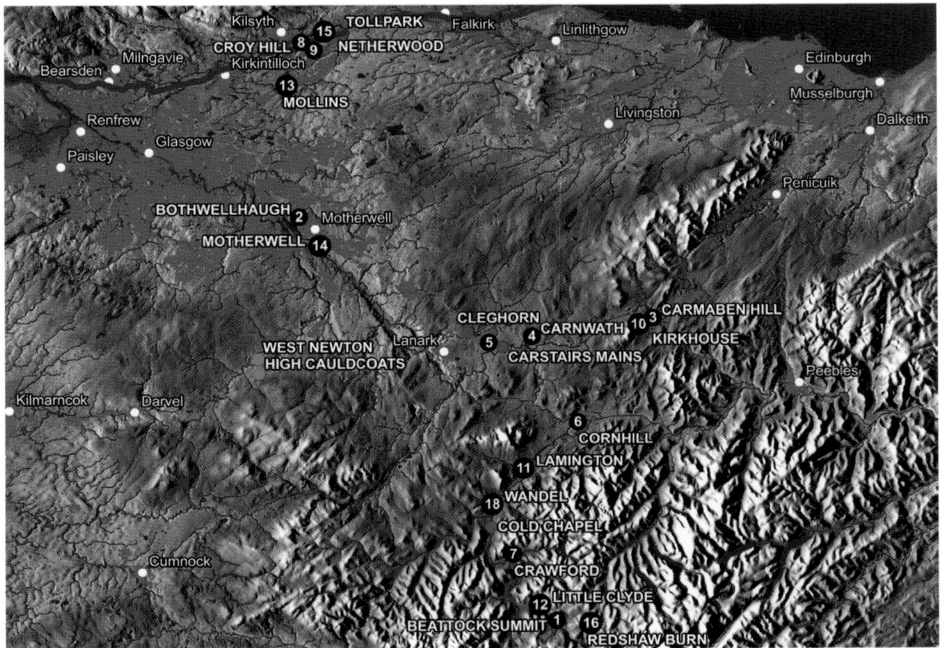

Bothwellhaugh

Fort | NS 730 577

The shores of Strathclyde Loch are the setting for this fort overlooking the water, where the South Calder Water flows into the loch. Upstanding remains were first noted in *The Old Statistical Account of Scotland* in the late 18th century but then seem to have been demolished at some point in the subsequent 70 years, as antiquarians at the end of the 19th century were unable to find the site. Of course, they may have been looking in the wrong places, as there are still some remains visible today.

The site was excavated in the 1950s, with archaeologists uncovering the rampart, which had a stone base with the top levels built from clay. The northeast and southeast defences consisted of two ditches, while there was only one on the other side. The entrances were noted, but not fully excavated, and it was also concluded that the interior buildings had been built from timber, with two possible construction phases.

The bath house was discovered near by and excavated in the mid-1970s, because it was at risk from water damage as the loch levels were raised. Subsequently, it was dismantled and relocated on slightly higher ground. Pottery recovered from the excavations gives an Antonine date for the structure.

Exploring

Bothwellhaugh fort and bath house are located within Strathclyde Country Park. While there is little to see of the fort – the southwestern and southeastern ramparts are visible as low mounds – the bath house, although no longer in its original position, is worth visiting. The remains that have survived are impressive and give a good indication of the layout of the building. The *frigidarium* (cold room), *caldarium* (hot room) and two *tepidaria* (warm rooms) along with the semi-circular plunge pool are all on display, while a fountainhead and a sandstone head of a goddess from the site are in the Hunterian Museum collection in Glasgow.

Carmaben Hill

Possible Tower | NT 109 469

St Joseph noted that Carmaben was the perfect location for a signal tower, because of the views from the site and because it is overlooking a Roman road. However, he was unable to find any archaeological evidence for such a site.

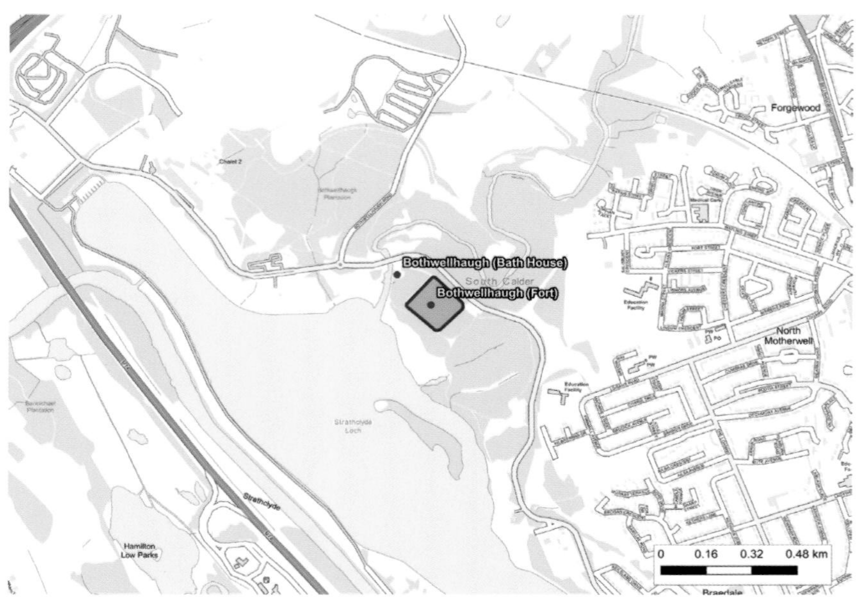

Carnwath

Bankhead – Camp I | NS 982 450
Bankhead – Camp II | NS 982 449
Bankhead – Fortlet | NS 971 449

Two camps have been discovered at Bankhead, one overlapping the other, although they do not appear to be contemporary with each other as they do not share defences, as is the case at other camps. Although only parts of the defences of Camp I have been identified, archaeologists believe that it covers an area of about 18 hectares, while Camp II is smaller, at 12.2 hectares.

The fortlet was also identified from the air, and appears to be guarding a crossing over the Lampits Burn. Most of the site has been destroyed, either by quarrying or by the former railway line, which cuts through the site. Archaeologists believe that it dates to the 1st century.

Castledykes

Fort | NS 928 442
Camp IA & B | NS 922 447
Camp IIA & B | NS 928 446
Camp III | NS 923 445
Camp IV | NS 931 445

Excavations by Anne Robertson in the middle of the 20th century revealed that the 3.2-hectare fort at Castledykes had three occupation phases, similar to the fort at Crawford. The first fort was from the 1st-century Flavian period. It was superseded by one from the Antonine period, which was abandoned and reoccupied at a later date. Much of the earlier fort had been destroyed by the later site, although Robertson did note one curious feature: an incomplete ditch outside of the eastern Flavian defences. A number of entrances were identified from the breaks in the ditch, which led Robertson to speculate whether they might have belonged to an early Agricolan site that pre-dated the Flavian fort.

The Antonine fort had a similar footprint and layout to the earlier fortification, although, as at Crawford, part of one ditch was filled in as the site was widened, while the remaining ditches were recut and the rampart expanded. Robertson thought that an annexe on the eastern side of the north part of the fort had been constructed at this time. The fort was then abandoned for a short period and subsequently reoccupied with little change to the structure, although the annexe appears to have been reduced in size. However, there is some evidence from aerial photographs taken in the 1980s that the annexe covered the whole of the north side of the fort, rather than just half of it, and that it may even have been physically linked to the riverbank.

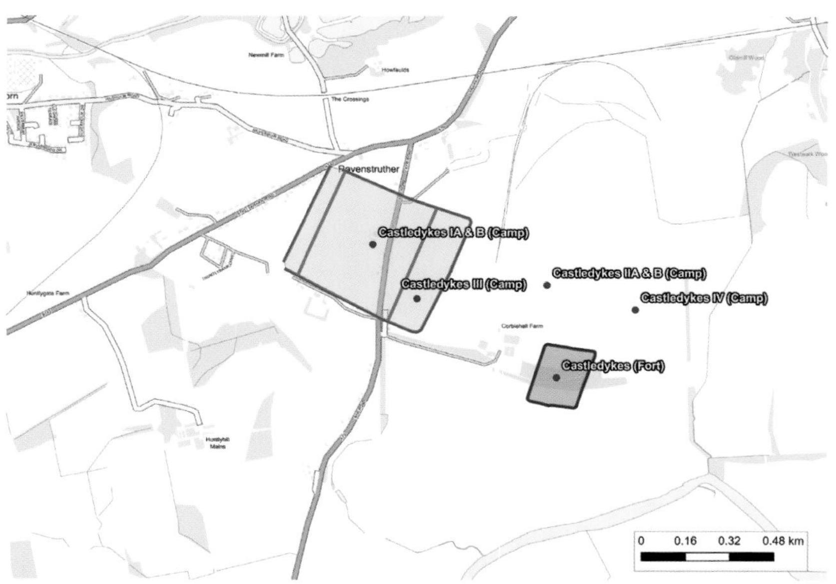

Exploring

The site is to the northeast of Lanark on the A70, the Ayr Road. Follow the road eastwards at the turn-off for Corbiehall. To get to the fort on foot, follow the track (which is a Roman road) through the woodland. Go past the turn-off on the left, and the western rampart will be ahead of you. The path turns slightly to the left around the centre of the fort, and then passes through the eastern rampart.

Cornhill

Camp | NT 021 357

Originally covering an area of around 17 hectares, the camp was later reduced in size to about 13.8 hectares. No datable evidence has been uncovered for the site.

Exploring

The camps can be found on a minor road between the A72 and the A702.

Crawford

Forts | NS 953 214
Camp I | NS 959 205
Camp II | NS 958 204
Camp III | NS 958 204
Camp IV | NS 958 204
Crawford Parish | NS 92 06

Crawford appears to have been an important location for the Romans, with four camps and a fort that was occupied during the Flavian and Antonine periods. Perhaps this is not surprising, given Crawford's location in a fairly wide, flat valley on the main route to the north from Carlisle. This also gives the site great views up and down the Clyde valley and control of anyone passing through the area.

The fort itself is one of the smaller military sites and was discovered in 1938 by St Joseph, who went on to excavate it in the 1960s. The excavations uncovered three periods of occupation, with three different forts constructed on the same site. The first fort, which dated to the Flavian period, had two ditches and faced south with internal timber buildings, which were dismantled, presumably when the fort was decommissioned. Archaeologists have found evidence of forts being deliberately burned down when they were abandoned, and the ramparts pushed into the ditch, however there is no evidence for this at Crawford, which suggests it was carefully dismantled when the army left the site. Due to similarities with other forts in the south, the excavators wondered if Crawford was a particularly early fort, constructed under Agricola in AD 80.

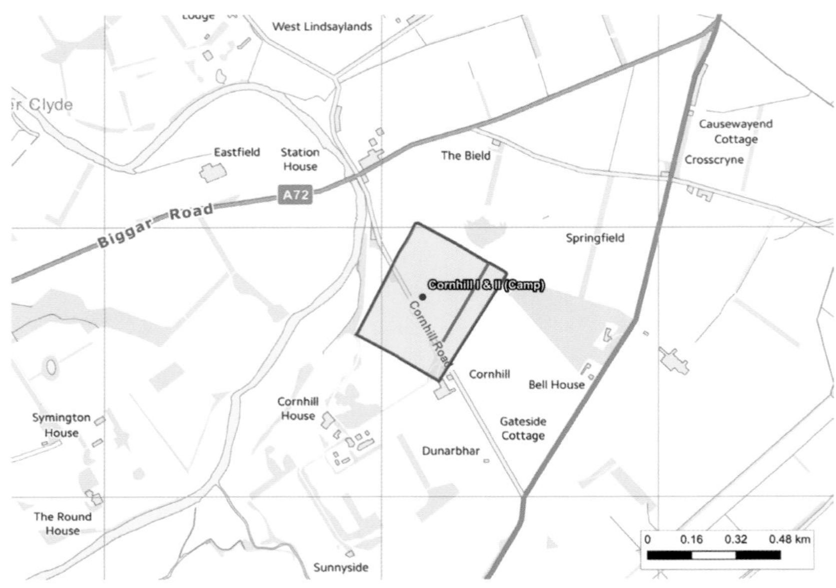

The second fort, built on the site of its Flavian predecessor, dated to the early Antonine period, and was similar in size to the previous one, although it was now rotated to face east. The internal buildings appeared to have been partially constructed from stone. After the site had been abandoned, the stone was robbed and used to construct nearby Crawford Castle (the ruins of which are visible just to the south of the fort). There appears to have been a brief respite before the construction of the third fort, which dated to later in the Antonine period. Two of the inner ditches were filled in, and the fort was widened, and a new outer ditch was created, while a new rampart was placed on top of the old ditches. To the north of the fort, a series of *lilia*, or shallow pits, were dug and probably filled with vegetation such as thorns, designed to slow down any forces running at the fort. These were similar to the *lilia* found at Rough Castle on the Antonine Wall. The internal buildings were not demolished from the last fort and were brought back into use with no apparent alterations, although there was some evidence of repair work. Following this period of occupation, the fort then appears to have been carefully demolished.

Exploring

The fort is just across the road from the medieval castle, although only the western part of the platform can be seen.

The fort area at Crawford.

Croy Hill

Fort | NS 733 765
Camp | NS 733 765
Fortlet | NS 732 764
Signal Platform (West) | NS 727 762
Signal Platform (East) | NS 728 762

With excellent views along the line of the Antonine Wall, a Roman presence at Croy Hill has been known about since the 18th century. Over that time, the site has been flattened and it was not until the 1920s and 1930s that George Macdonald began to investigate it.

The ditch of the Antonine Wall with the fort at Croy Hill in the distance.

Macdonald's excavations uncovered most of the site and recorded that the defences were built from turf, that there were three ditches on the west side and two on the south, and that the northern rampart was part of the Antonine Wall. He also recorded a lined well that had been covered over by the construction of a corner tower. Underneath the fort, Macdonald found the remains of a double ditch, which he interpreted as belonging to a possible fortlet. Archaeologists in the mid-1970s suggested a Flavian date for the site as it seemed similar to a structure on the nearby fort of Bar Hill. However, re-analysis of the possible fortlet has since indicated that it may have been the remains of a construction camp for the wall during the Antonine period.

A separate, confirmed fortlet, to the west of the fort, was uncovered during excavations in the late 1970s. The fortlet was adjoining the Antonine Wall and seemed to have been constructed at the same time as the wall, rather than one or the other being built first and then the other being added on. The fortlet was built in an area of shallow soil, so the entrance was slightly off-centre because of the bedrock, and the defensive ditches were themselves cut into the rock.

There are two signal platforms on the wall, which were semi-circular in shape, with a stone or bedrock base and layers of turf on top. The platforms most probably (but not definitely) had a beacon on top and were used for signalling and communicating with other parts of the wall and nearby military sites.

Exploring

The site is worth visiting for the views alone, particularly westwards along the Antonine Wall to the fort

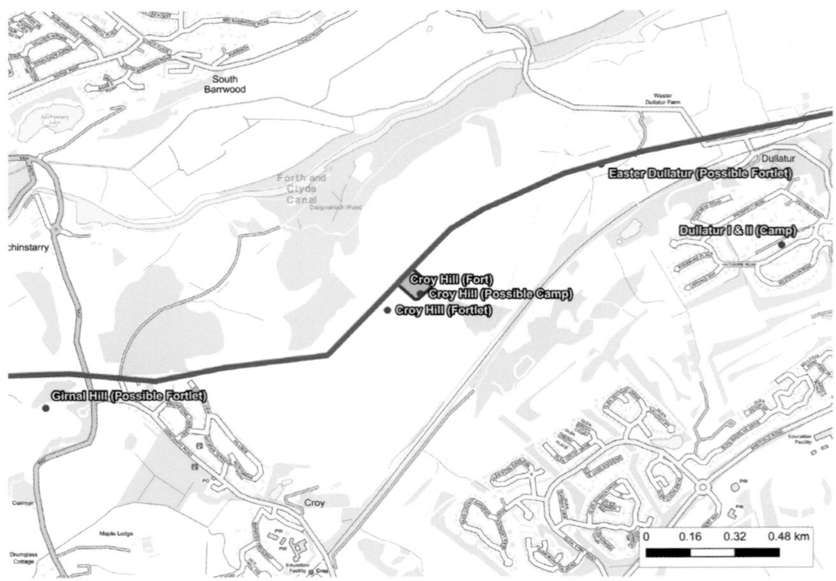

at Bar Hill, although there is nothing to see of the Croy Hill fort. The easiest approach is via the John Muir Way, which follows the towpath of the Forth and Clyde Canal as far as the road, Cadger's Heugh, just north of Dullatur. The path crosses the canal and then heads up Croy Hill along the line of the Military Way to the fort. The fortlet is west of the fort, and on the line of the wall.

Dullatur

Camps | NS 746 767
Easter Dullatur Fortlet | NS 740 770

The camps have been excavated on several occasions during the 20th century, most recently in 1998 in advance of housing development. Prior to this, Keppie excavated the site in the 1970s and confirmed the presence of two camps, an inner one and an outer one, with the latter being the earlier of the two.

Kirkhouse

Camp | NT 098 462

The camp at Kirkhouse was discovered in 1983 and is located alongside the presumed line of the Roman road. It covers an area of around 16 hectares.

Exploring

The camp is located alongside the modern A702, believed to follow the line of Dere Street, which heads towards Inveresk. It is possible that the road over-lies part of the southeastern defences.

Lamington

Camp | NS 977 307
Camp | NS 977 309
Fortlet | NS 977 307

The fortlet was discovered through aerial photographs taken by RCAHMS in the late 1970s. The entrance was not clear, and there are no remains to be seen on the ground. It is yet to be examined by LiDAR or geophysical survey and may give up more of its secrets if such investigations do take place. Like the fortlet, the camps were identified from the air, and there are no traces of either camp on the ground.

Little Clyde

Camp | NS 994 159

Little Clyde is another camp that is located at a convenient stopping point on the route northwards into Scotland. The site has not been excavated to any

great extent, although there have been patches of modern development on and around the site, such as the construction of a pipeline which went through the camp in the 1990s. No Roman features were recorded at the time.

Exploring

There are two ways to reach Little Clyde. Head to the fortlet at Redshaw Burn and continue on the track following the Roman road, which eventually arrives at the camp. By road, turn off at Junction 14 on the M74 and take the A702 northbound. Go under the motorway and take an immediate right on to the B7076, following alongside the M74 for about three miles. By the phone masts, the road will cross over the motorway; take a left before this, on to the track running behind the masts. Carry on for just over a mile, and take the first left, heading towards the forest. The Roman road carries on the line of the modern track past the Weigh Station and becomes a path heading up towards Redshaw Burn. Before the forest is a field boundary. Follow this to the other side of the trees and look for a track between the two lots of woodland; follow this and the ramparts will be visible on your right, past the first plantation. The northern corners, as well as the ditch and rampart, are still visible.

Mollins

Fort | NS 713 718

The area around Mollins fort vanished under the expansion of the M80 in the early part of the 21st century. Originally identified from cropmarks in the late 1970s, at only 0.4 hectare it is one of the smaller forts in Scotland, and has a single ditched annexe on its western side. The site was excavated shortly after its discovery by Gordon Maxwell and William Hanson, who dated the fort to the 1st century and concluded that it was likely that the site was deliberately destroyed in the same period.

Ahead of the expansion of the M80, archaeological evaluations took place around the fort, which included excavation and survey to the south of the site itself. The only evidence of Roman activity came from a single find – a stone quern. Further evaluations took place between 2009 and 2011, when the area was dug in advance of work on the motorway, but again there was a lack of Roman features and no artefacts were recovered.

Exploring

The site is located at the junctions of the M80, M73 and the A90 at Mollinsburn.

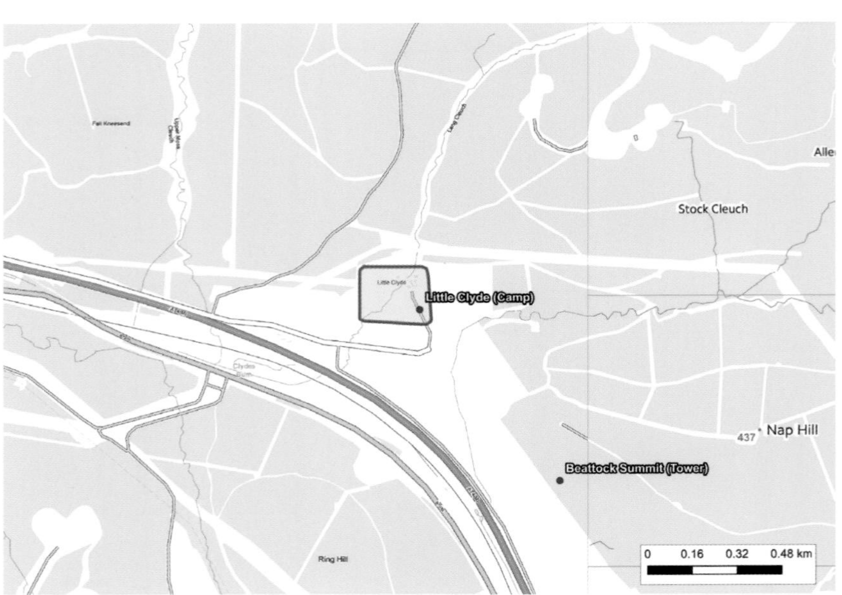

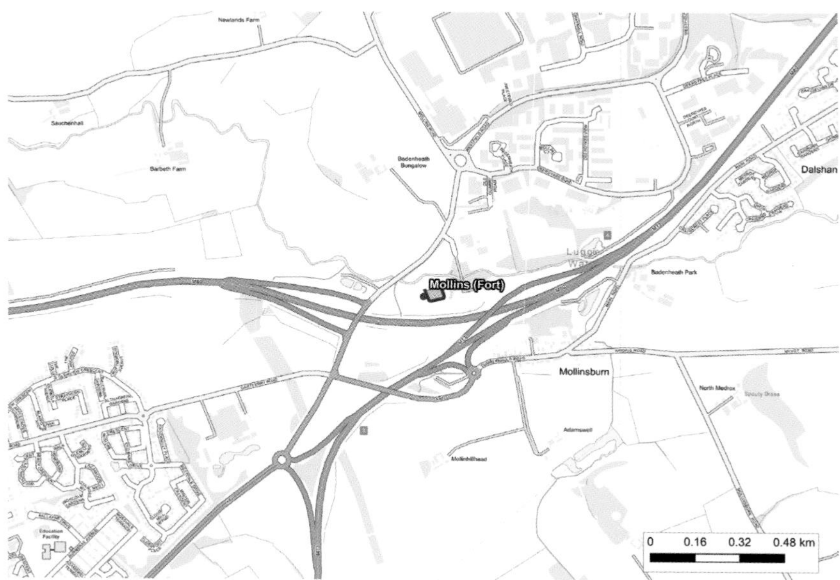

Motherwell

Unknown | NS 748 557

An 18th-century account refers to a Roman fort or camp on land near what is now Airbles cemetery. The description was of a ditched enclosure of around 0.1 hectare. If it was Roman, it would have been a small fortlet.

The area is big enough to accommodate a small fort or possibly a camp, but modern development and the railway line have interfered with the site. While a number of excavations were undertaken in the middle of the 20th century, and there were watching briefs ahead of development in the 1990s, no Roman artefacts were uncovered.

Netherwood

Possible Platform | NS 770 777

A possible tower at this location is mentioned by Sibbald in the 17th century. Excavations in 1979 revealed a platform connected to the Antonine Wall. Its function is unknown.

Redshaw Burn

Fortlet | NT 030 139

Discovered from the air in 1939, the fortlet guards the road heading north from Carlisle, almost running parallel with the modern M74. The fortlet has good views down the valley of the Evan Water as the road itself climbs around 365 metres.

Erosion from the burn has partially destroyed the defences, but archaeologists believe the fortlet had double ditches in places, although on the northwest side there is a single ditch. The fortlet also appears to have had a partial annexe on the northeastern side. The site has not been excavated, but there has been speculation that it was occupied in the 2nd or 3rd centuries. The similarities with Wandel fortlet in terms of size (both are around 0.8 ha) suggest that they were probably both occupied at the same time.

Exploring

The defences of the site are still visible on the southern side of the Roman road (now a track), with the rampart being visible in places. The site is surrounded by woodland, and the fortlet is visible in the clearing. From junction 15 on the M74 by Moffat, head north on the A701, parking just before Tweedshaws at the small layby. There is a footpath just before this into the forest, which takes you up Errickstane Hill, where the path joins the course of the Roman road by a small pond. The road passes the fortlet (*see* overleaf).

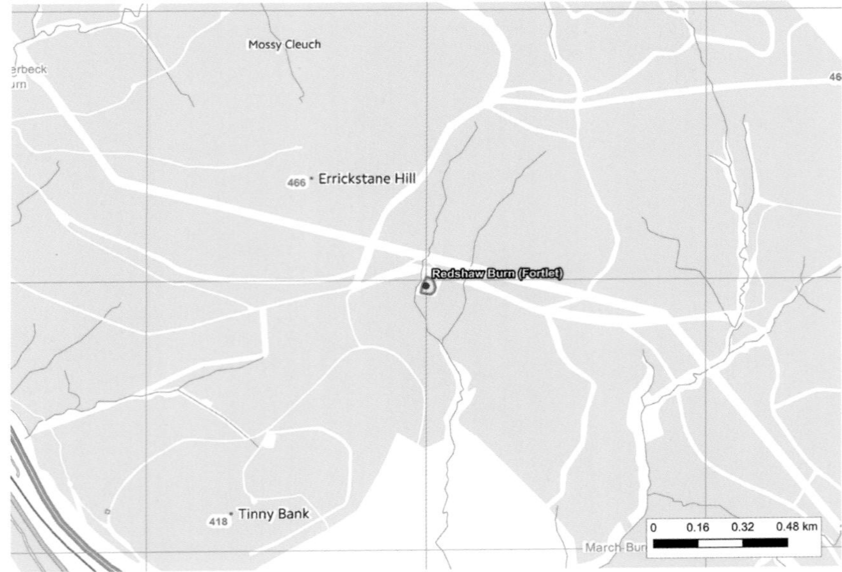

Tollpark

Camp | NS 778 774
Possible Fortlet | NS 77 77
Tower | NS 77964 77924

In 1959, a circular cropmark was identified from the air, with the suggestion that it could be the site of a Roman tower. Some archaeologists speculated that it was actually the site of a barrow, but when the site was dug by Woolliscroft he found Roman glass as well as a track that connected it to the Military Way.

Tollpark was predicted to be the site of a fortlet attached to the Antonine Wall by Hanson and Maxwell; however, when Keppie and Walker investigated the site in 1982, they found no evidence for it.

The camp was identified from cropmarks by St Joseph and excavated in 1998 in advance of development. Unfortunately, this failed to detect any Roman archaeological deposits because of early industrial developments on the camp site.

Wandel

Camp | NS 944 267
Fortlet | NS 944 268

Wandel plays host to both a fortlet and a temporary camp. The fortlet has been extensively eroded by farming, but the site was excavated in the 1960s, when it was noted that it was surrounded by a single ditch and next to the Roman road, although the entrance was not discovered. It was very similar in shape to the nearby fortlet at Redshaw Burn, so archaeologists have speculated that the two fortlets were built and in use at the same time.

The temporary camp is to the south of the fortlet, and was excavated in 1970, when the rampart was uncovered. No datable remains were discovered.

Exploring

While the fortlet is no longer visible, parts of the camp can still be made out, such as the southern and eastern parts of the ramparts. From the M74, take the A702 north from Junction 13 (by Abington Services), keeping on the A702 at the roundabout with the A73. Cross the River Clyde at Clyde's Bridge, then go over the railway bridge. The fortlet is in the field immediately on the right, with the Roman road running parallel to the railway line. The camp is in the adjacent field to the south. The remaining ramparts are at the far end of that field, and partly into the field beyond.

Westerwood

Fort & Possible Fortlet | NS 760 773

The fort at Westerwood has been known about for

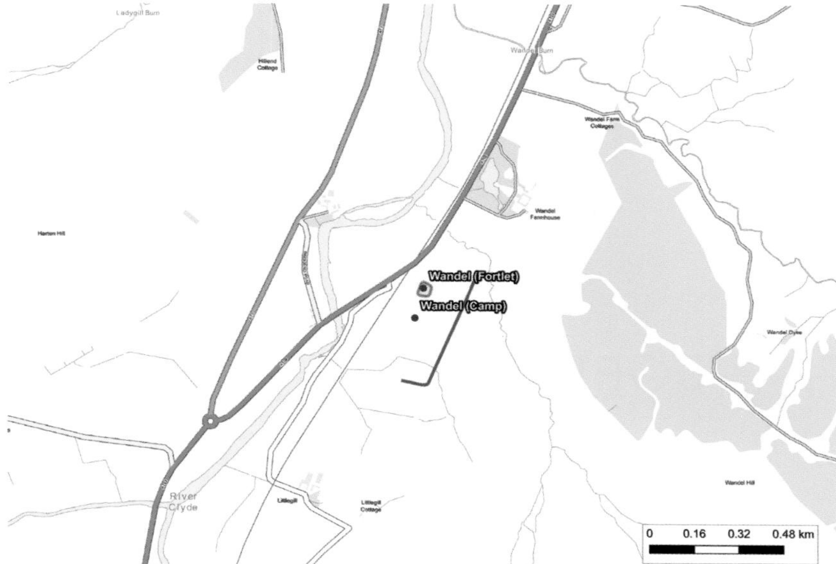

several hundred years. The first excavations, which took place in the 1930s, confirmed that the fort was attached to the Antonine Wall. The evidence indicated that the wall was finished first and then the fortification was linked to it.

Further excavations took place in the 1970s, and in 2006 a geophysical survey of the site revealed both Roman and post-Roman features, although the construction of the adjacent golf course appeared to have damaged some of those outside the fort.

The Other Sites

Carstairs Mains (Camp | NS 947 443)

This camp was originally seen from the air. Only parts of defences have been identified and the southern and southeastern sections remain undetected. Additional cropmarks, which are not clearly linked to the known defences, have led Jones to speculate that the site could cover an area of up to 17 hectares.

Cleghorn (Camp I | NS 903 454 – Possible Camp II | NS 910 458)

A number of cropmarks have been noted around the camp at Cleghorn, making it difficult to interpret the site, although it was excavated by St Joseph. However, archaeologists have disagreed on whether or not there is a Roman camp here.

Cold Chapel (Camp | NS 935 249)

The camp at Cold Chapel was discovered in the mid-1980s, and is close to a number of other camps at Carlops, Cornhill and Kirkhouse. The camp has not yet been fully surveyed.

Garnhall (Camp I | NS 785 780 – Camp II | NS 780 779)

The camps were discovered by St Joseph and have since been extensively excavated in advance of modern construction on both sites.

High Cauldcoats (Possible Camp | NS 692 414)

Cropmarks seen in 1989 showed a possible rounded corner along with two sections of ditch, which may indicate a Roman camp. The site is yet to be further investigated.

West Newton (Possible Camp | NS 692 430)

A series of cropmarks spotted in the early 1980s indicated a camp at West Newton, although it is yet to be confirmed through excavation or geophysical survey.

PART SIX: THE SOUTHEAST OF SCOTLAND

Chapter 18

SCOTTISH BORDERS

Dere Street was the main Roman road into Scotland from the legionary fortress at York, passing though the Scottish Borders – a route that remained relevant well beyond the fall of the Empire. Its importance throughout the Roman occupation is evidenced by the significant number of temporary camps from the different periods that have been located along it. The various forts in the region were also key to the activities of the camps, particularly the sire at Newstead, which was not only the largest fortification in Scotland for a time, but was also rebuilt on four occasions, and has yielded evidence of a substantial population living near by.

Brownhart Law

Fortlet | NT 790 096

Positioned by Dere Street, the main Roman road into Scotland, and first identified by St Joseph in 1945, the fortlet was excavated the following year. It affords excellent views of the surrounding area, so much so that St Joseph argued that its primary function was

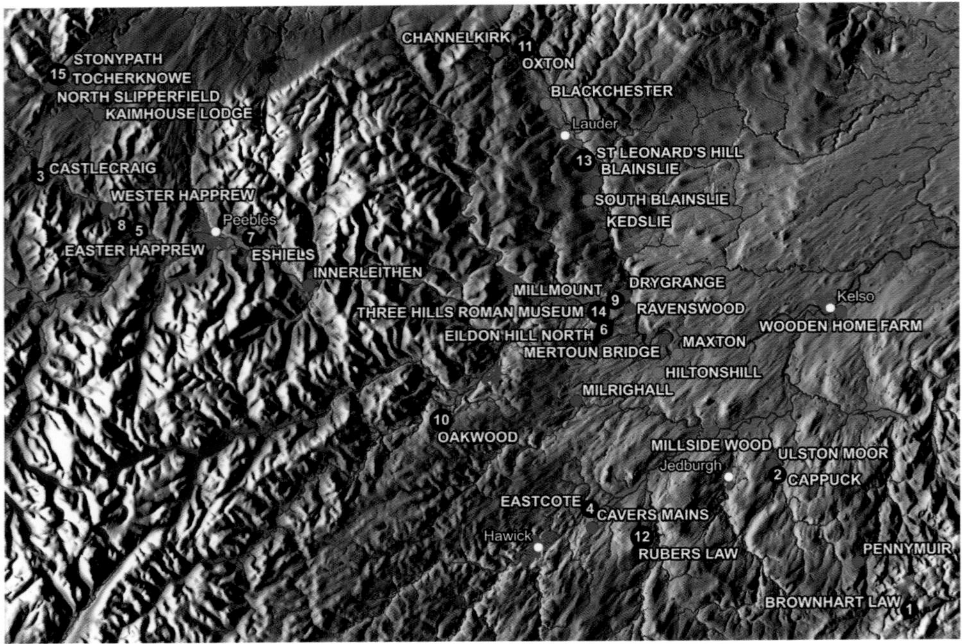

to communicate with the nearby tower on Rubers Law rather than with traffic on Dere Street.

Cappuck

Fortlet | NT 695 212
Camp | NT 699 209

The fortlet and camp at Cappuck are not only located along the line of the Roman road, but are also very close to the camps at Millside Wood and Ulston Moor. Positioned at the bottom of a hill, the fortlet guards the crossing over the Oxnam Water and was first excavated by Laidlaw in 1886. The excavation came up with evidence for internal structures, as well as an inscription by the 20th Legion who had constructed the fort. It was not until 1911, when Miller excavated the site, that the extent of the defences was revealed. Richmond followed this up in the 1940s with a more thorough examination of the fort, concluding that it had been occupied twice in the Flavian period, and then reoccupied on two occasions during the Antonine era. He argued that the inscription uncovered by Laidlaw would have come from one of the Antonine occupation periods.

The camp was identified during aerial reconnaissance in 1958 by St Joseph, but has not been further explored.

Key Dates

1886: Laidlaw undertakes the first excavation of the site, uncovering an inscription noting the 20th Legion had built the fort
1911: Miller excavates the fortlet uncovering sections of the defences and internal buildings
1949: Richmond begins further exploratory excavations
1958: The camp is identified from the air by St Joseph

Exploring

Cappuck is located around three miles to the north-east of Jedburgh. Heading south through the town, take the first left after crossing the Jed Water (opposite the car park) and follow Oxnam Road, taking a right at the fork after a mile. After a mile and a half, take the left turn just after Pleasants Bridge, and go on for just under a mile. The fort is after the farm at Cappuck and the camp is on the right-hand side of the road, to the west of Sourless Plantation.

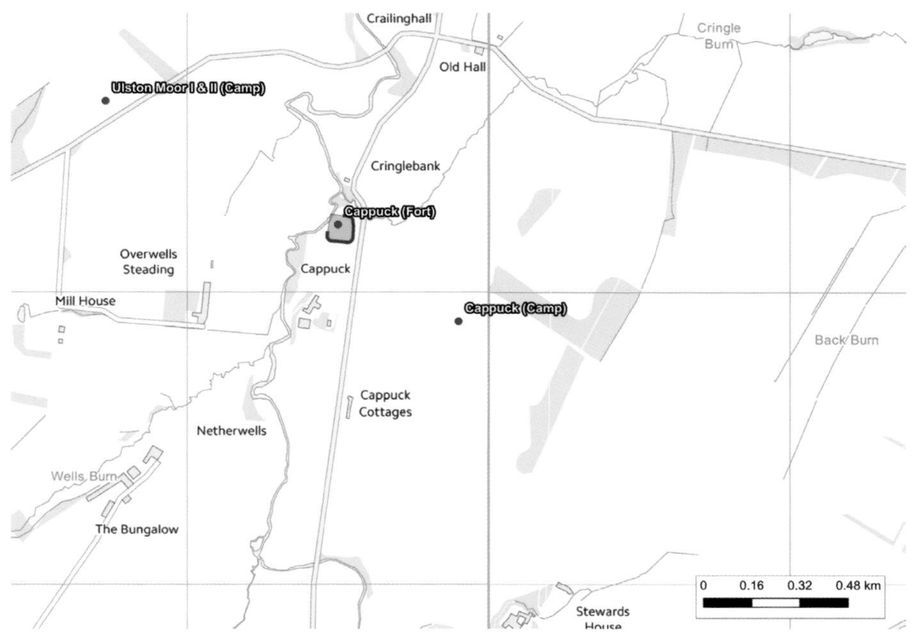

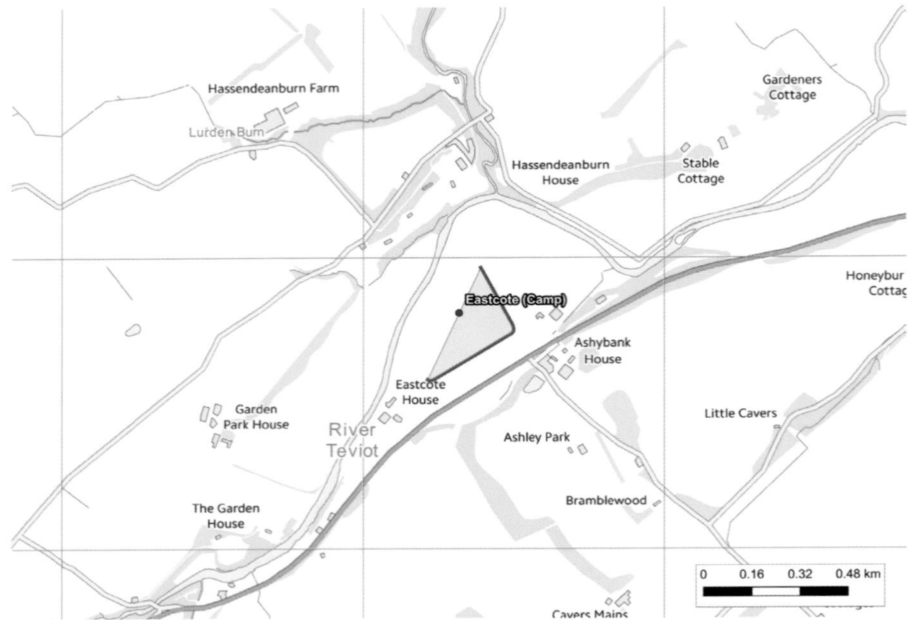

Castlecraig

Camp I | NT 125 445

Camp II | NT 125 445

The site was identified by St Joseph from the air in the 1960s, with Camp II set inside Camp I. The former is around 3.3 hectares in size, while the latter is 21 hectares. Only part of the defences of both sites have been identified and a watching brief in 2009 failed to locate any archaeological remains.

Eastcote

Camp | NT 543 178

The camp at Eastcote was constructed next to the River Teviot, which has eroded the eastern side of the site. It was first seen from the air by St Joseph at the beginning of the 1960s.

Exploring

Eastcote is located to the northeast of Hawick, on the A698. The site is about a mile outside of the town. There are no remains to be seen on the ground.

Easter Happrew

Fort | NT 194 401

Identified from aerial photographs in 1955, the fort at Easter Happrew was excavated by Steer the following year. Steer's excavations confirmed the unusual defences, consisting of only a single ditch and turf rampart. He also noted that the gates were not opposite each other, partly because the fort was rhomboid in shape.

St Joseph, when recording the site from the air, noted an annexe and a series of buildings to the east of the fort, which showed up as cropmarks. He speculated that these marks could indicate the presence of a *mansio*.

Artefacts indicate that the fort was occupied during the 1st century, and then abandoned in favour of a new fort constructed on the other side of the Lyne Water.

Key Dates

1955: The fort is identified from aerial photographs
1956: Steer excavates the site

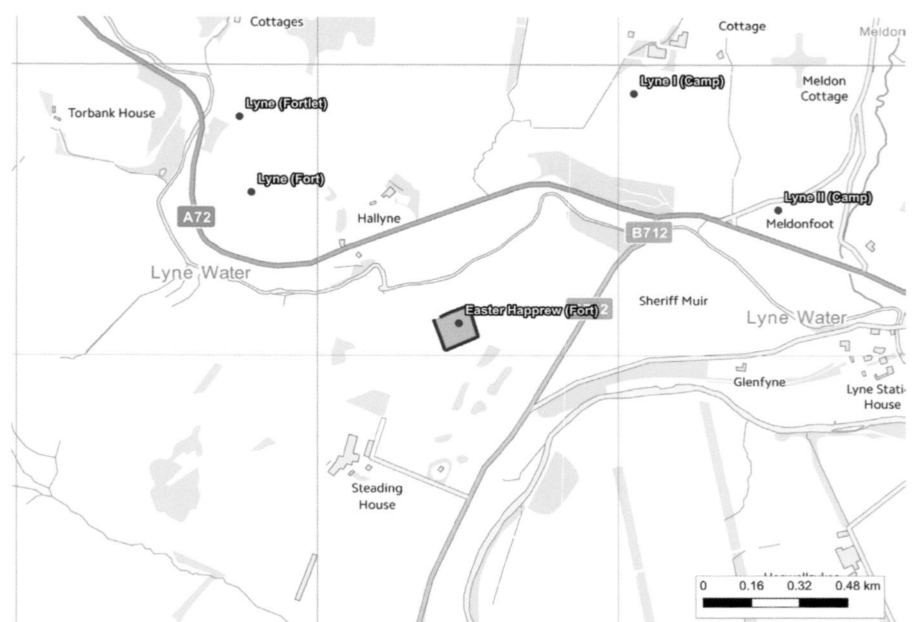

1960s: St Joseph records several buildings to the east of the fort

Exploring

Easter Happrew is to the east of Peebles, on the A72, by the junction with the B712.

Eildon Hill North

Tower | NT 554 328

Eildon Hill North is home to a number of archaeological sites, including a substantial hillfort occupied before and after the Romans, as well as a number of Iron Age hut circles. In the 1950s, the RCAHMS was surveying the hillfort and noted a previously unrecorded circular ditch feature, which they proceeded to excavate in 1952 and 1953. This revealed a Roman tower, similar in design to those found along the Gask Ridge in Perthshire. Steer, the excavator, also found fragments of Roman roof tile. This would be unusual for a wooden tower in Scotland, but Rivet has suggested that the tile could have come from a later stone tower, possibly dating to the Antonine period, located near by.

Eshiels

Camps | NT 281 395

Located to the east of Peebles and on the north bank of the River Tweed, the camps of Eshiels lie

Eildon Hill North from the site of Newstead.

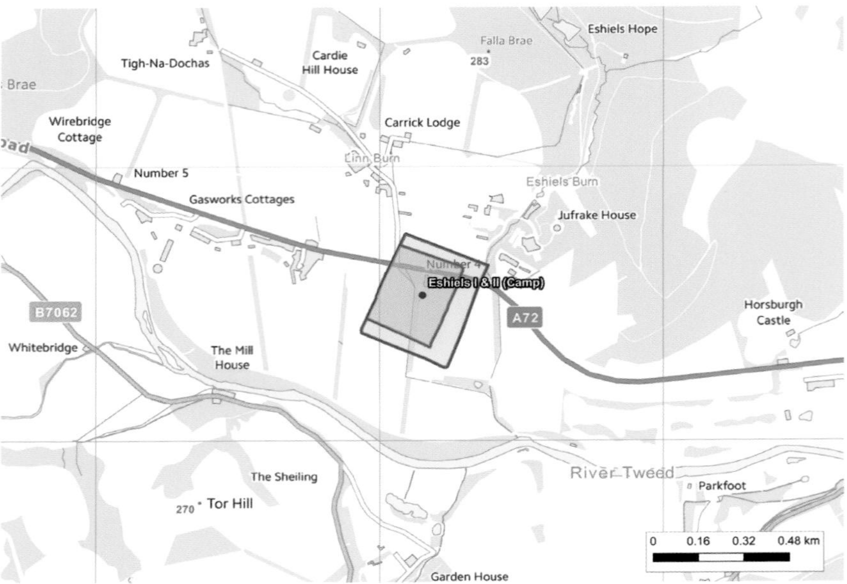

nestled one inside the other. Recorded by St Joseph during his programme of aerial reconnaissance, the camps share defences on the western side, which demonstrates that they are not contemporary with each other.

Exploring

Located to the east of Peebles, the camps are bisected by the A72. There are no visible remains on the ground.

Lyne

Fort | NT 187 405
Camp I | NT 200 409
Camp II | NT 205 405
Fortlet | NT 187 408

The sites at Lyne are located where two river valleys meet, one east–west and another from the south. No road has been identified here, but the positioning of the Easter Happrew fort implies that there may have been a route approaching a crossing point over the Lyne Water, meeting the known Roman road, which heads east–west.

The fort is located by a bend on the river and would have afforded good views to the east and west. First noted by Sibbald in the 17th century, and planned by Gordon in 1726 and later by Roy, the fort was first excavated by David Christison in 1900. Christison provided a detailed history of the site, and his research revealed the extent of the defences, along with evidence for two annexes – one on the north side and another on the south. From 1959 to 1963, Steer and Feacham undertook more extensive excavations, uncovering a number of internal buildings. The excavations revealed parts of the *principia*, granaries and the *praetorium*, constructed from red sandstone, while other structures on the site were built of timber. Archaeologists have speculated that the fort was occupied for a brief period during the reign of Antoninus Pius.

The camps were both recorded from the air by St Joseph, but two decades apart. Sections of the camp ditches were excavated between 1974 and 1977, with evidence of pottery fragments indicating a possible 1st-century date.

Key Dates

1901: Christison initially excavates the fort
1959–63: Steer and Feacham undertake further excavations of the fort
1974–77: Excavation of parts of the camp ditches

The site of the fort at Newstead, known as Trimontium to the Romans.

Newstead

Fort | NT 569 344
Camp I | NT 574 341
Camp II | NT 574 342
Camp III | NT 574 342
Camp IV | NT 570 337
Camp V | NT 567 337
Amphitheatre | NT 571 346

Newstead, near Melrose, guards the point where Dere Street crosses the River Tweed. It was a long-occupied and important site to the Romans, with not only several forts built on top of each other, but also a number of camps, annexes, an extensive settlement and even an amphitheatre.

Newstead, or Trimontium (meaning 'the place of the three hills'), as the Romans called it, was suspected as a Roman military site since the 18th century, when the Rev. Milne of Melrose described Roman remains near by. The claim was repeated in *The Old Statistical Account of Scotland*, but it was not until the 19th century, during construction of the railway, that altars and carved stones were uncovered, sparking much archaeological interest in the site. Influenced by the discovery of a Roman building found in 1904, the Society of Antiquaries of Scotland, under James Curle, began excavations the following year. Multiple phases of construction were uncovered in the forts, as well as details of the camps near by. Subsequent excavations took place under Ian Richmond in 1947, although these were much more limited.

The two excavations revealed that there had been four forts and phases of occupation on the one site – two Flavian and two Antonine. The earliest fort, rhomboid in shape, is believed to have been constructed around AD 80 from timber. There has been little excavation of the buildings from this period. Coins, found in context, have been dated to AD 86 and were in mint condition, leading the excavators to conclude that the site must have been abandoned by AD 90. This fits in with the general dating for the abandonment of other forts in Scotland.

The second Flavian phase of occupation began shortly after the abandoning of the earlier fort. Construction of the new fortification saw the destruction of the earlier ramparts and buildings, although some stretches of the former were included in the new defences. The new fort was rectangular and, at that period, the largest military site in Scotland, the legionary fortress at Inchtuthil having been abandoned by this time. There was also evidence that outside the fort the bath house and a possible *mansio* had been built. Some archaeologists have speculated that the fort was destroyed at the end of this period, possibly by enemy hands – the buildings showed evidence of having been burned down and armour and weapons found during the excavations were damaged. The excavators suggested that the site was abandoned around AD 100.

The first phase of Antonine occupation began around AD 140, using the previous Flavian ramparts

The site of Camps I, II, III and VII at Newstead.

but creating new ditches, and re-orientating the fort to face east. Excavation revealed a number of the internal buildings, in particular the central range, the granaries and *principia,* although the site of the *praetorium* was unexcavated. Unusually, the remains of armour for legionary soldiers and auxiliaries were discovered. The fort was then abandoned briefly before being reoccupied again, with the rampart being reused from the previous occupation and the ditches being recut.

In recent years, a number of geophysical surveys have taken place across the site, as well as exploratory excavations and field walking, which have indicated that there may have been industrial workings within the annexes. These may be related to the cavalry unit that Richmond has suggested may have been based at Newstead. Indeed, recent analysis of animal bones has indicated the presence of significant numbers of horses on the site.

At least seven camps have been identified at Newstead, which adds to those suspected and confirmed at the nearby sites of Ravenswood and Millmount, as well as one on the opposite bank of the Tweed. Not all of the defences of the camps are known. With Curle having excavated part of Camp I and ascribing a Flavian date, St Joseph's aerial work has done much to improve knowledge of the camps. Although the number of cropmarks, combined with the known sections, makes interpretation difficult, Rebecca Jones is one researcher who has given a good account of

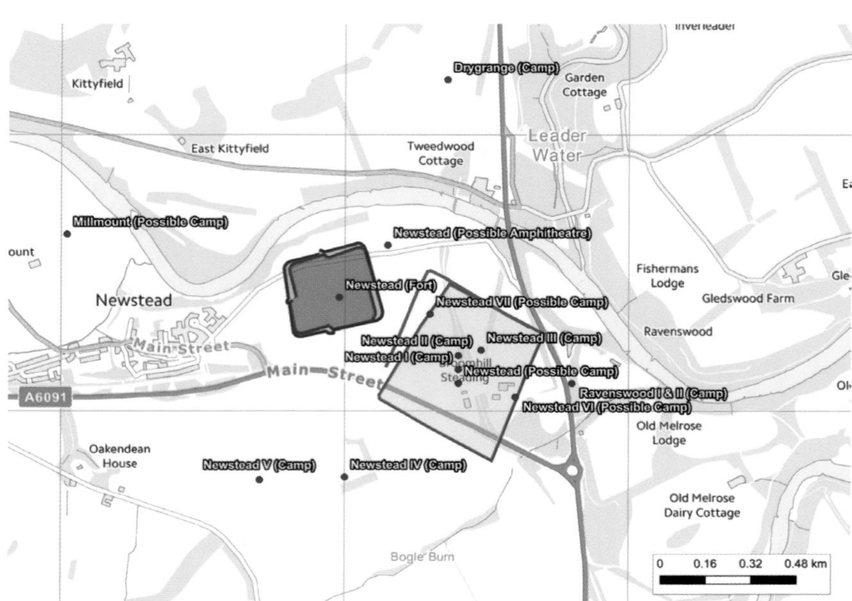

their chronology, in her book *Roman Camps in Scotland*.

The Three Hills Museum (*see* below) in nearby Melrose charts the history of this important site and offers frequent guided tours.

Exploring

The sites at Newstead are located to the east of the village of Melrose. The best location from which to see the various sites is the pedestrianized road that runs across the top of the fort, and is located off the B6361. A trip to the Three Hills Museum is recommended beforehand.

Oakwood

Fort | NT 425 249
Camp | NT 424 254

Located in the middle of the Scottish Borders, and no doubt protecting the Roman route through this part of the region, the fort and camp were both identified from St Joseph's aerial photographs taken in 1949. The views from the fort site were noted by St Joseph as being particularly good. Indeed, he concluded that, by using the tower at Eildon Hills North, soldiers at Oakwood would have been able to signal to the fort at Newstead.

The fort was excavated in 1951 and 1952 by Steer and Feacham, who found evidence of two occupation phases, with the first dating to the 1st century. The first phase noted that the fort faced east and was surrounded by a double ditch, with a third ditch occurring only on the south side. Unusually, the gates were set back from the front of the rampart by about 10 metres. The excavators speculated that the western gate had a timber frame above it, known as a fighting platform and similar to structures that are depicted on Trajan's Column. There was some indication of a guard tower in the base of the eastern gate tower. The unusual design of the gates (being set back from the ramparts) does suggest that the towers were a later addition, and put in after the ramparts. The fort was reduced in size at some point, which may be why the towers are set back, although this idea would not necessarily fit in with the findings of the excavators. Steer and Feacham suggested that the early phase was built around AD 80, but acknowledged that the pottery implied a date of about AD 86.

The second phase saw the layout staying the same, but the defences being strengthened and improved. The excavators suggested that this phase was abandoned no later than AD 100, while an annexe was located and believed to date from this phase.

The camp was excavated by Steer and Feacham at the same time as the fort, with small trenches dug across the defences to confirm the size, which was calculated at 13 hectares. Blocks of clay were used to stop the ramparts from slipping into the ditches, and it has been suggested that the camp was built to house those constructing the fort.

Exploring

The fort and camp are to the southwest of the town of Selkirk, just off the B7009. The sites can be reached by taking the minor road off the B7009 at Inner Huntly. The fort is on the right after about half a mile, with the camp on the opposite side of the road behind the trees.

The ditches of the fort are visible as slight dips, while the northern side of the camp defences can be seen as a slight rise (*see* overleaf).

Oxton

Fortlet | NT 490 546

Located close to the camp at Channelkirk, this small fort has three annexes on the southeastern, northeastern and northwestern sides and guarded the Roman route from the legionary fortress at York into Scotland. It was first identified during aerial reconnaissance in 1956, and fragments of Antonine pottery have been found within the fort during agricultural works. No excavations have taken place to indicate whether it was occupied during any other period, although that does seem possible given its positioning on this strategic route.

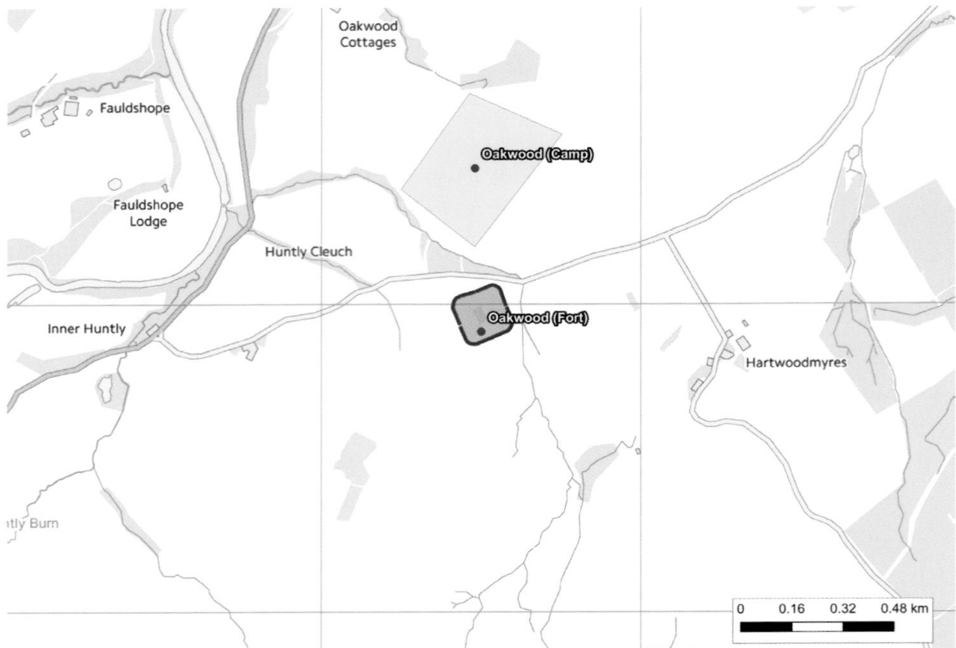

Rubers Law

Tower | NT 580 155

One of the highest peaks in the Scottish Borders, Rubers Law is hardly a surprising choice as the location for a Roman tower. A native fortification on the summit was recorded and sectioned by Alexander Curle at the beginning of the 20th century. During his work, Curle noted extensive reuse of dressed Roman sandstone, used throughout the defences, leading him to conclude that the fort must be post-Roman. He went on to suggest that the stone came from another, unknown Roman signal tower. This was emphasized by a number of artefacts found in the local area. It seems likely that, if there is a Roman tower built of stone on the hill, it may date from the Antonine period, as earlier structures were built of timber.

Recent research into Roman signalling by David Woolliscroft has demonstrated that signals were only effective if the person receiving them was a maximum of about three and a half miles away. Archaeologists have therefore debated whether the stones were from a Roman signal tower, or were in fact from a different type of building such as a shrine or temple.

St Leonard's Hill

Camp | NT 548 455

The largest known and confirmed Roman camp in Scotland, and the second-largest encampment found in the world to date, St Leonard's Hill covers a massive 70 hectares. Discovered by St Joseph during aerial reconnaissance in 1948, the camp was constructed to house the substantial invasion force that was led by the Emperor Septimius Severus in the 3rd century. Parts of the site have been surveyed with magnetometry, with possible ovens or latrines located on the northeast side of the camp.

Three Hills Roman Museum

The Ormiston, Market Square, Melrose TD6 9PN | Entry Charge
www.trimontium.org.uk | @TrimontiumTrust
Opening Times (seasonal. Opens on request out of season) | Mon–Sun 10:30–16:30

Three Hills may be a small museum, but that is certainly no reason to pass it by. Crammed full of information and artefacts relating to Roman Newstead, it is one of the best local museums in Scotland, and even includes a replica of the Trimontium Helmet, an ornate helmet mask discovered locally, which would have been worn at ceremonial events by a commanding officer.

There has been a programme of redevelopment at the museum, so it is worth checking out the website in advance for the latest information.

Tocherknowe

Fortlet | NT 141 526

The fortlet, which guards the crossing point of Dere Street over the Lyne Water, was first postulated by Alexander Gordon, who noted the presence of a Roman site near West Linton in 1726. It was rediscovered by Maxwell in the 1990s while undertaking an aerial survey for the RCAHMS. Maxwell followed up the discovery with excavation of the site, identifying a double ditch surrounding the fortlet. Unfortunately, the site had been damaged by ploughing and there were no archaeological features recorded in the centre of the fortlet.

The Other Sites

Blackchester (Possible Camp | NT 513 504)

Located between the Leader Water and Dere Street, this 14-hectare site was located from the air in the early 1990s, and has not yet been further explored.

Blainslie (Camp | NT 552 442)

Identified by St Joseph, cropmarks indicate that the site either has an annexe on the southern side or is next to a second camp.

Cavers Mains (Camp | NT 548 167)

Located next to the River Teviot, the camp was identified by St Joseph in the 1960s. However, only some sections of the defences have been located.

Channelkirk (Camp | NT 475 546, Channelkirk House – Possible Camp | NT 480 545)

Two camps were located during aerial reconnaissance in 1969 and 1973. Both share sections of defences, although the second camp is the smaller of the two. An antiquarian account details a further camp near Channelkirk House, but there is no conclusive proof to confirm the existence of the fortification, and archaeologists are continuing to debate whether or not there is a camp here.

Drygrange (Camp | NT 573 352)

The camp, located almost opposite the Newstead complex, was identified by Maxwell flying over the site in the 1970s. It covers an area of at least 16.5 hectares, and is still to be explored on the ground.

Hiltonshill (Possible Camp | NT 60 29)

The Old Statistical Account of Scotland details an account of a Roman camp in the area around Hiltonshill. The camp is yet to be rediscovered.

Innerleithen (Camp | NT 329 361)

The site was identified from aerial photographs taken in the 1960s. Sections of the defences are still to be identified, so the size of the camp is unknown.

Kaimhouse Lodge (Camp | NT 167 498)

Kaimhouse Lodge camp was revealed during aerial reconnaissance and parts of the defences are believed to lie under the B7059.

Kedslie (Camp | NT 556 400)

Another site identified by St Joseph in 1976, during his extensive aerial survey programme. The camp covers an area of 7.2 hectares. Jones has identified a further cropmark in close proximity to the site and speculates that it may belong to an earlier phase of the camp, reducing it in size.

Maxton (Possible Camp | NT 614 304)

Located on the south bank of the River Tweed, a camp was indicated by cropmarks recorded by St Joseph. However, Jones is sceptical that it is Roman in origin, given that it has only been recorded once, and because the shape of the cropmark is more precise than would be expected for a Roman site.

Mertoun Bridge (Camps | NT 604 316)

Both camps were found by St Joseph in the 1960s, one larger than the other. Jones has noted an additional cropmark that runs between the two camps and may indicate an additional occupation phase or encampment.

Millmount (Possible Camp | NT 560 346)

In 1961, St Joseph reported cropmarks that may have been part of a camp. The site has not been further explored or confirmed as being Roman.

Millside Wood (Camps | NT 691 222)

Both camps were identified by St Joseph, with the first one covering an area of almost 20 hectares. The smaller site lies inside the first camp and covers 2.4 hectares. A third possible camp, or possibly an annexe, lies to the northwest of the second camp.

Milrighall (Camp | NT 536 268)

This camp was identified by RCAHMS during aerial reconnaissance. Covering an area of around 14 hectares, it is assumed to date to the Flavian period.

North Slipperfield (Camp | NT 130 520)

Another site identified through aerial photography, the camp has not been excavated and some sections are underneath a golf course. A watching brief in 2009 found no Roman remains.

Pennymuir (Camp I | NT 754 139, Camp II | NT 756 138, Camp III | NT 756 144, Camp IV | NT 758 139)

Three confirmed camps have been located at Pennymuir, although there may be a fourth, which has shown up in aerial photographs, but has not been confirmed through excavation.

Ravenswood (Camp | NT 578 341)

First discovered in 1991, the camp is located near the complex of sites at Newstead. The camp was subsequently confirmed through excavation by St Joseph, with two phases of construction recorded. Geophysical survey in 1995 confirmed that the camp initially covered an area of 3.15 hectares and was then reduced to 2.5 hectares.

South Blainslie (Possible Camp | NT 545 427)

Noted by Maxwell when flying over South Blainslie in 1986, the camp has not been excavated but shows signs of being Roman. It may lie on the line of the road heading towards Newstead.

Stonypath (Camp | NT 144 532)

Sections of this camp were seen from the air by Maxwell in 1979. The rampart survives in places to a height of around 1 metre, with parts of ditch also visible.

Ulston Moor (Camp | NT 687 216)

The site at Ulston Moor was seen from the air in 1955. Archaeologists have speculated that it has two occupation phases, with the site being reduced in size at some point.

Wester Happrew (Camp | NT 172 423)

Wester Happrew camp was identified in the 1990s by RCAHMS and covers an area of almost 6 hectares. No entrances have been seen in the aerial photographs and the site has not been confirmed as Roman.

Wooden Home Farm (Camp | NT 741 338)

The camp was seen in aerial photographs taken in the 1970s by RCAHMS. However, St Joseph questioned the Roman attribution after examining more photographs. Excavation by Maxwell in the 1980s confirmed that the ditch belonged to a Roman camp, and this was supported by subsequent analysis of new photographs of the site.

PART SEVEN: THE NORTH OF SCOTLAND

Chapter 19

PERTH AND KINROSS

Perth and Kinross has the largest and most diverse collection of Roman remains in Scotland, including the massive legionary fortress at Inchtuthil and the chain of small towers stretching along the Gask Ridge. The area also has its fair share of forts and camps, including Ardoch, which is one of the best-preserved turf forts in Britain, if not the world. Further north is the fortlet of Kaims Castle, another spectacularly well-preserved site. As well as Roman fortifications, there is the Roman quarry at Gourdie, watched over by a small Roman camp with six curious ditch-like features, which may have formed the foundations of a triumphal arch.

Abernethy (Carey)

Camp | NO 173 164

Conveniently positioned overlooking the River Earn, near where it flows into the Tay, the camp at Abernethy may have been protecting a crossing point over the Earn, although there are no fording points recorded locally. To the south, it would have been

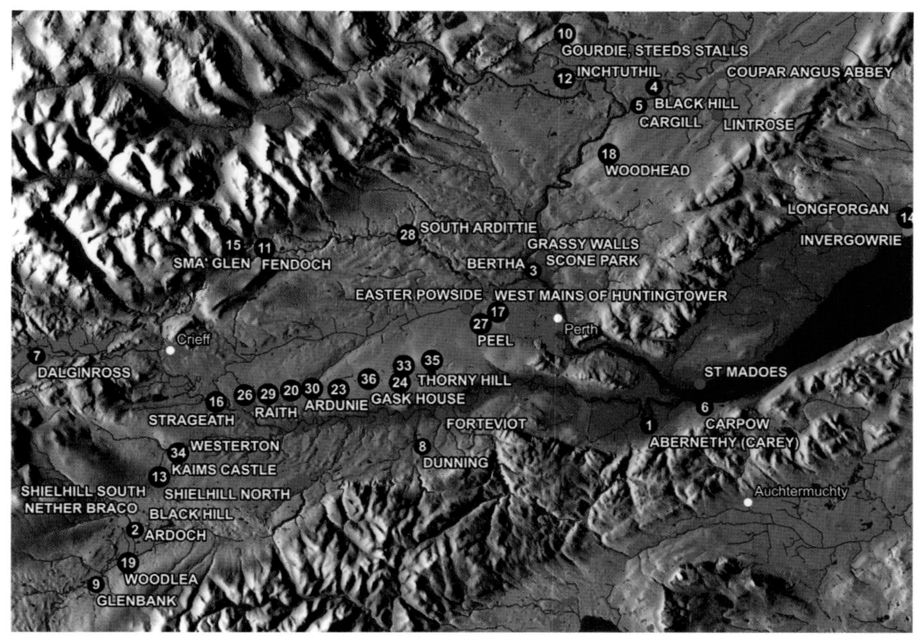

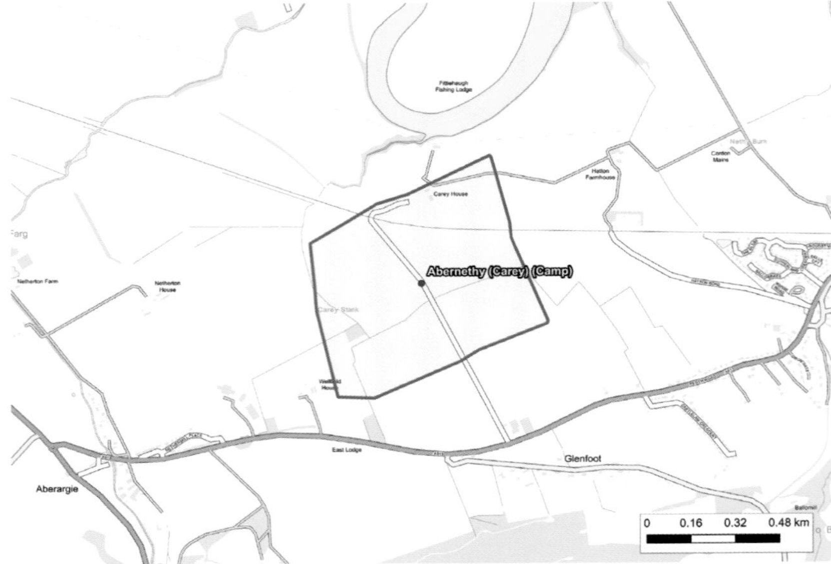

overlooked by the Ochils, in particular Ballomil Hill and the pre-Roman fort at Castle Law.

The fort was first recorded by St Joseph, who followed up the identification from the air with a brief excavation of a section of ditch, where he recovered a piece of 1st-century pottery. The large (and probably later) fort at Carpow is only two miles away, located on the Tay, just after the meeting point with the Earn.

Key Dates

1971: St Joseph identifies the site during aerial reconnaissance

Exploring

The camp is located between the villages of Aberargie and Abernethy, alongside the A913.

Ardoch

Fort | NN 839 099
Camp I | NN 842 108
Camp II | NN 839 109
Camp III | NN 838 105
Camp IV | NN 837 106
Camp V | NN 840 102
Tower | NN 845 107

Strategically located to the east of the River Knaick, just north of where it joins the Allan Water (the main tributary of the Forth), this is the heart of Roman Scotland, a place where soldiers from the Flavian to the Severan periods passed through. Ardoch itself is arguably the best-preserved Roman site in Scotland, if not Britain, and a must-see for any Roman enthusiast. There are few Roman sites where it is still possible to stand in front of original defences and see them almost as they were 2,000 years ago. The area must have been important to the Romans as there are a number of military structures in the immediate vicinity, including two forts (and possibly a third, all on the same site), at least five camps and a tower. In addition, a number of other cropmarks have been identified, which imply that there may be further sites yet to be discovered.

At 127 metres high, with good views of the surrounding area, the fort has been known since at least the 18th century, when it was first excavated by Christison and Cunningham, in 1898. The fort that is visible today is the second on the site. The earlier fort was much longer and subsequently shortened when the innermost ditches on the north side were added, creating the later (and smaller) fort. The early excavation indicated that the internal buildings had been rebuilt on at least two occasions. The finds suggested that the site had been active during both the Flavian

The fort ditches at Ardoch.

and the Antonine periods. Subsequent surveying of the site in the 1990s revealed a number of additional buildings and the possibility that what was originally believed to have been an annexe was actually a separate feature and possibly unconnected to the fort. The outline of the building that can be seen in the middle of the fort is a later structure, possibly a chapel that was constructed long after the Roman period.

In the 17th century a tombstone was uncovered near the site, which recorded a soldier (probably during the Flavian period) who was a member of the *cohors I Hispanorum*, the Cohort of Spaniards.

To the north of the fort site are at least five camps, first noted by Sibbald in the early 18th century before being formally recorded later. The camps vary greatly in size. Camp I is the largest, at around 52 hectares, while Camp II is 27 hectares, Camp III is 5.3 hectares, Camp IV is 11.8 hectares and Camp V is 4.3 hectares. The camps are generally overlapping and, together with a lack of significant finds, this makes it difficult to date which camp came first and when it was occupied. However, archaeologists generally agree that Camp I is probably Antonine, given the size, while Camps II and V are earlier than I. The overlapping suggests that Camps III and IV are likely to pre-date I and II.

Exploring

Ardoch is well worth a visit, not only to see the fort, but also to have a look at part of the visible remains of the camps. The fort is to the north of the village of Braco, on the A822. Park at the north end of the village, just before the bridge turns to the right and crosses the River Knaick. Carry on over the bridge and look for the path up to the fort, straight in front of you. The path takes you into the south end of the fort; carry on to the far end to see the most impressive defences.

The best-preserved camp is the first one, which can be reached by carrying on past the fort and after about half a mile take the left on to the B827. The preserved section of camp is immediately on the right (*see* overleaf).

Part of the rampart and ditch defences of one of the (many) camps at Ardoch.

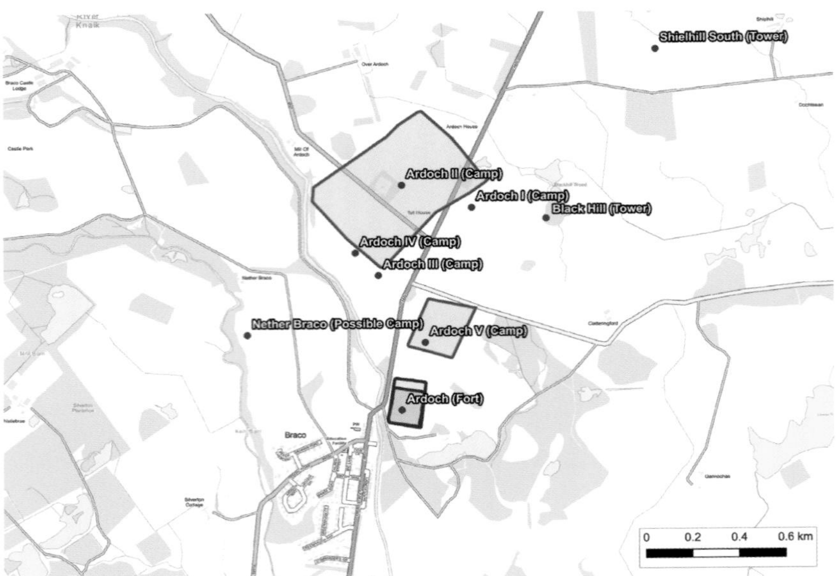

Bertha

Fort | NO 097 268

The fort at Bertha was built at the point where the River Almond flows into the Tay, where the Tay was crossed by the Romans. The fort itself is on low-lying ground and may have been prone to flooding, something which still happens to the area around the fort. Callander produced an early plan of the outline of the fort in 1919, which, due to the positioning of the southern gate, indicated that the site faced northeast. However, as has been noted by Woolliscroft, the site has never shown up particularly well in aerial photographs and it was only with geophysical survey in the 21st century that the outline was clearly mapped.

While the fort was previously assumed to have been occupied only in the 1st century, St Joseph speculated that, as there are distinct differences in the two identified ramparts on the north and south sides, the fort may have been reduced in size at some point. Woolliscroft analysed a number of field-walking finds previously collected by the Cumbernauld Historical Society during the 1970s and identified a number of Flavian as well as Antonine pottery fragments, so the site may actually have been reoccupied after the 1st century.

Key Dates

1757: Maitland identifies parts of the fort and the nearby Roman road

1745: Roy records sections of the defences, although

The fort site at Bertha. A few depressions in the ground are probably part of the defences.

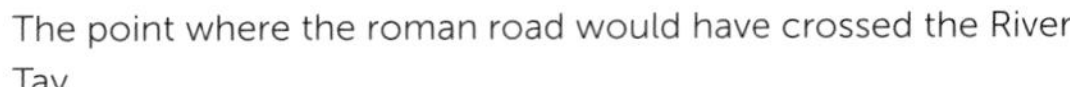

The point where the roman road would have crossed the River Tay.

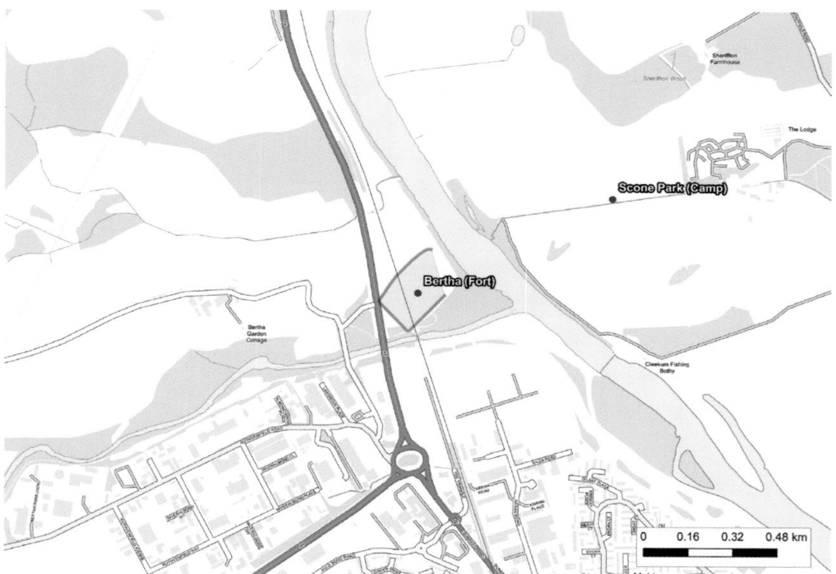

speculates that some parts have been lost due to erosion and flooding by the Tay
1795: *The Old Statistical Account of Scotland* notes the discovery of wooden remains from what is assumed to be a Roman bridge across the Tay
1917: The site is planned by Callander, although his conclusions differ from those before him
1949: Crawford plots the fort and the course of the bridge across the river based on his projection of the line of the Roman road
2008: Geophysical surveys undertaken on site reveal the defences of the site and possibly an annexe

Exploring

The fort at Bertha is next to the A9, just to the north of Perth. From the roundabout where the A912 meets the A9, head north. After a quarter of a mile the road crosses over the River Almond – the fort is on the right and can only be accessed from the southbound carriageway. Park by the field entrance and head underneath the railway tunnel.

Black Hill

Tower | NO 176 391

Located to the northeast of the fort at Cargill, the tower at Black Hill was first excavated by Abercrombie, who confirmed that the plan of the site was broadly similar to other Roman tower structures in the area. Abercrombie found iron nails, which he thought indicated the presence of a wooden tower on the site. It was re-excavated by Richmond in 1939, who uncovered evidence of postholes, confirming that the site was occupied during the Flavian period.

Key Dates

1795: The mound is noted in *The Old Statistical Account of Scotland* as being artificial
1903: The mound is excavated by Abercrombie who finds limited evidence of Roman occupation
1939: Richmond excavates the site revealing postholes which implies occupation during the Flavian era

Cargill

Fort | NO 166 379
Fortlet | NO 163 376

Located a stone's throw from the tower at Black Hill, the fort and fortlet at Cargill are constructed on a hillside near the confluence of the Isla to the north and the Tay to the west. Unusually, the fort is overlooked by a hill to the south, which may have been close enough to put the interior at risk if it was attacked.

The fort was identified from the air by Bradley in

The fortlet at Cargill visible as a cropmark running left to right in the centre of the hill, near the summit.

the 1940s and then appears to have been forgotten about until St Joseph flew over the site in 1977, recording the ditches and parts of the annexe. A limited excavation to confirm its Roman origins was undertaken by Maxwell and St Joseph in 1980 and 1981. They confirmed that the fort faced northwest towards the river, and possibly a crossing point. Aerial survey work undertaken by Woolliscroft and Hoffmann (2005, 2006) identified the *via principalis*, indicating that the fort is likely to face northwest, although it would be orientated towards an area that appears to have been an annexe for the fort. The fort has a Stracathro-type gate so is assumed to be Flavian.

Artefacts found during excavation indicated that the site was abandoned around AD 85, a date reflected in coin finds noted by Woolliscroft in 2005.

The fortlet was not identified until the 1940s, when Bradley photographed cropmarks indicating Roman structures on the site. The defences were confirmed by St Joseph, who flew over the site in the 1950s and identified the ditches and entrances, and the area covered by the fortlet. Excavations in 1965 confirmed the defences, but also noted a lack of interior buildings, as the evidence had been ploughed out. As no internal features have been identified from the air or from the trial trenching, it is not possible to be more specific about the orientation of the fortlet. It was presumed to have been of Flavian date, but this was not confirmed until work undertaken by Woolliscroft and Hoffmann (2003), when shards of late 1st-century glass were discovered during field walking. A shard of mid-2nd-century glass was also uncovered during the same exercise.

Key Dates

1941: The fort and fortlet are photographed from the air by Bradley

1955: St Joseph confirms further details of the fortlet defences

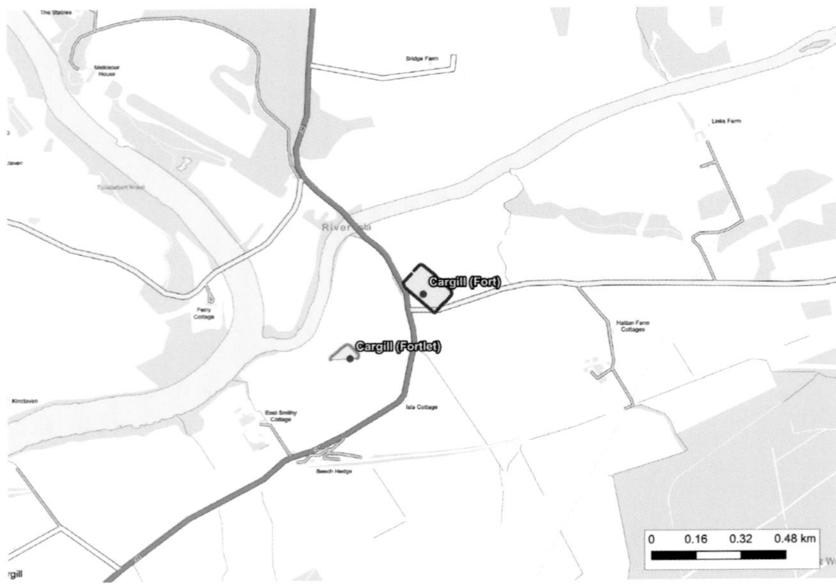

1965: St Joseph excavates the fortlet
1977: St Joseph re-records the fort from the air
1980–81: A partial excavation of the fort is undertaken
2005 and 2006: Aerial survey by Woolliscroft shows some internal features of both sites

Exploring

Both sites are located by the village of Cargill, to the west of Coupar Angus. From here, head north on the A923, crossing the Isla, then take a left on to the A984. After around two miles, at the crossroads with the A93, take the left on to the A93, heading south. After crossing the Isla (the bridge has traffic lights), the fort is on your left and the fortlet just past this on the right, although the cropmarks of the latter can only be seen from the river looking back.

Carpow

Fort | NO 207 178
Camps | NO 209 176

The fort, which is sometimes referred to as a fortress, is located on the banks of the Firth of Tay and was most likely situated here to aid the shipment of supplies further inland. While the bath house of the fort was known about in the early 1940s, it was not until St Joseph flew over the site in 1943 that details of the fortification, along with an annexe, came to light. Excavations in the early 1960s focused on the central area of the site, and the eastern gateway was uncovered in 1963. Excavations between 1964 and 1968 identified sections of the ramparts on all four axes and confirmed that the site extended to around 11 hectares. Artefactual evidence uncovered from the area of the fort indicates an occupation date of the early 3rd century, with some speculation that the site was under construction in AD 210 and may have been abandoned by AD 215.

Both camps were identified by St Joseph from the air, with Camp II noted in 1968 and Camp I in 1971. Both have been subjected to limited excavations to confirm their Roman origins. St Joseph noted that the ditch of Camp II cut through the backfilled ditch of Camp I, indicating that it was later.

Key Dates

1943: St Joseph flies over the site charting the defences
1968: St Joseph records Camp II
1971: Camp I is identified from the air
1961, 1962: Excavation of the *principia* and a possible bath house
1964–79: Excavations reveal site plan including gates, ramparts, ditches and internal building

Dalginross

Fort | NN 773 210
Camp I | NN 773 209
Possible Camp | NN 774 207

There are two forts at Dalginross, one inside the other, both of which are on a level plain. The surrounding area is not particularly defensive, although the forts do make use of their position next to the Water of Ruchill, which runs to the west and joins the River Earn to the north. Field-walking finds, which were collected by the Cumbernauld Historical Society in the 1970s, indicate that the site was occupied during both the Flavian and Antonine periods. While archaeologists have not been able to work out which fort was occupied first, Dalginross I has parrot-shaped entrances, implying that it is Flavian.

This camp is presumed to be Flavian on the basis of the Stracathro-type gate and because it is adjacent to

Looking northwest towards the forts at Dalginross.

The site of Dalginross camp.

a fort (Dalginross) of this date. Rogers speculated that it was conceivable that the fort could also have been Antonine. He offered no datable evidence, instead indicating that the defensive ditch has been recut at some point, which could have been done within the Flavian period. Stracathro-type gates have been identified for the site, indicating a 1st-century date.

Exploring

The sites are to the south of the village of Dalginross, which is next to Comrie. The modern road cuts through the camp, while the forts are untouched.

Dunning

Camp | NO 025 150

The camp at Dunning is first recorded by Macfarlane in 1723, who wrote about a trench, or enclosure, which could contain several thousand men. In the 1940s, Crawford went in search of the trench. He managed to locate it, but thought that it may have been a dyke to alleviate flooding, although he remained open to the idea that it could belong to a camp. It was not until the 1970s, when St Joseph flew over the site, that further sections of the defences were traced and then confirmed through selective excavation.

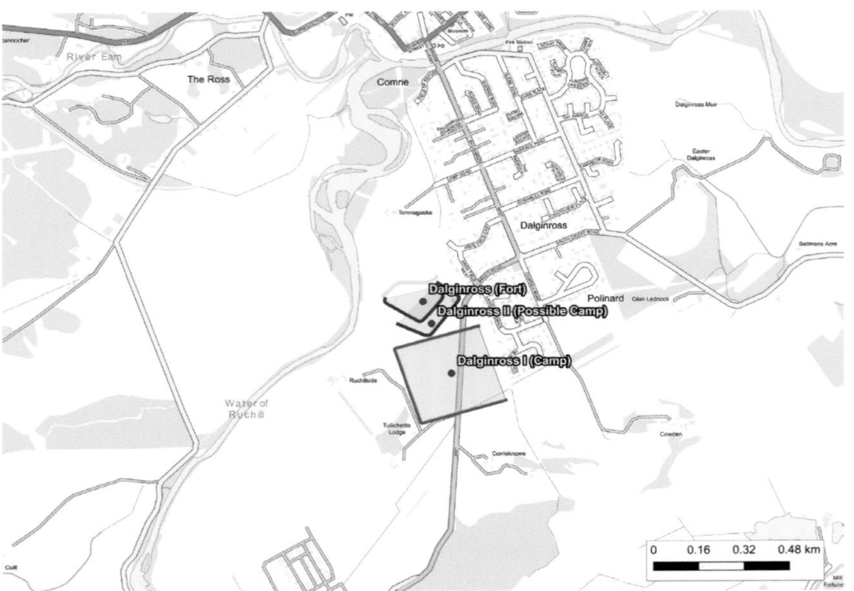

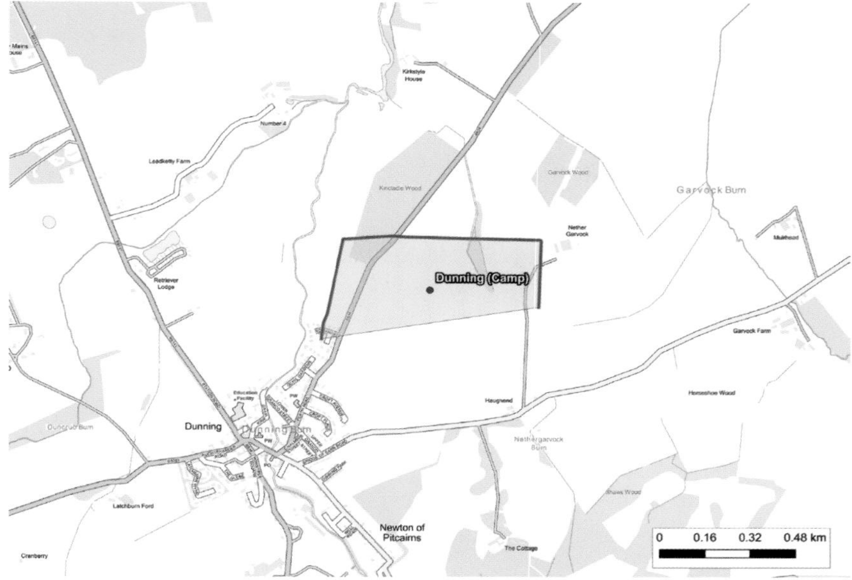

In 1988, a trench was opened up to examine the northern rampart and ditch in advance of a pipe being laid through the site. The ditch was recorded as being 3 metres wide and almost a metre deep and had been open to the elements long enough for about 20 centimetres of silt to have built up in the bottom. Further excavations in advance of development in 1992 and 1998 revealed the defences, but several watching briefs in 2009 failed to note any features. In 2014, excavations by the University of Glasgow re-examined sections of the defences, confirming that they may have been rebuilt on a similar line to the original rampart and ditch, possibly indicating that the camp was reoccupied for a second period.

Key Dates

1723: What would later be identified as the camp ditch is mentioned as a trench that could contain thousands of men
1940: Crawford rediscovers the trench as a ditch and bank, which he suspects is agricultural but suggests could be Roman
1970: Ordnance Survey visit the site, identifying further sections of the defences
1972: St Joseph records further sections of the camp from the air and goes on to excavate
1988: Excavation in advance of insertion of a gas pipe examines a section of the northern defences
1992: Further excavations in advance of development
2014: More excavations take place on the defences
2015: Geophysical survey of part of the camp takes place

Exploring

The camp is located to the northeast of the village of Dunning. Part of the northern ditch and rampart can be seen in the wood, with a *titulus* visible as a low mound outside the camp defences alongside the B234.

Glenbank

Fortlet | NN 812 057

The fortlet is situated on a hill, making use of the natural ridge along which the Roman road was constructed. To the north is the Allan Water and immediately east is the Glassingbeg Burn; the Todhill Burn is to the west of the site. The site was first discovered from the air in the early 1980s and excavated in 1983, confirming its size and its single entrance on the north side. Geophysical survey by Woolliscroft and Davies in 1997 revealed little detail of the interior. This was followed by excavation in the

The site at Steeds Stalls, with some of the 'stalls' visible in the mid ground, in the cut grass.

following year, which came up with evidence for a substantial four-post timber tower over the entrance, but no evidence of internal structures other than a single posthole. It was speculated that such evidence had been destroyed by ploughing.

Gourdie (Steeds Stalls)

Camp | NO 1151 4271

Gourdie is home to two Roman sites: the camp at Steeds Stalls, located on top of the hill overlooking the legionary fortress at Inchtuthil; and, further down the hillside, a quarry used by the Romans in Inchtuthil's construction.

Steeds Stalls has been known about since at least the 18th century, appearing in both *The Old Statistical Account of Scotland* and *The New Statistical Account*. Identified as Roman from an early date, a series of at least six 'stalls' or circular, pit-like structures are visible on the ground at the site. Their purpose is not clear but archaeologists have suggested that they may be kilns associated with the quarry, horse stalls or the foundations for a triumphal arch. In the 1940s, Bradley flew over the site and identified the presence of a square camp, with the stalls within the boundaries of the fortification. Curiously, there does not appear to be an entrance to the site and there is a cropmark through the middle of the camp, indicating it was divided into two halves (with no breaks).

At the base of the hill is a quarry that has been identified as Roman and was used in the construction of the legionary fortress, which is about a mile to the south. The stone was used in the construction of the defences and for the foundations of some of the buildings. Many archaeologists assume that the quarry and the camp on the hill above were in use at the same time.

The quarry at Gourdie.

Exploring

Gourdie is located to the north of the village of Spittalfield, which is itself between Caputh and Meiklour. The site is located up a small road that leads to the Mains of Gourdie farm. The quarry is along a track and visible from this. The camp is on the top of the hill and can be reached heading up the hill beside the quarry (it is extremely steep in places). The quarry is not fenced off, so do be careful when approaching it from the camp.

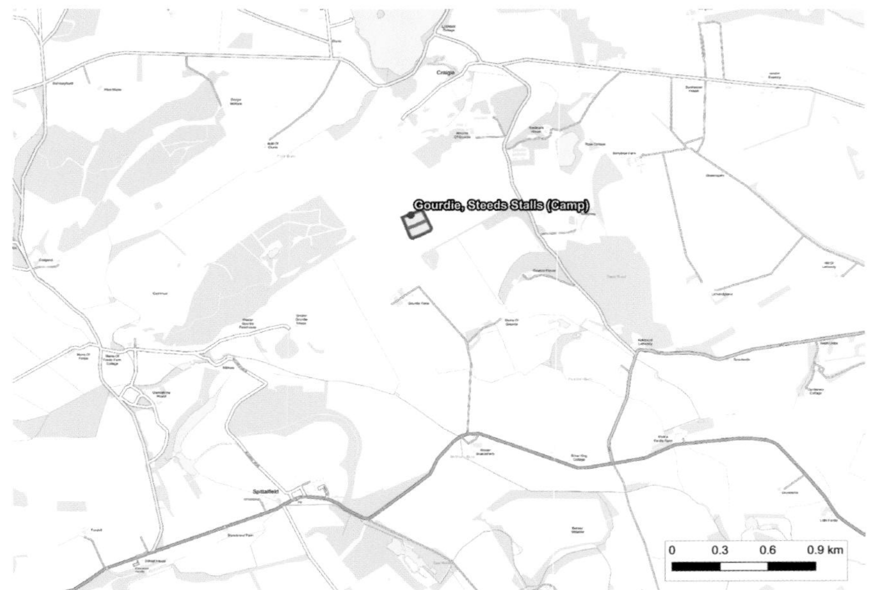

Fendoch

Fort | NN 919 283
Redoubt & Possible Camp | NN 916 287
Possible Fortlet | NN 911 278

The fort at Fendoch is a prime example of the Romans taking advantage of the natural environment when constructing their fortifications. The site here is built on an outcrop, taking up the whole of the area, with the internal layout of the fort adapted slightly in order to fit. However, the defence is much poorer on the southwest side, which is overlooked, putting the interior at risk in event of an attack on the fort from the hillside.

The site is first noted in *The Old Statistical Account of Scotland*, which records the remains of the fort, even noting that the ditches are six feet deep in places. It seems to have been Colonel Shand who first suggested that the site may have had Roman origins, but it was not until Richmond and McIntyre began looking into it in the 1930s that this was confirmed. Their excavations revealed that the fort was surrounded by a turf rampart and a single ditch, with an additional ditch on the eastern side. To the east of the fort was an annexe, while pottery recovered dated the site to the latter half of the 1st century.

The fort platform at Fendoch in the middle distance.

The site was geophysically surveyed at the beginning of the 21st century with the results confirming the plan of the interior originally proposed by Richmond and McIntyre. The survey also confirmed the presence of the annexe, and the possibility of a bath house to the southwest of the fort, although this has not been confirmed through excavation.

The possible fortlet was discovered by Allan who recorded the dimensions. To date the site has not been excavated, so archaeologists are not certain that it has Roman origins, but it does seem well positioned to guard the route through the area.

The camp and adjacent redoubt (a mini camp) were recorded as early as the 1770s when they appeared on an early map of the area. Neither has been confirmed as Roman, and Richmond and McIntyre have speculated that the redoubt was actually an indigenous site, a view that was shared by Crawford when he examined the site.

Key Dates

1778: The redoubt and camp are first noted on an early map
1795: *The Old Statistical Account of Scotland* notes the location of an old encampment
1830s: The camp is recorded
Late 18th century: Colonel Shand suggests that the site at Fendoch is Roman
1935: Richmond and McIntyre begin investigations into Fendoch
1936–38: Richmond and McIntyre begin a series of excavations that reveal the plan of the fort, as well as many of the interior buildings
1984: Allan records a possible fortlet on the ground to the southwest of the fort
2003: Geophysical survey confirms the shape and layout of the fort, as well as the annexe, and reveals the location of a possible bath house

Exploring

Fendoch is located to the north of Crieff, where the A822 meets the B8063. Turning on to the latter road, the fort is to the right, but only really visible at the top of the hill. The fort is worth visiting, just to see the outline of the site and the views of the surrounding area, although cattle are usually grazing in the field.

The redoubt is to the left off the main road, near where the powerlines cross overhead. Slight traces of the defences are visible as a low rise.

The fortress at Inchtuthil covers 20 hectares.

Inchtuthil

Legionary Fortress | NO 125 397
Camp I | NO 116 393
Camp II | NO 119 394

Located on a raised natural platform, the fortress and camps at Inchtuthil were well protected from any potential attackers, although the fortress was more vulnerable to the elements, with river erosion to the northern defences. The Tay runs around the eastern and southern sides of the peninsula, although there is some indication that the river has changed its course and may have originally run to the north of the fortress, causing the erosion. The fortress would have been the base of operations in this part of Scotland and was constructed with the purpose of being the northern headquarters of the army. It is one of the larger legionary fortresses, covering an area of some 20 hectares; this makes Inchtuthil bigger than its nearest equivalent – the Roman fortress that is now the city centre of York.

The earliest reference to Inchtuthil dates to 1526, when Hector Boece referred to the site as a Pictish town in his *Scotorum Historiae*. Most of the later antiquarians have discussed the site, including Roy, Maitland and Pennant. The first serious plan of the site was drawn by Roy in 1755, although a few decades after it was published (in 1795), the site had already been altered by agriculture. In 1901, John Abercromby undertook an excavation of parts of the fortress on behalf of the Society of Antiquaries of Scotland. This covered the *via principalis* and several features outside of the fortress, including the so-called redoubt or eastern compound. More extensive excavations took place between 1952 and 1965, with Richmond and St Joseph uncovering evidence of internal buildings such as the *principia*, the *praetorium*, granaries and barracks. They found that some buildings had not yet been built and there were gaps where there should have been structures. Richmond and St Joseph concluded that the fortress had been deliberately dismantled before construction of the interior was completed. Although they extensively excavated the site, they did not dig the whole area of the fortress. However, they did publish a plan of the anticipated layout based on their knowledge of other sites.

From 2009 to 2011, Woolliscroft and Hoffmann of the Roman Gask Project undertook magnetic and resistance surveys of the fortress and some of the surrounding features. The results confirmed Richmond and St Joseph's plan of the site and revealed evidence of a potential smaller camp at the south-western end of the peninsula. The investigations by Richmond and St Joseph, and later Woolliscroft and Hoffmann, have indicated that the *principia* building does not fill the space allocated for it. Indeed, it is much smaller and appears to be on a marginally different alignment to the rest of the fortress, so may be part of an earlier fort. Alternatively, it may have been built as a temporary structure, with the intention

The surviving eastern ditch at Inchtuthil fortress.

of being replaced when the rest of the site was completed. Early datable evidence for the legionary fortress at Inchtuthil was uncovered by Richmond and St Joseph during their early excavations. The pottery indicated a Flavian date. Datable evidence uncovered during later work has confirmed this.

The camps were identified from the air in the 1950s. It has been suggested by archaeologists that Camp I was constructed by a reconnaissance force for survey as it is sited on the highest point of the peninsula, and there has been speculation that Camps II and III were labour camps to house troops while the fortress was being built. Both camps are presumed to be Flavian in date due to their proximity to the 1st-century legionary fortress, although there have been no datable finds.

Key Dates

1526: Historian Hector Boece refers to Inchtuthil as a Pictish town
1755: General Roy plans the Inchtuthil plateau
1757: Maitland notes the presence of a Roman station in the vicinity of the mansion house at Delvin
1901: Abercrombie undertakes first excavations of the fortress
1952–65: Richmond and St Joseph undertake extensive excavations of the site, revealing many internal features
1957: St Joseph identifies the camps from the air
2009–11: The Roman Gask Project undertakes geophysical surveys of the entire site

Exploring

The site at Inchtuthil is vast and well worth exploring to get an impression of how big the fortress would have been. It is best approached from the Delvine side. Heading west from Meikleour on the A984, take a left at the junction with the B947. Follow the track for about three miles, past the farm and carry on up the slope when it takes a turn to the right (at

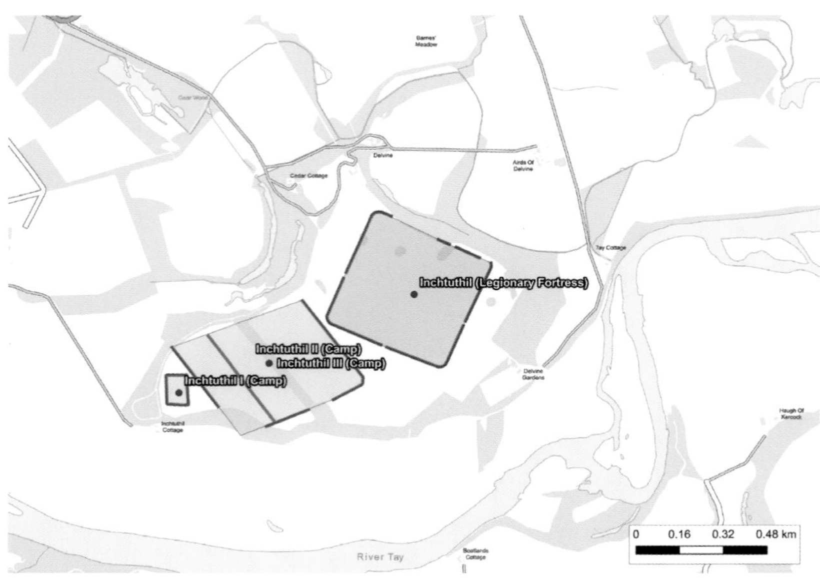

Delvine Gardens) and becomes a grassy track. Park in front of the fence and the fortress is in front of you.

Cross the stile and you will be on the edge of the fortress and on the line of the *via principalis*. Cross over the causeway (this is the *porta principalis dextra*). The fortress extends to the gate at the far side of the field. To the right are the best-preserved section of ditches, but it is possible to make out other slight indentations along the line of the ditches elsewhere on the site.

There are no remains of the camps to be seen on the ground. The field containing the fortress is often being grazed by cattle, so caution is urged when on site. The fields containing the camps are home to pheasants and visitors should avoid these parts of the peninsula during shooting season.

Kaims Castle

Fortlet | NN 860 129

Kaims Castle, originally referred to as 'Camps Castle', was known to antiquarians, with both Gordon and Roy writing about the site. It was excavated at the beginning of the 20th century by David Christison, who established that the site was unusual in having a rectilinear rampart with the ditches curvilinear and a single entrance. The interior had a cobbled or paved surface, and there was no evidence of postholes to indicate timber buildings or structures inside.

The fortlet at Kaims Castle.

Although there was a lack of datable finds, archaeologists believe the site dates to the 1st century because it is a key part of the Flavian frontier. Steer speculated that it may have been reoccupied during the Antonine period.

Exploring

Kaims Castle is on private land, but access is freely given if permission is asked from the friendly owners who live at Kaims Lodge, the house in front of the fortlet. Parking is limited in the vicinity, but there is some space on the opposite side of the road from the Lodge.

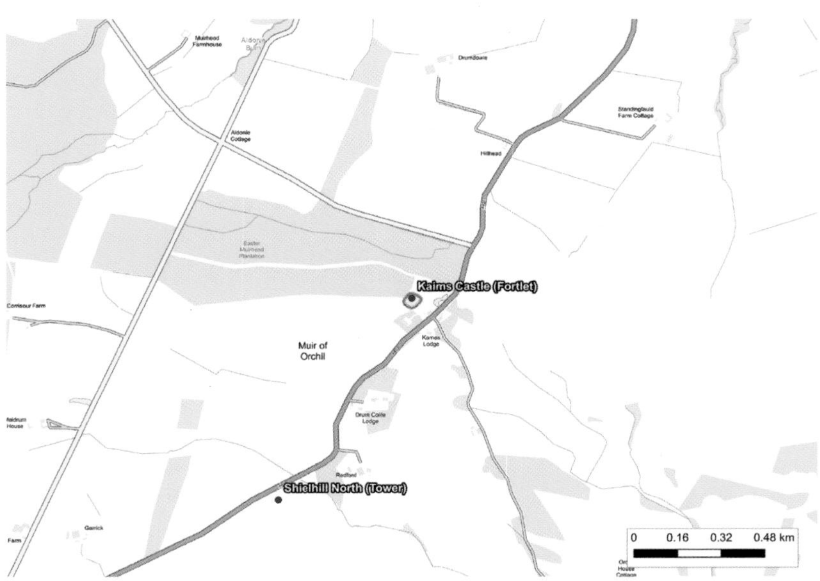

Mylnefield

Possible Fort | NO 339 303

Aerial photographs taken by Crawford in 1949 showed a series of cropmarks revealing the rounded corner of a rampart. It has been suggested by Mechan that this could be the camp recorded by Maitland in 1757. Maitland's site was located somewhere near Dundee, and could just as easily be the one at nearby Bullion.

Sma' Glen

Possible Tower | NN 908 285

Located by the fort at Fendoch, this tower is positioned on a rise, with good views north (up the Sma' Glen) and southwest towards Crieff. The mound shares similarities with other tower structures on the Gask Ridge – it is circular with an inner ditch enclosing a central area – although there is no obvious entrance, leading some archaeologists to suggest it is not of Roman origin. Until the site is further explored, its Roman credentials remain questionable.

Strageath

Fort | NN 898 180
Camp (Strageath Cottage) | NN 890 180

Located next to the River Earn, the fort probably guards a crossing point on the route northwards, while also protecting the southwestern end of the Gask Ridge chain of fortifications.

Antiquarians have been aware of the fort since the 17th century, with Roy planning the fort and earthworks to the west of the site. These were subsequently recorded by Crawford, who saw them when he visited the site in the 1940s. He went on to note that, in the intervening years, agricultural activities had significantly eroded the site and reduced the earthworks.

The site was extensively excavated by Frere from 1973 to 1986, with large sections of the internal layout of the fort uncovered. The excavators found evidence that the site had three phases of occupation, one Flavian and two Antonine. The Flavian-period fort was constructed some time around AD 80 and then abandoned by AD 87, while the second phase (Antonine I) began in AD 142. The fort was abandoned between AD 155 and 158, and then reoccupied about AD 158 (Antonine II). Archaeologist Nick Hodgson has questioned whether there was a second phase, instead arguing that the fort may have been refurbished rather than abandoned and reoccupied.

The camp was originally discovered from the air in 1969, but went unnoticed at the time. It was not until a decade later that Maxwell flew over the site, confirming the discovery, and subsequently followed this up with a limited excavation, confirming that the camp was Roman and covered an area of 13.5 hectares.

The site at Strageath, with the fort platform visible in the background, just in front of the trees.

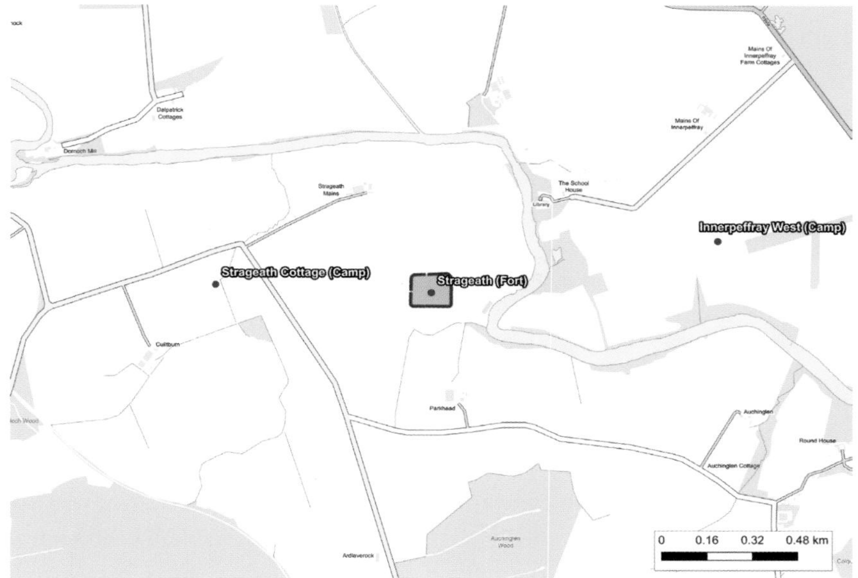

Key Dates

1793: Roy plans the fort at Strageath, including a number of earthworks west of the site
1973–86: Frere extensively excavates the fort, revealing multiple phases of occupation
1979: The camp is spotted from the air by Maxwell and confirmed shortly afterwards through excavation

Exploring

Strageath is located to the northeast of the village of Muthil. In the village, take Station Road to the right of the church. Follow the road to the end, taking a left at the T-junction. Carry on for just under a mile, heading down the slight slope and passing the entrance to Parkhead farm on the right. The fort site is in the field on the right.

The fort platform is clearly visible in the field, just in front of the line of trees. The road ahead goes on to cut through the site of the camp, although there are no visible remains.

West Mains of Huntingtower

Tower | NO 071 246

In 1985, Maxwell reported the discovery of a possible tower site near the farm at West Mains of Huntingtower. The tower was next to the projected line of the Roman road and appeared to resemble other similar sites on the Gask Ridge. The tower was subjected to geophysical survey by David Woolliscroft of the Roman Gask Project in 1997, and followed up by excavation. Although smaller than most other sites, with the defences having a radius of 16.8 metres, the tower had the usual rampart and ditch arrangement with room for a tower in the centre. There was evidence of two or three structural phases, and an indication that the tower was built on top of a roundhouse. There was a single entrance facing northwest, and evidence that the tower was deliberately demolished at the end of occupation. Unusually, there was no evidence of demolition through burning the site, as has been recorded at some of the other tower sites.

No datable finds were excavated, but, given the proximity to the other Gask Ridge towers, and the similarities in design to these, West Mains is likely to date to the Flavian period.

Woodhead

Tower | NO 1433 3463

The tower at Woodhead was first recorded on aerial photographs taken in 1969, having shown up as a double-ditched enclosure. It was surveyed by the Roman Gask Project in 2010, and subsequently excavated. This revealed that the ditches were V-shaped and that there was a single entrance. Evidence for postholes was excavated, indicating that there was a tower in the centre of the site.

Although no datable artefacts were recovered, archaeologists believe this was a Roman tower.

Exploring

The tower is located to the southwest of Coupar Angus. Head southwest on the A94 from the town, and take the last road on the left when passing through the village of Birrelton. After a mile and a half, pass the farm at Myreside and the tower is located at the top of the track before it turns right to Parkhead Farm.

Woodlea

Tower | NN 8304 0716

The tower was seen in aerial photographs of the area taken by Maxwell in the mid-1980s. It was subsequently excavated by David Woolliscroft around a decade later, confirming the tower was surrounded by an unusually shallow V-shaped double ditch with a single entrance. There was also evidence of four postholes, indicating that there was a tower, but no datable finds were recovered. The site is likely to date to the Flavian period because of its position as part of the Gask Ridge frontier.

The Other Sites

Coupar Angus (Possible Camp | NO 223 397)

Maitland described a site with a double rampart and ditch arrangement on three sides that was gradually being destroyed by agriculture. By the time of *The Old Statistical Account*, most of the site had gone. While Maitland claims that the site was Roman, Crawford suspected that what had been seen were the boundaries of the Abbey at Coupar Angus.

Easter Powside (Camp | NO 056 245)

Seen from the air in 1979, cropmarks at Easter Powside have indicated the presence of a camp. Excavation in 1998 by the Roman Gask Project indicated the ditch had a V-shaped profile, suggesting it was Roman, but there were no finds to confirm this.

Forteviot (Camp | NO 03940 17530)

Another camp identified from the air in 1951, and

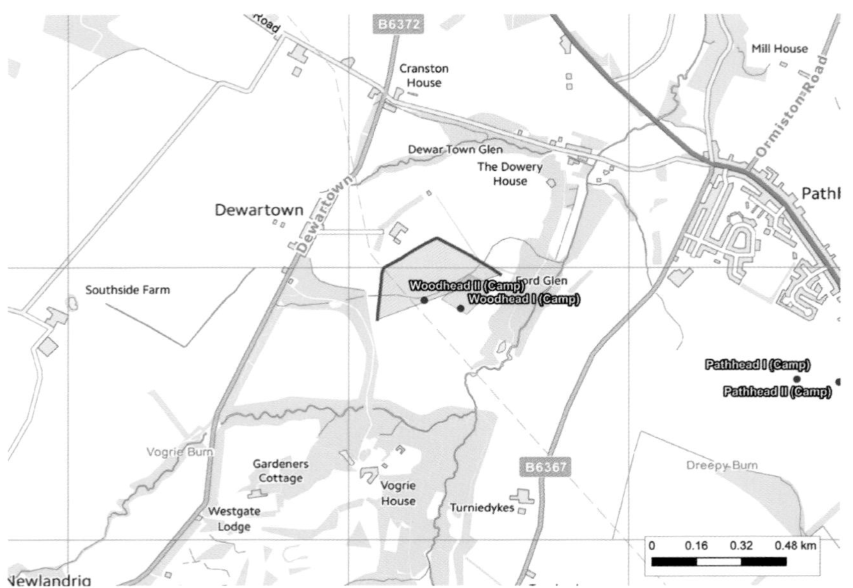

excavated the following year. Subsequent aerial photographs have recorded a small annexe on the southwestern side. St Joseph has speculated that the camp dates to the Severan period, although a coin of Hadrian was found at a nearby farm in 1829.

Gask House (Camp | NN 990 190)

Originally recorded in 1789 and then forgotten about until 1960, traces of the camp have since been destroyed by forestation.

Grassy Walls (Camp | NO 1050 2800)

Bisected by the 1st-century Roman road that runs northwards across the 52-hectare site, the camp at Grassy Walls is opposite the fort at Bertha. Archaeologists believe it was constructed during the Severan period.

Innerpeffray (East Camp | NN 915 180, West Camp | NN 908 181)

Horsley was the first to record earthworks at Innerpeffray, but these were forgotten until St Joseph recorded the camps from the air. There are some indications that he may have noted an additional two camps in the area, but evidence for this is questioned by some archaeologists.

Invergowrie (Possible Camp | NO 344 298)

Early antiquarians wrote about a Roman site in the vicinity of Invergowrie, but this remained lost until Maxwell identified cropmarks in the 1980s. Excavation in advance of development in 2016 failed to find any archaeological evidence for the camp.

Lintrose (Camp | NO 220 376)

Discovered in 1754, and recorded by Roy in 1755, the upstanding remains had been significantly eroded by agricultural work by the time Crawford examined the site, in the 1920s. The camp covers an area of almost 26 hectares and was built in the Severan period. The ramparts survive in a few places up to 6 metres wide and almost 1 metre high.

Longforgan (Camp | NO 298 303)

Identified from the air in the 1960s, the camp has an annexe and covers an area of about 26 hectares, indicating that it dates to the Severan period. Limited excavation in 2014 confirmed the ditch had an ankle breaker while there were no internal features noted.

Nether Braco (Possible Camp | NN 832 102)

In the mid-1960s, St Joseph recorded a cropmark that was identical to the corner of a Roman camp. No further evidence was visible in the images, so the site has not been confirmed as Roman, but St Joseph noted that the immediate area was ideal for a camp.

Scone Park (Camp | NO 104 271)

Like its larger neighbour (Grassy Walls), the camp at Scone Park sits opposite the fort at Bertha, and to the south of the line of the Roman road. The 24-hectare site was identified from the air and subsequent excavation confirmed the Roman origins. Today, most of the camp lies under Scone Racecourse.

St Madoes (Camp | NO 208 195)

The camp was discovered during aerial reconnaissance in 1967. Only parts of the defences have been located, but Jones speculates that the camp probably encloses an area of about 2 hectares and may have been protecting a route across the Tay. The site sits opposite the fort at Carpow.

The Gask Ridge Towers

Stretching across Perthshire, the Gask Ridge is arguably the earliest Roman land frontier in the world, comprising a series of Roman forts, fortlets and towers spaced at intervals along the Roman road that heads northeast from the central belt. Archaeologists are not sure where the road terminates.

The main chain of fortifications runs north from Ardoch to Strageath, before turning northeast, where the bulk of the towers are. Most of the towers have been explored either through geophysical survey or

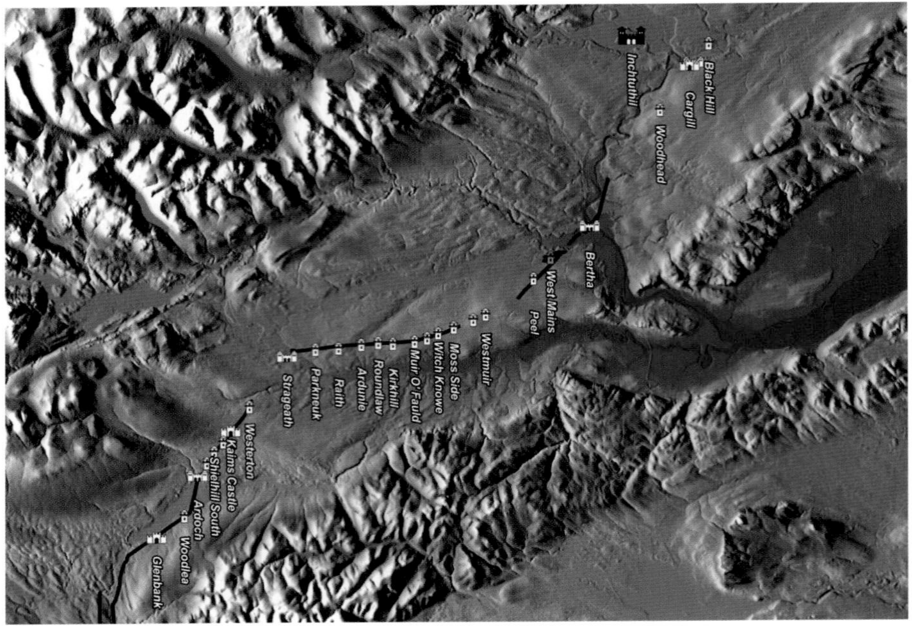

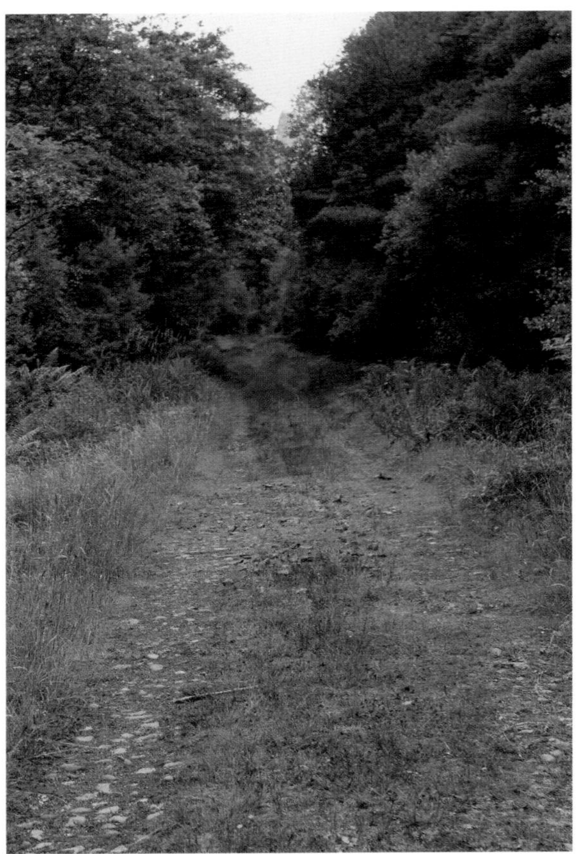

The old Roman road running along the Gask Ridge.

excavation, and follow a similar pattern of a central wooden tower structure enclosed by a defensive rampart/ditch arrangement. Their purpose would have been to guard the road and maybe also to act as signal points.

Most of the recent archaeological work on the frontier has been undertaken by David Woolliscroft and Birgitta Hoffmann of the Roman Gask Project (www.theromangaskproject.org), which has been working in this area for over 20 years. The project uses a variety of techniques, such as geophysical survey, aerial photography and excavation, to identify and explore sites. To date, the team has surveyed every fort north of the Forth–Clyde isthmus, including the fortress at Inchtuthil, as well as a number of smaller sites.

The research that Woolliscroft, Hoffmann and their volunteers have undertaken has proved invaluable to the understanding of the Romans in Scotland and archaeologists have much to thank them for. Their website has the most up-to-date information on many of the sites on the Gask Ridge, including the towers, while most of the older excavations are covered in the *Proceedings of the Society of Antiquaries of Scotland*.

The remains of the tower site at Muir O' Fauld. The ditch is visible as a mossy patch which turns to the left in the background.

Exploring

Most of the towers exist in the landscape as low mounds, but a handful are slightly more impressive. The best way to see the main group is by travelling along the line of the original Roman road. From the village of Auchterarder, head north on the B8062 for two miles, taking the right crossing over Kinkell Bridge. Carry on this road for about two miles until you enter the forest and the road takes a sharp left then right. Park up and follow the track through the forest to the west. After a quarter of a mile, the remains of the Muir O' Fauld tower will be on the left. The site is cared for by Historic Scotland and gives a good indication of the remains of a tower site.

Back on the main road, drive east along the line of the Roman road. The various towers are interspersed on either side for the next mile or so before the road joins the A9 just southwest of Perth.

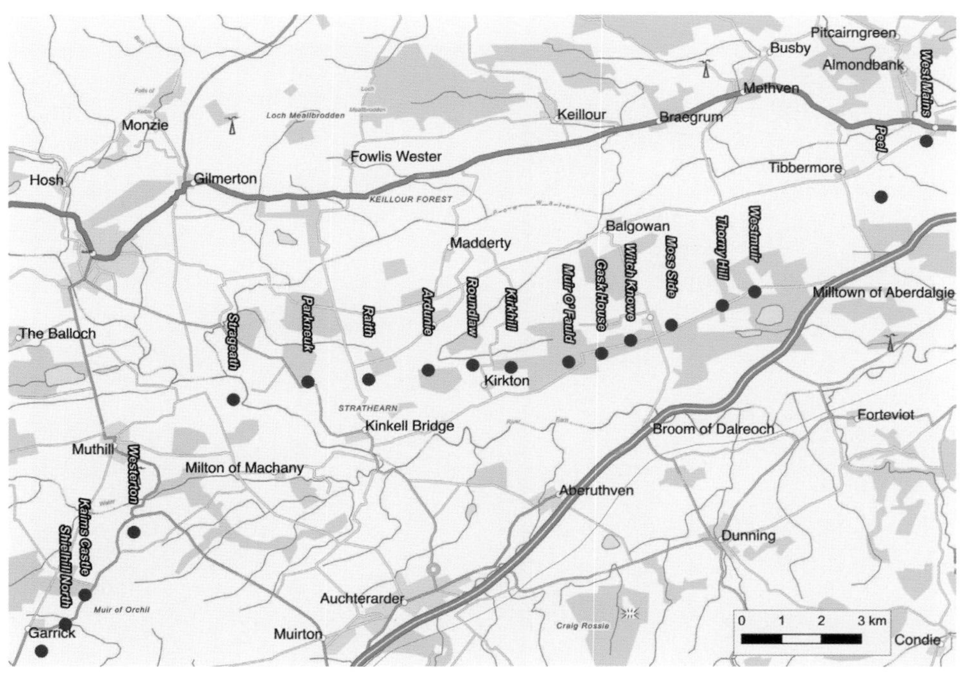

Chapter 20

DUNDEE

If there was ever a Roman fort or camp in the vicinity of Dundee, it is more than likely to have been obliterated by the growth of the modern city. Other than a handful of coins, there is no evidence of Roman activity in the area, with Bullion being the one possible exception.

Bullion

Possible Camp | NO 350 310

Knowledge of this camp comes from William Maitland, describing in 1757 a square enclosure surrounded by a ditch and rampart, which was subsequently ploughed out of existence. Archaeologists question whether or not this was a Roman site, given a number of contradictions in the original account. The exact location is now lost, although Crawford thought he had identified the site, but could find no trace of the camp.

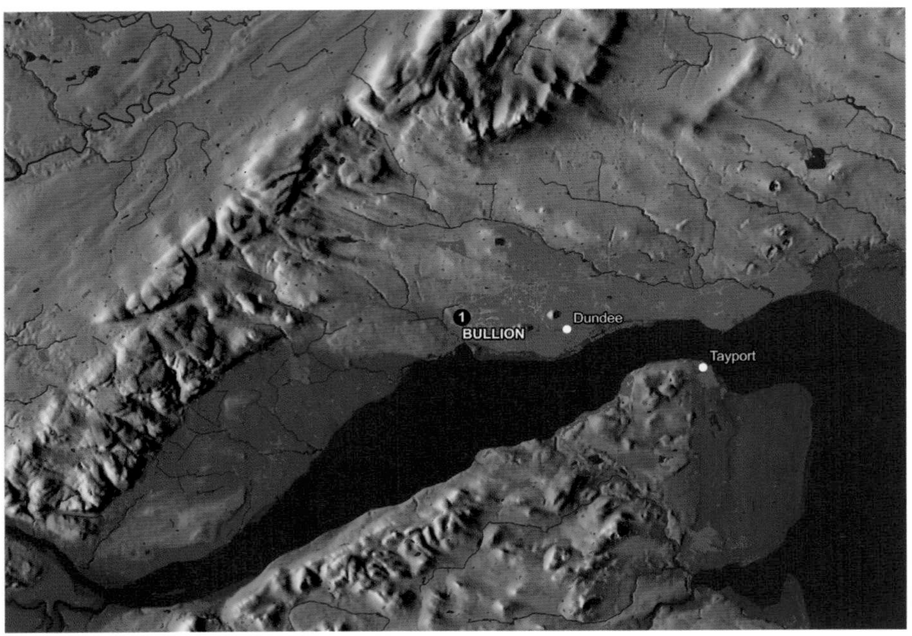

PART EIGHT: THE NORTHEAST OF SCOTLAND

Chapter 21

ANGUS

FOR A BRIEF PERIOD IN THE LATE 1ST CENTURY, Angus was the most important place in Roman Scotland as construction began on the legionary fortress at Inchtuthil. Intended to be the centre of military operations in the north, its completion would have seen Scotland become a fully fledged part of the Empire, but the site was never completed. Around 20 years after building began, Inchtuthil was abandoned as the army headed south to fill the vacuum left by soldiers dispatched to Germany to quell various uprisings. They left behind them a fascinating snapshot of Roman frontier life.

Cardean

Fort | NO 289 460
Camp | NO 299 462

The fort and camp at Cardean were constructed next to each other, and may have been occupied during the same period, as seems to have been the case at Inverquharity and Stracathro.

The camp was discovered and excavated by St Joseph in the 1950s, although he was unable to find parts of the southeastern defences, which should have been in the Crow Wood. He speculated that this was because he was excavating in the gateways rather than

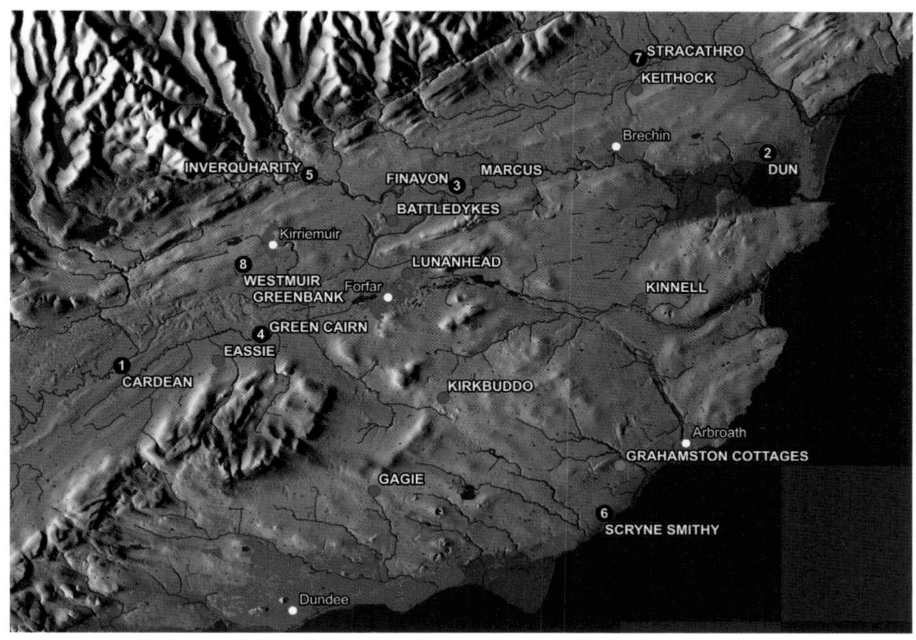

The fort at Cardean is now a potato field.

where the ditches should have been. He went on to propose that there was a second camp located within the original camp. More recently, Rebecca Jones has re-analysed St Joseph's original aerial photographs and has suggested that, while some of the cropmarks are clear, others are less regular and less Roman-like, and that further excavation is needed to confirm what the site is.

St Joseph also excavated the fort, suggesting that, because the defences varied in size, rather than being uniform, there may be two forts on the site. However, there was no material evidence to support this. Anne Robertson, who subsequently undertook large-scale excavations of the fort between 1968 and 1972, concluded that the site was only occupied for a single period and abandoned just after AD 86.

Key Dates

1777: General Melville notes the existence of the fort
1939: The fort is spotted from the air
1951: St Joseph undertakes an aerial survey of the site
1955: St Joseph discovers the camp while taking aerial photographs and also records internal layout of the fort from the air
1966, 1967: Robertson undertakes limited excavation of the fort

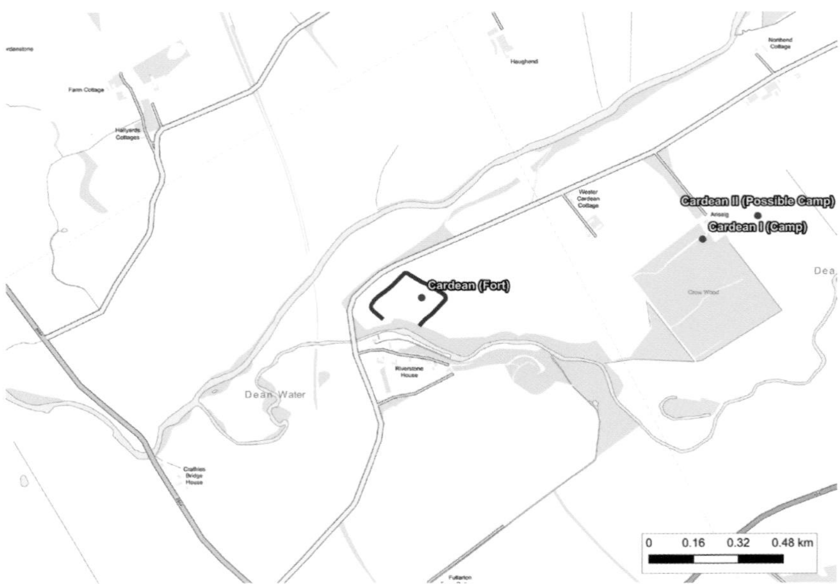

1968, 1970–75: The Scottish Field School, under Anne Robertson, undertakes extensive excavations of the fort
1972, 1974: St Joseph undertakes limited excavations on the camp
2001: Field walking, metal detecting and resistivity surveys are undertaken on the fort and annexe
2010: Magnetometry survey of fort takes place

Exploring

There are no remains of the fort to be seen, but some of the camp defences are still visible, including a possible *titulus*, which appears as a low rise on the southeastern side of the camp. Various ditches are visible in the Crow Wood, although some of these are for drainage and not connected to the fort. The Crow Wood can be reached via the path running on the northern side of the Dean Water.

From Meigle, follow the A94 towards Coupar Angus. After the village, take the B954 signposted for Alyth (on the right), but, rather than head down this road, take the minor road immediately to the right (signposted Cardean). After a mile, pass over the Dean and park just over the bridge. Follow the river path, which will pass below the fort and on to the Crow Wood.

Dun

Camp | NO 689 595

One of the biggest challenges facing archaeologists is identifying the coastal sites from which the Roman navy, the *Classis Britannica,* would have operated. Tacitus tells us that Agricola sailed his fleet around Britain to prove it was an island, so those ships would have needed to shelter. We also know that, when the army invaded a new area, it was provided with support from the fleet. These sites are yet to be discovered, but Dun seems to be a likely candidate. There is a lack of evidence for a harbour, but boats may have been beached rather than docked.

It is likely that Montrose Bay was much more accessible in the Roman period than it is today. The site was discovered by St Joseph during aerial reconnaissance, which he followed up with excavation. This located the defences and also turned up a single fragment of Samian pottery dating to AD 70–90, in a ditch underneath some silt, giving a 1st-century date to the site.

Key Dates

1970: St Joseph discovers the site from the air
1974: St Joseph excavates the defences
1990: The site is partially excavated by Rogers

The camp at Dun is on a flat plain overlooking Montrose Bay.

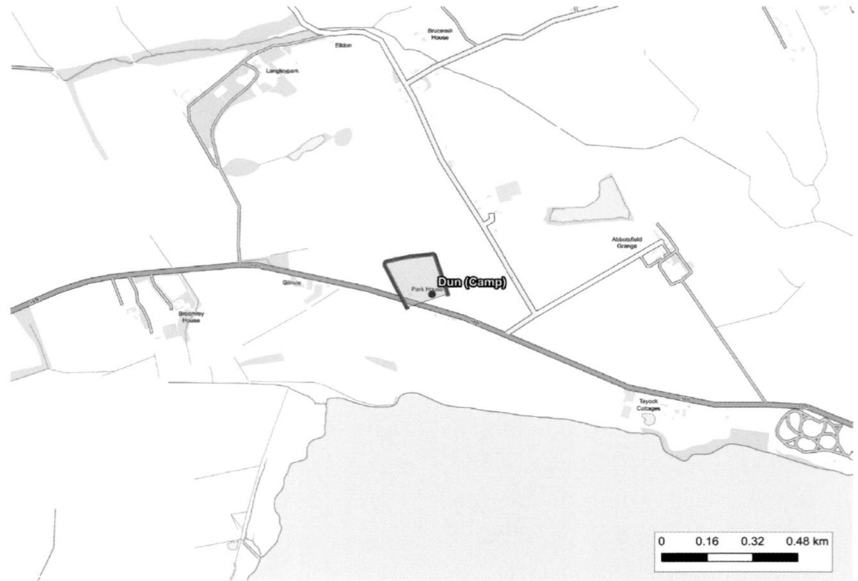

Exploring

Bisected by the A935, the site shows nothing on the ground, although aerial photography indicates a much more complicated history than initially thought. It is about a mile east of the House of Dun, a National Trust for Scotland property. Take the second road on the left after heading east from the House of Dun, where you can park on the verge. It is also possible to walk around part of the bay to reach the site, but it can be muddy and there are moving sands. Check the tide times, as the water coming rapidly into the bay will restrict access.

Finavon

Possible Fort | NO 49 57
Camp | NO 496 574

The camp was located from the air in the early 1960s by St Joseph, who then excavated the defences and confirmed the size of the site to be 16 hectares.

In the 1970s, St Joseph speculated that there was likely to be a missing fort in the area because there was a large gap in the chain between Cardean and Stracathro. Finavon, next to the River South Esk, was thought to be the most likely location although he was not able to find any cropmarks in the immediate area. In the early 1980s, a fortlet was found to plug the gap, but that was over at Inverquharity rather than at Finavon.

Key Dates

1962: The camp is identified by St Joseph
1965: Further defences are seen from the air
1966: St Joseph undertakes partial excavation of the defences
1987: The eastern ditch of the camp is excavated in advance of road widening
2009: A watching brief on the camp finds no Roman remains

Green Cairn

Cairn | NO 38 48

Glamis Castle is the location for this apparent Roman cairn, which was excavated in 1707, when the diggers uncovered an urn containing a number of Roman coins. No more details about the cairn and what was found have survived, so it is not clear whether there were bones or evidence of a cremation. It is not known either whether the coins were a bribe or belonged to a soldier.

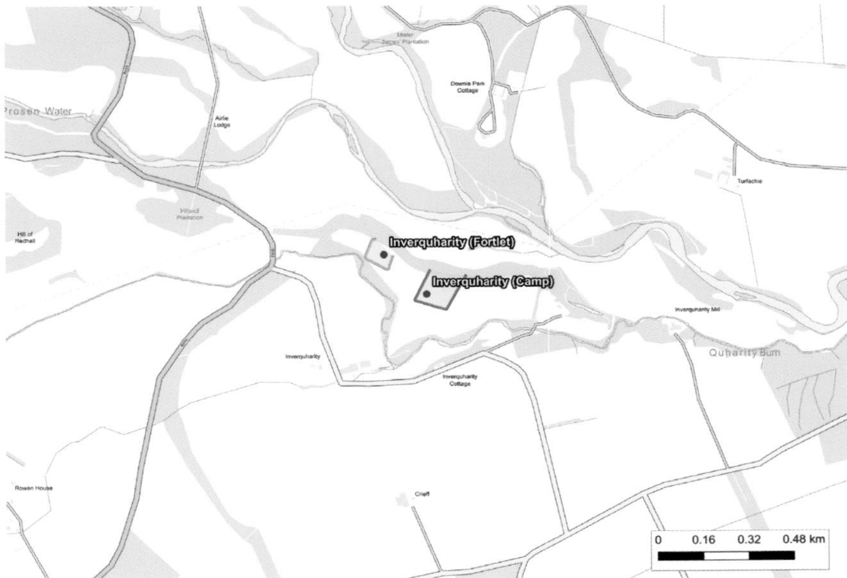

Inverquharity

Camp | NO 406 580
Fortlet | NO 405 581

Inverquharity is home to two very different Roman sites: a camp and a fortlet. Located on a hilly outcrop, the fortlet was first spotted from the air in 1983, although it appears to have been known about in the 18th century, when Sir Robert Sibbald, the Astronomer Royal wrote about a place called 'Innercaritie'. Sibbald did not provide a description of the location, but suggested that it dated to the Severan period, although he did not provide any evidence to support this.

Archaeologists firmly believe that both sites at Inverquharity are from the 1st century, basing this conclusion on their size, the Stracathro-type gates, and the proximity to other early fortifications. Both sites were identified in the early 1980s, with the fortlet appearing to have two annexes. David Woolliscroft and Birgitta Hoffman of the Roman Gask Project undertook a geophysical survey of the fortlet and part of the camp in 2002. They found that the ditch of the annexe crossed the fortlet's own ditches, indicating that the sites were not in existence at the same time. They also found evidence indicating the existence of four roundhouses and a souterrain. However, without excavation, it is not possible to say whether these were built before or after the Roman army had arrived in the area.

Key Dates

1707: Sibbald records Roman activity at a site called 'Innercaritie', which may be Inverquharity
1983: Maxwell identifies the fortlet or small fort from the air
1984: Maxwell discovers the camp during aerial reconnaissance. The defences are subsequently partially excavated
2002: Geophysical survey of the fort and parts of the annexe and camp reveal the defences of the former

Exploring

The camp and fortlet are located in fields surrounded by woodland. Although there are a few depressions in the ground, there is nothing to indicate any of the features of either site.

From Kirriemuir, head north through the town (towards the golf course), until you join the B955, then head east for a mile, past Muirhouses Farm. Go on for another mile, past a minor road marked 'Inverquharity' on the right. Immediately next to this is a layby at the entrance to fields, where you can park.

Take the right gate and follow the stream, then head on to the hill and the fortlet is in front of you. The field itself is not accessible because of barbed wire, and there can be cattle grazing. If you take the left gate at the layby you can follow the track down to the river and see the erosion, which has swept away part of the fortlet platform of the site (which is behind you on the hill).

Scryne Smithy (East Haven)

Possible Site | NO 588 366

Two ditches and a rounded corner were identified as cropmarks by Maxwell in 1983. It is possible that this is a Roman camp or fort, but no further work has taken place to confirm this.

Stracathro

Fort | NO 617 657
Camp | NO 613 656

Like Inverquharity, Stracathro is another Flavian site, which has a camp and a fort that date to the Flavian period but may not have been occupied at the same time. Archaeologists have not been able to say which was constructed first because, unlike at Inverquharity, the camp and the fort do not overlap. The fort was constructed on a headland, where the land drops away steeply to the river valley, although the northern side of the site has been severely affected by erosion.

The camp was first identified by St Joseph in 1955, and he went on to discover the fort two years later. To date, it is the most northerly known Roman fort, not only in Scotland, but in the world. On excavating the fort defences, St Joseph uncovered part of the southeastern ditch and postulated that the gate on that side was actually the *porta principalis dextra*, and that the site faced either northeast or southwest. However, in 1969, Anne Robertson excavated part of the field outside the church boundary wall, which had been earmarked for expansion of the graveyard. She uncovered the remains of a Roman period building, which she interpreted as being part of a barrack block and implying that the fort faced northwest–southeast. In 2012, the Roman Gask Project team undertook an extensive geophysical examination of the fort and part of the camp. The results showed some of the internal features and the gates and defences. Pottery and gate design have indicated a Flavian date for the camp and fort.

As well as the Roman features, the geophysics indicated traces of the early medieval church that lay on top of the fort site and is quite possibly where John Baliol capitulated to Edward I of England, renouncing the mutual protection treaty that Scotland had with France in 1296.

Although there is little to see on the ground of the

IN MEMORY
OF THE MEN
BELONGING TO
THE PARISH
OF STRACATHRO
WHO FELL IN
THE GREAT WAR

The church at Stracathro, which is on top of the fort.

camp or the fort, the 19th-century church that sits on top of the site is worth a visit, as is the extension to the cemetery that was excavated by Robertson. In the field next to the layby opposite the church, the field slopes down to the Cruick Water. To the east of the fort lies Brawl's Well (NO 619 658), a natural well that was used for healing in the 18th century and possibly before that. It is now overgrown but may have originally supplied the fort and possibly even a bath house with fresh water; the bath house would have been located just outside the fort.

Key Dates

1955: The camp is identified from aerial photographs
1960: Aerial photographs of the site show clear defences
1967: St Joseph excavates the northwest gate of the camp
1969: Robertson undertakes excavations on the fort in advance of cemetery expansion
2000: A cropmark of a circular enclosure, possibly a roundhouse, is identified to the immediate east of the camp
2008: A magnetometry survey of the fort and annexe reveals further details
2012: Extensive geophysical surveys reveal the defences and some internal features

Exploring

Stracathro can be found heading south on the A90 from Stonehaven. Take the first left immediately after passing the Stracathro services. Follow the road for a mile to the T-junction, turn right and on to the church. The fort is under the church and in the surrounding fields. The fort ditch is under the track to the houses at Smiddyhill.

Westmuir

Possible Signal Tower | NO 364 524

The site was identified through RAF aerial photographs as a dark ring that could indicate a signal tower. The site is next to the Roman road that runs along the Gask frontier, which makes it a likely suspect.

Key Dates

1965: St Joseph records a circular mark during aerial reconnaissance, noting similarities with two other nearby towers. He also notes its proximity to the Roman road

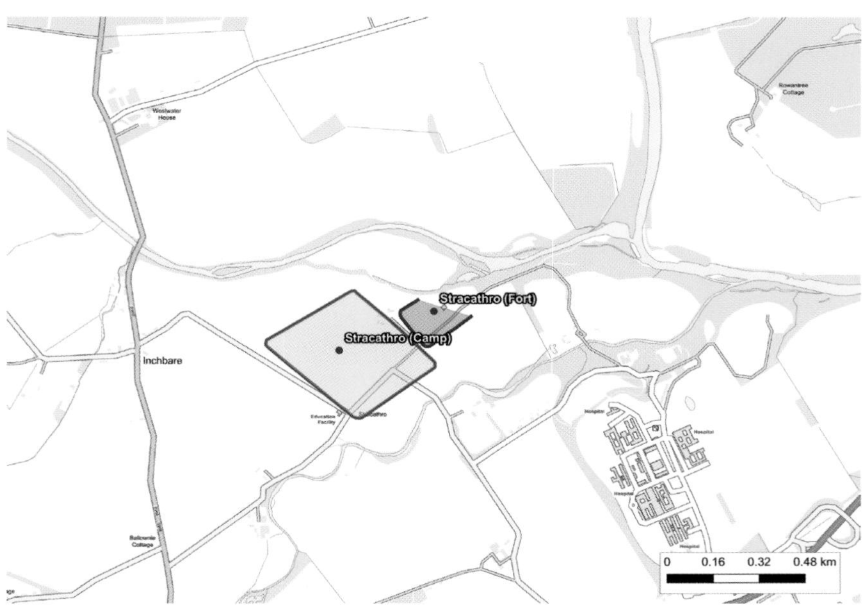

The Other Sites

Battledykes (Camp | NO 459 554)

There are a number of early accounts that record the existence at Battledykes of a camp that was assumed to be Roman. However, St Joseph, when examining the site from the air in the second half of the 20th century, concluded that the site appeared to be native rather than Roman.

Eassie (Camp | NO 351 466)

Archaeologists speculate that the 25-hectare camp at Eassie was constructed as part of the campaigns of Septimius Severus in the 3rd century. While excavations in 1968 located the ditches, subsequent work in 1970 noted that the ditch was not the traditional V-shaped feature associated with Roman fortifications.

Gagie (Camp | NO 448 383)

Gagie camp was discovered from the air, with the ditches being subsequently excavated. However, they were notably small and flat-bottomed, unlike regular Roman camp defences, leading some archaeologists to question whether this is a military installation.

Grahamston Cottages (Possible Camp | NO 600 399)

Several cropmarks seem to indicate the presence of a large camp in the vicinity of Grahamston Cottages, with the northern ditch being around 90 metres and the western 80 metres. The other sides of the possible camp have not yet been identified, and the site is yet to be excavated.

Greenbank (Possible Camps | NO 370 499)

In 2008 aerial reconnaissance by David Woolliscroft of the Roman Gask Project identified two rectilinear features, both of which had rounded corners, implying possible Roman camps. No excavations have yet taken place to confirm what they are.

Keithock (Camp | NO 610 638)

Located next to the Cruick Water, and a short distance from the fort and camp at Stracathro, Keithock is a 25-hectare camp that is thought by archaeologists to belong to the Severan campaigns. The camp has six gates, with four *tituli*, and an annexe on the northwest side of the camp.

Kinnell (Camp | NO 613 505)

Found in 1968 from the air, Kinnell camp was subjected to limited excavation to confirm whether it was Roman. In 2005, the site was part of a series of excavations in advance of quarrying, although the excavators found no evidence of datable Roman features.

Kirkbuddo (Camp | NO 490 442)

First recorded in 1754, and formally planned a year later by William Roy, the standing remains were fairly substantial, with the site having six gates and an annexe on the southern side. Today, some visible remains can still be seen in the nearby Whig Street Wood, with the rampart still standing at around a metre high, and the ditch 1.5 metres wide in places. One of the surviving *tituli* can be seen on the southwest side of the camp.

Lunanhead (Camp | NO 468 521)

This camp first appears on a 1794 map, where it is shown covering an area of 87 hectares. Archaeologists agree that this is likely to have been an error on the part of the map maker. The site has been investigated in the 20th century by several archaeologists, including Crawford, St Joseph and the Ordnance Survey, all of whom noted different parts of the defences. None of them seemed to match up with the 18th-century map.

Marcus (Camp | NO 511 580)

Marcus is likely to have been constructed as part of the 3rd-century Severan camps. The camp was around 27 hectares and had an annexe and *tituli*, several of these are still visible on the northwest side of the site.

Chapter 22

ABERDEEN AND ABERDEENSHIRE

Not only is Aberdeenshire home to some of the most northerly Roman camps in the world, but it is also the area most closely associated with the battle site of Mons Graupius, the big showdown between the invading Romans and the native Caledonians. Around the time when the battle took place, a series of Roman camps were constructed along the edge of the Highlands, across Aberdeenshire and on to the Moray coast, part of a plan to invade the northern part of Scotland and bring it under the control of the Empire. It was a plan that was never fulfilled as trouble on the German frontier resulted in troops being relocated from Britain. The north was abandoned by the Romans, never to be fully conquered again, no matter how hard they tried.

Aberdeen

Aberdeen, located at the mouth of the River Dee and with a natural harbour for shipping, is exactly the sort of spot where the Romans would have established a fort. However, if there was a Roman fort there, it has long been forgotten about and built on. The 2nd-century astronomer and mathematician Claudius Ptolemy, based in Alexandria, Egypt, drew up a map of Roman Britain that included a fort known as 'Devana' at the place where Aberdeen now sits. Although there is no archaeological evidence to suggest any buildings in the area, there have been a number of coins found around the city, as well as other objects such as pins and fish hooks recovered from the Dee near Duthie Park. In addition, a nearby

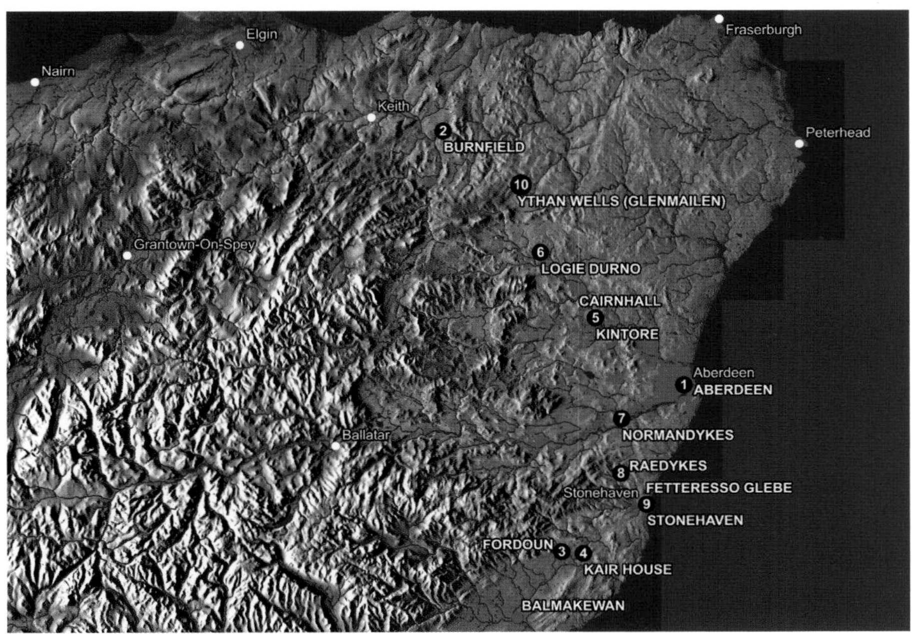

The Battle of Mons Graupius

One of the most enduring mysteries of Roman Scotland, the battle of Mons Graupius took place in the 1st century and was the culmination of Agricola's campaigning in Scotland. Many books and academic papers have been dedicated to detailing this great battle, and in particular where it happened, with most scholars believing that it took place somewhere in the northeast, although a range of sites across Scotland have been proposed as the location of the battle site.

All the information concerning Mons Graupius comes from a single source: Tacitus, and his semi-biographical work on his father-in-law, Agricola. In his account of the battle, Tacitus devotes pages to the speeches given by Agricola to his troops, and by Calgacus (the leader of the Caledoni) to his men, although, strangely, when Tacitus goes on to describe the battle, neither character features in the action. It is also the only battle that is mentioned by name that occurs in the book.

To date, there are no artefacts or other types of archaeological evidence to indicate that a great battle ever took place in Scotland. That is not to say that Mons Graupius did not take place, but it may not have been the substantial skirmish that Tacitus details. Was he being a bit fanciful? He gives the number of Caledoni ready to do battle as 30,000. In fact, the archaeological evidence may indicate a more peaceful existence, with indigenous roundhouses frequently located next to forts, while excavations at brochs, such as East Coldich in Stirling, have revealed evidence for trade, with Roman beads and glass being found.

While many archaeologists have tried to locate the battle site, Mons Graupius remains elusive, despite serious academic study and profiling of the numerous potential sites. Until artefacts such as damaged armour, slingshots and other weaponry or significant damaged human remains are recovered, it seems likely that Scotland's most famous battle site will remain lost in the mists of time.

hearth at Shiprow has been dated to between 2 and 128 AD.

Key Dates

1832: Coin of Domitian found
1890: Coin of Constantine the Great and Constans found
1970: Coin of Constantine I found
1984: Coin of Licinius I found

Burnfield

Camp | NJ 540 476

Identified in the early 1980s, the site has been subjected to limited excavation to confirm its Roman origins. Only small sections of the defences have been located, indicating that the site was probably 12–16 hectares in size.

Key Dates

1982: Site identified from the air by Ralston
1982: Limited excavation of defences by Ralston and St Joseph

Fordoun

Possible Camp | NO 732 769

Looking at a map showing the 1st-century camps in the north, there appears to be a missing site between Stracathro and Normandykes (the camps at Balmakewan and Keir House probably date to the Severan period). Camps were normally constructed one day's march from each other, around 20 kilometres, but in this instance, the camps are 33 kilometres apart – a challenge for even the Roman army!

The earliest record of a Roman camp at Fordoun comes from the Reverend Alexander Leslie, who wrote *The Old Statistical Account of Scotland* for the area in 1801. Leslie noted the camp before it was ploughed out of existence. In 1850, James Know's *Map of the Tay Basin* included a plan of the camp at Fordoun, which would have been one of the largest in Scotland. Today, there are no traces of the camp and very little evidence to indicate it ever existed.

Fordoun: the site of one of Scotland's largest Roman camps?

Key Dates

1793: General Roy suggests that there should be a Roman fort in the vicinity of Fordoun
1792: *The Old Statistical Account of Scotland* gives an account of a Roman camp in the area
19th century: Coin of Trajan found near Fordoun House
1850: Knox draws a six-gated camp on his *Map of the Tay Basin* covering Fordoun
2015: Archaeologists field walking the site fail to find any Roman artefacts

Exploring

While there may not be a camp at Fordoun, there is a well-preserved moated site near by (NO 735 770). Originally identified as being the headquarters of the fort, it is actually a medieval moated farmstead, with ditches 5 metres wide and 2 metres deep in places. Although overgrown, it can be accessed with caution via the turf causeway on the northern side. Head through the farmyard, following the track between the two sheds. The moated site is up a slight rise and in the clump of trees ahead.

Kair House

Camp | NO 767 767

At around 50 hectares, the camp at Kair is one of the larger sites, and likely to date to the Severan campaigns of the 3rd century. The location is strategically important, commanding excellent views of the immediate area, as well as down the Mearns

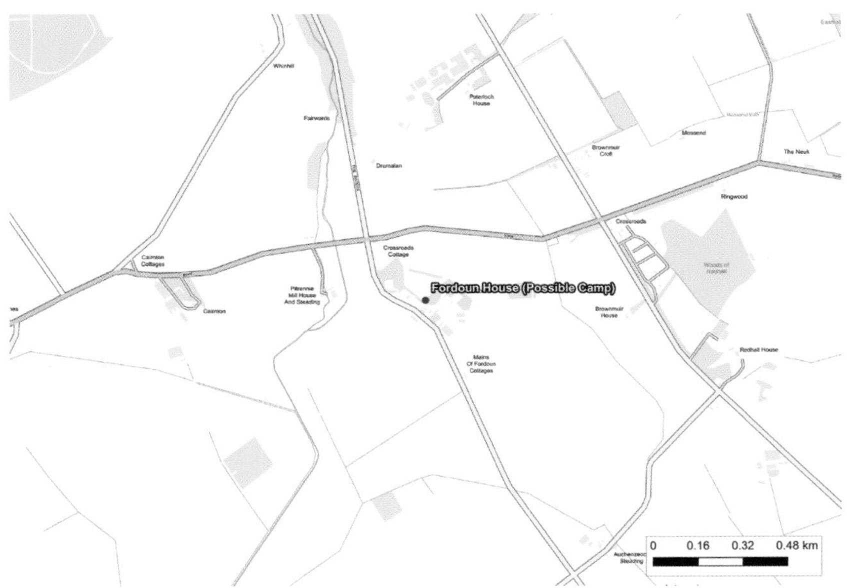

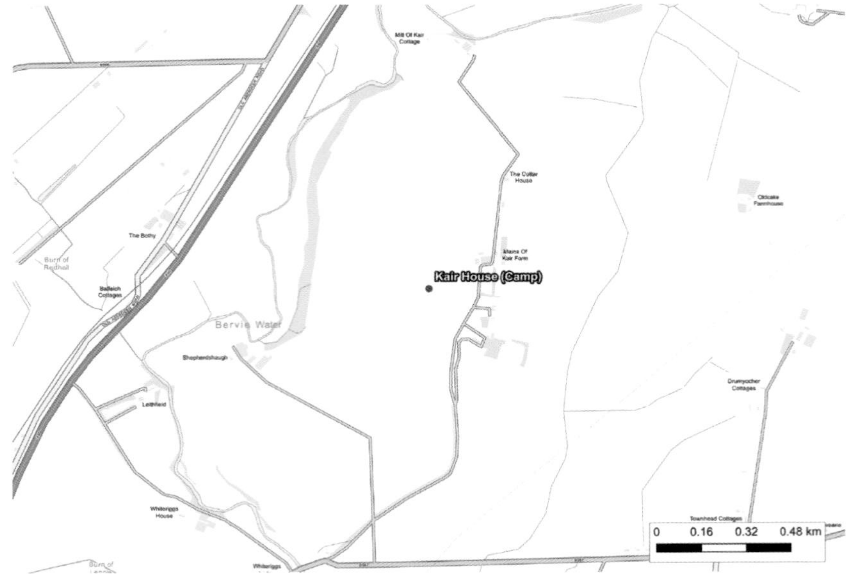

to the south. There is some speculation amongst archaeologists that, because of the good views, and its location almost halfway between Stracathro and Raedykes, there may be an older camp underneath. However, no evidence has yet been discovered to support this theory.

Key Dates

1793: General Roy suggests that there should be a Roman fort in the vicinity of Kair House
1945: The site is discovered by St Joseph during aerial reconnaissance
1959: Quern stone fragments are found within the camp but believed to be post-Roman
2003: Watching brief during development finds no internal features of the camp
2011: Watching brief during wind turbine construction failed to find any Roman features or artefacts

Exploring

Heading northbound on the A90, take the right turn on to the B967 near Fordoun, then take the third turning on the left. Cross over the bridge over the Bervie Water and follow the road for a mile, past Kair House, and through the farmyard and stop near the wind turbine. The rampart can be seen ahead of you, and in the trees to the right.

The camp is now farmed, although there are some features to be seen on the ground, with 18 metres of rampart visible as a mound in a field to the north-east of Kair House, with a further 10 metres visible in the trees.

Kintore

Camp | NJ 787 162

The camp at Kintore is one of the most-explored Roman sites in Scotland, with archaeologists having managed to excavate around 85 per cent of it in advance of modern development. Today, the A96 cuts across one side of the site and most of the rest of the camp is covered by housing. The site was first noted in the 1860s by Alexander Watt but was not formally recorded until 1867, when Captain Courtney of the Royal Engineers noted that the visible remains had been significantly reduced in the intervening years.

The camp was subject to extensive excavations during the late 20th and early 21st century in advance of development. While work in 1984 confirmed the defensive ditches, it was the excavations between 1996 and 2004 that revealed the most about the camp, with over 180 ovens and more than 60 Roman rubbish pits full of pottery, burnt grain and animal bones. The work on Kintore has given archaeologists an insight into life on the edge of the Roman empire. The archaeologists also uncovered signs of life pre-dating the arrival of the Romans, including Iron Age round-houses, pottery, several semi-circular cropmarks, and a series of nine, substantial postholes. These were arranged in such a way that they may have formed part of a prehistoric timber circle, which would have been in use long before the Romans arrived in Aberdeenshire.

The camp at Kintore now lies under a modern housing estate.

Key Dates

1868: Captain Courtney records the site
1950: Aerial survey of the site by St Joseph
1984: Excavation of the camp ditch by Shepherd
1996, 1997, 2000, 2001, 2002, 2003, 2004: Extensive excavations across the site in advance of the construction of the A96 bypass and building development

Exploring

Kintore is located off the A96, around 14 miles northwest of Aberdeen. Due to the modern development, there is nothing to be seen on the ground.

Logie Durno

Camp | NJ 698 271

Logie Durno is around six miles northwest of Inverurie and was discovered in the mid-1970s. It is one of the largest camps in Britain, at 57 hectares, which is about the same size as 141 football pitches or 57 rugby fields. Constructed on a hillside with a difference in height of 35 metres from the lowest point to the highest, the site takes advantage of the natural contours of the land and so is not the typical playing-card shape of Roman camps. The northern defensive ditch turns 20 degrees north on the long axis, which creates a kink at one end of the site.

Although camps of this size are generally associated with the Severan campaigns, Logie Durno is assumed to be Flavian because of the closeness of other Flavian camps – Kintore is about nine miles to the south and Ythan Wells is about seven and a half miles northwest. Bennachie is also close by and a prime contender as the site for Mons Graupius,

where the last stand of the native Caledoni took place against Agricola. St Joseph was a strong proponent for Logie Durno being the Roman encampment for the battle, arguing that a number of local hills match the description of the battle site. While there is no archaeological evidence to support this claim, there are at least six native hillforts surrounding the camp, although these have not yet been dated.

Key Dates

1975–77: St Joseph identifies the site from the air. Sections of the defences are excavated

1978: St Joseph argues that Logie Durno hosted the Roman army on the eve of Mons Graupius

Exploring

Only part of the defences has been identified, and while there are no remains to be seen on the ground, there is some speculation that a very low rise on the northeastern side of the site constitutes the remains of the rampart. However, this is yet to be confirmed through excavation.

The site is accessible on foot. Heading west through the village of Whiteford, take the second left at the school and head on for a mile until passing the farm at Logie Durno. About 500 metres on from this are a handful of houses on the right, at Easterton. This is the inside of the southwestern perimeter of the camp. A path opposite Easterton heads into the woods and on to the defences of the site. The possible rampart is visible further along the road from Westerton Cottages.

Normandykes

Camp | NO 829 993

Positioned on a ridge, with commanding views of the surrounding countryside, Normandykes takes advantage of the landscape and its natural defences. The camp has been known about since at least 1795, although at the time it was believed to have been constructed by Viking raiders, and it was not until 1807 that a Roman date was put forward for it. The dating for the site was confirmed in the 1930s by

The camp at Normandykes was built on the ridge.

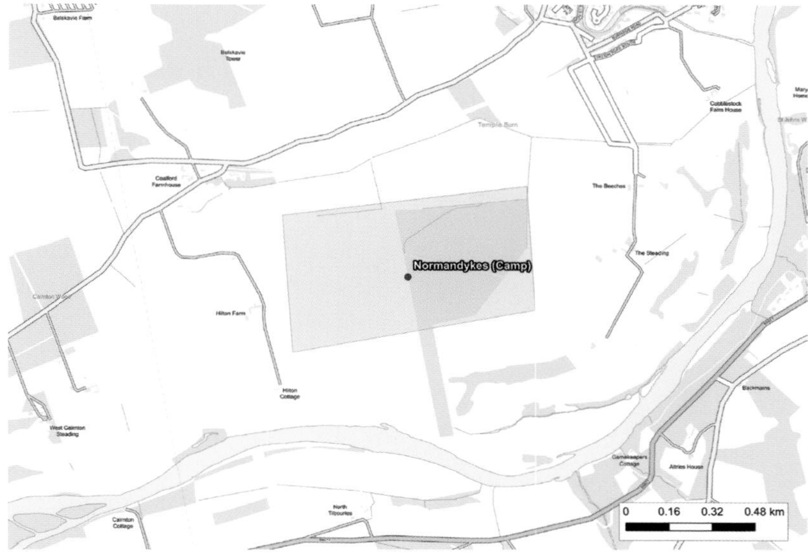

Richmond and McIntyre, although their excavations were never published. Further work took place in 1949 and 1971, and then in 2006, when a number of ovens and hearths were revealed, which were likely to have been Roman.

Key Dates

1795: The camp is recorded in *The Old Statistical Account of Scotland* and ascribed to the Norman period
1801: Colonel Shand notes that Normandykes is a Roman 'station'
1935: Richmond and McIntyre undertake limited excavations of the site
1998: A watching brief fails to record any pre-19th century finds
2006: Excavation reveals ovens but fails to locate the defences

Exploring

While there is not much to see on the ground, there are pleasant walks in the vicinity of the ridge, as well as through the camp itself. To the east of the camp is a well, marked on the Ordnance Survey maps (and now a patch of boggy land). In the 1860s it was known as the 'Roman Well', but by the 1900s it was being called 'Norman's Well'. The site is partially covered by a plantation, and some of the original rampart still exists as part of the northern boundary of the forested area.

Raedykes

Camp | NO 841 902

If there was ever an award for the most untypical or peculiarly shaped Roman camp, then Raedykes would surely win. Within the camp defences is an entire hill, and at least one of the defensive ditches is cut through solid rock rather than earth. The ramparts differ considerably in width and height in various places and, more importantly, there does not seem to be any source of fresh water near by. It certainly breaks all the rules of the 4th-century guide on how to be a good soldier, written by Publius Flavius Vegetius Renatus; his perfect camp has to have fresh running water, should not be overlooked by hills (so the enemy cannot fire into it), and should be built on a level plain. While the site at Raedykes is not perfect, it seems to have been the best spot in the local area to construct a camp, despite having a hill in the middle of it.

The builders made extensive use of the natural topography, creating a camp that is distinctive in shape, like a rectangle with one corner stretched to a point. The defences cover an area of about 39 hectares, and there is almost a 40-metre difference in heights between the highest and lowest parts of the

The camp at Raedykes covers all of the hill in the background.

Part of the rock-cut ditches which form part of the eastern defences of Raedykes.

camp. Garrison Hill, which sits within the perimeter of the camp, would have restricted views from the site, but the highest point affords good views out to the coast, including south to Stonehaven, where there may have been another Roman site.

The site is first mentioned in 1757 in William Maitland's *History and Antiquities of Scotland*, and a few decades later George Brown and Mr Barclay of Urie declared that it must have been the encampment for Mons Graupius, which they argued took place at the nearby Kempstone Hill. In 1831, John Stewart suggested that the site may have been built by the Caledoni trying to replicate the Roman style. It was not until the early 20th century that George Macdonald investigated the site and noted inconsistencies in the defences. In 1949, OGS Crawford noted additional earthworks outside of the camp to the south (which may have nothing to do with the Roman occupation).

The camp is believed to date to the Flavian period because of the proximity of other possible Flavian camps (Stracathro, Kintore and Normandykes), and because *tituli* have been recorded at the eastern entrances. However, some archaeologists have questioned the dating, as there is a lack of datable finds from the site. St Joseph suggests that the site may have been occupied in the Antonine or Severan periods; coins from the latter have been found just over a mile away.

Key Dates

1757: Raedykes is detailed by Maitland who believes it is associated with Mons Graupius
1792: Barclay describes Raedykes in relation to Mons Graupius
1831: Stuart claims that Raedykes is a poor attempt by the Caledoni to replicate a Roman encampment
1914: Macdonald excavates part of the camp, including the defences
1949: Crawford visits Raedykes and notes additional earthworks to the south of the camp

Exploring

From Stonehaven, head northwest on the A957, crossing over the A90. After four miles, cross over the Cowie Water and after a mile take the right, carrying on for half a mile. When the road turns sharply to the right, go straight on to the minor track. On the right are the earthworks noted by Crawford, which may have formed an outer defence. On the left is Garrison Hill. Where the track bends to the left, park on the side and carry on up the track on foot, where a section of rock-cut ditch is visible in front of you. The site is marked on the Ordnance Survey map.

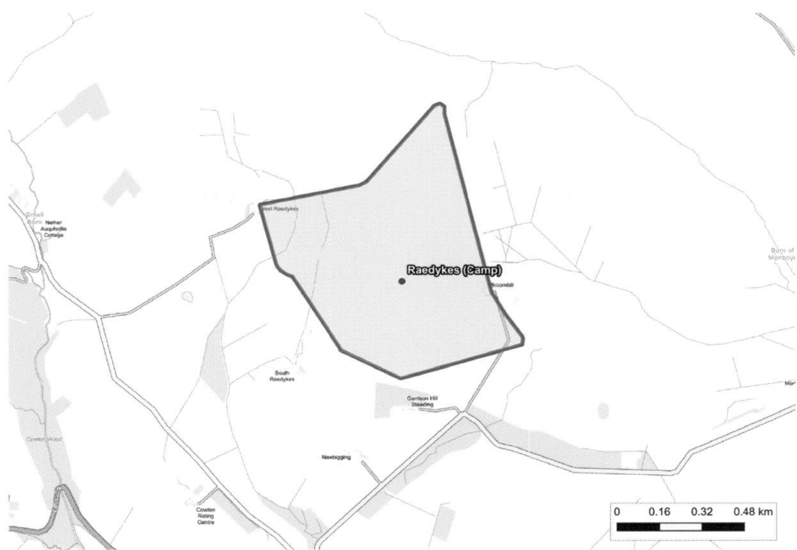

Stonehaven

Possible Site | NO 87 85

Like Aberdeen, Stonehaven would have made an ideal location for a Roman site because of the natural topography, as well as the easy access following the river inland, and the harbour. It is also the one of the only sheltered beaches on the northeast coast. However, also like Aberdeen, there is little evidence for Roman activity in the area. Of course, an absence of evidence does not necessarily mean the Romans were not here, and the expansion of the fishing village in the 18th and 19th centuries may have obliterated any features. St Joseph suspected a fort in the vicinity of Stonehaven, while Shepherd Frere, a prominent Romanist, noted that the line of Flavian forts running along the edge of the Highlands appeared to be heading towards the sea, and Stonehaven would have made a natural end to this chain. Unlike Aberdeen, there have been no reports of Roman coins being found in the town.

Ythan Wells (Glenmailen)

Camp I | NJ 655 381
Camp II | NJ 660 384

There are two camps at Ythan Wells, both located fairly near to the source of the River Ythan. Archaeologists believe that both camps date to the Flavian period, although they were occupied at different times, with the smaller, 13-hectare camp being built on top of part of the larger (44-hectare) one. The camps are not ideally located, being overlooked by hills to the northeast, which could have let the enemy have the advantage and fire into the sites.

The larger camp was recorded in the 1780s by Captain Shand, with Mr McRonald drawing up a site plan in 1789 and a more formal recording being made by William Roy four years later. The site was excavated in the early 20th century by Francis Haverfield and George Macdonald, who noted that the rampart still existed in places up to 2.3 metres, although this had been reduced to its foundations when OGS Crawford visited only a couple of decades later. The smaller camp was discovered in 1968 by St Joseph who was trying to photograph the larger site. Both sites are dated to the Flavian period because the larger camp

Site of the larger camp at Ythan Wells.

has a Stracathro-type gate and they are close to other sites of this period.

Key Dates

1785–86: Captain Shand records Camp I
1789: McRonald plans Camp I (published by Roy in 1793)
1913: Macdonald excavates Camp I
1949: Crawford visits the site and identifies some of the defences on the ground
1951, 1957: St Joseph photographs parts of the defences of Camp I from the air
1968: Camp II is identified from the air by St Joseph and both camps are excavated and found to overlap
1974: Northern camp defences are identified
1978: Further aerial photographs reveal more of the defences

Exploring

The site is close to the hamlet of Wells of Ythan (NJ 633 384), as it appears on some local signs. The hamlet is on a crossroads, so head east for about a mile until the road curves to the left at the Glenmallen farm. The larger camp is on the hill on the right, with a field boundary marking the southern extremity of the camp.

The Other Sites

Balmakewan (Camp | NO 6657 6667)

Noted in 1807, the camp was not further explored until the 1960s when it was examined through aerial photography, which indicated that the site covered an area of 46 hectares. Given the size of the camp, it was probably constructed during the Severan campaigns.

Cairnhall (Possible Camp | NJ 784 175)

At Cairnhall, just to the north of the camp at Kintore, a single linear cropmark was seen in the 1970s. St Joseph subsequently excavated the cropmark, uncovering a ditch that was similar to typical Roman camp defences. However, as only one ditch has been discovered, Cairnhall's status as a Roman camp is only tentative.

Fetteresso Glebe (Possible Camp | NO 8681 8651)

William Camden noted a camp at Fetteresso Glebe in 1722, and a plan of the site was published in 1785. Just two decades later all traces of the site had vanished. The plan of the site showed a long, thin fort, which Crawford decided in 1949 was more likely to be a native site. Today, the fort lies under a housing estate, keeping its mysteries safe.

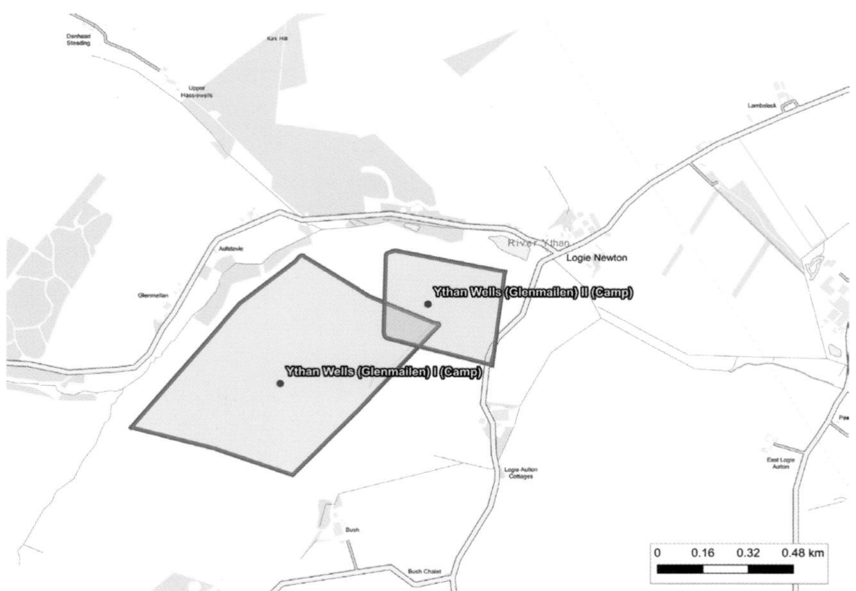

PART NINE: THE HIGHLANDS OF SCOTLAND

Chapter 23

MORAY

The Moray coast is home to the most northerly and last known site in the Roman Empire. Bellie is at the end of the chain of fortifications starting on the Clyde and running through Stirling, Perthshire, Angus and Aberdeenshire before ending here on the edge of the Highlands. There are a few tantalizing hints that the Romans may have travelled beyond Moray (*see* the Highlands section).

The range of fortifications in Moray is limited, with the sites being briefly occupied camps, but they do give archaeologists a limited glimpse into the Roman army on the edge of the Empire.

Auchinhove

Camp | NJ 461 517

The most northerly confirmed Roman camp in Scotland (Bellie is slightly further north, but may not be Roman) is located on a gentle rise in the valley of the River Isla. It is unusually close to two other camps, which are believed to date to the same period: Muiryfold, less than two miles away, and Burnfield, which is five and a half miles away. Camps are usually a day's march apart, which indicates that these sites are either closely connected, perhaps being in use at the same time, or that archaeologists are wrong and the camps were occupied at different times. As

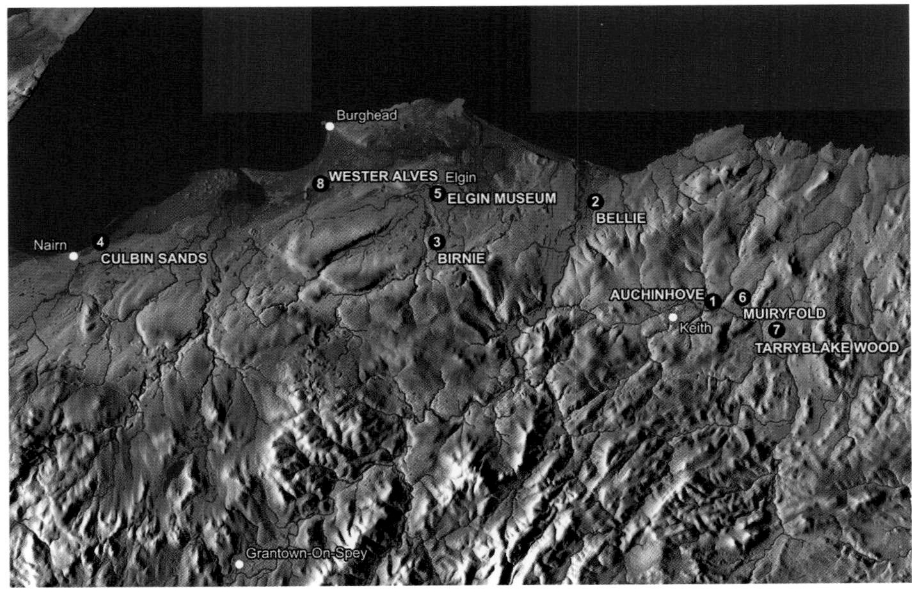

The camp at Auchinhove.

the Auchinhove entrance is parrot-beak in style, St Joseph argued that it dated to the Flavian period.

The camp itself has left no visible traces, except the cropmarks visible from the air that led to the site's discovery in 1949. Subsequent aerial photographs a few years later helped to identify the eastern, western and southern defences, leading the surveyors to conclude that the northern ditch was likely to be located under the modern road.

Exploring

Travelling east on the A95, the site is on the right, just past the farm of Auchinhove, opposite the turn-off for the B9018. There is a group of houses by the turn-off where you can park and look south towards the camp.

Bellie

Camp | NJ 355 611

Bellie could be the most northerly Roman site in Scotland, and indeed anywhere, but the evidence is inconclusive. It could be the last of a chain of Flavian sites, which ends abruptly on the banks of the River Spey, or it could be more recent. The site seems to have been noted twice in the 18th century, but efforts between the world wars to trace the place mentioned in the accounts drew a blank.

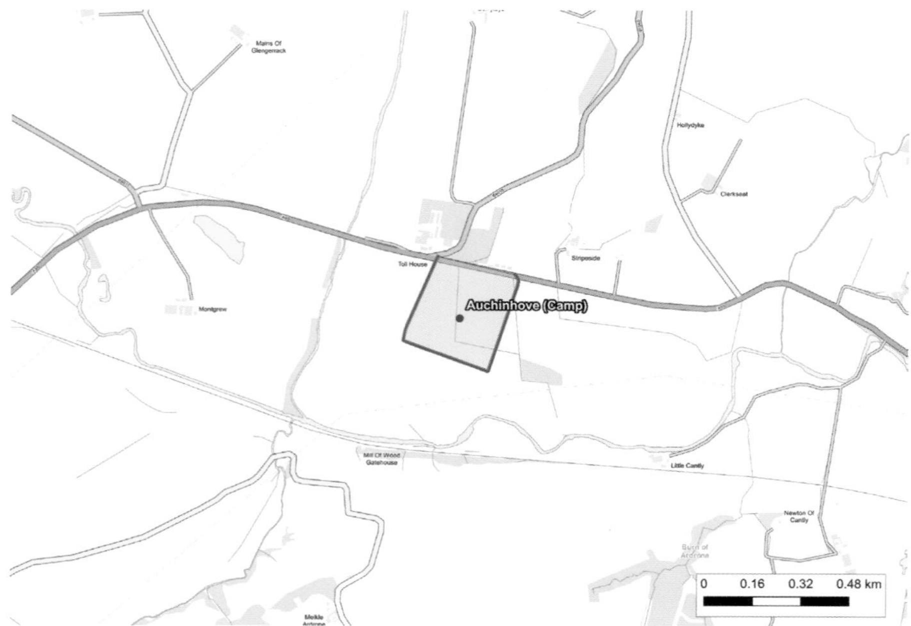

One of the sites for the possible Roman camp at Bellie.

It was not until the deployment of aerial photography that a number of cropmarks were seen, in 1943. This led St Joseph to excavate the site in 1967. He uncovered what he thought were the defensive ditches of the camp, although subsequent re-analysis of his excavation plans have indicated that the ditch is not particularly Roman in shape. Subsequent work by archaeologists has identified possible ditches of a camp, although each project appears to have put the site in a slightly different location, making it difficult for everyone to agree on where exactly the site is. Rebecca Jones has re-examined the aerial photographs and identified a potential defensive ditch cropmark to the north of the old church of Bellie. Jones has re-examined St Joseph's original work and has argued that the features excavated do not have outstanding Roman characteristics.

Exploring

The three different sets of ditches identified can be found by heading westwards out of Fochabers on the A98 and taking the right exit on to the B9104. After a mile or so, the road turns sharply to the left. Carry straight on, rather than turning, past the cemetery. Follow the road beyond the cemetery and you will be driving on a minor road through a field; this is the edge of the 'official' camp at Bellie.

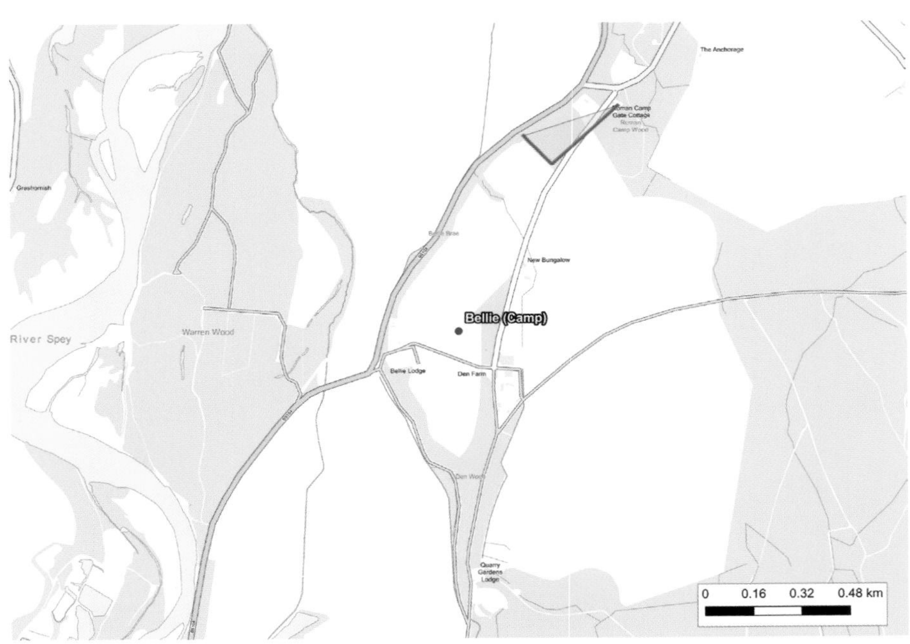

Birnie

Possible Roman site (on map) | NJ 210 574
Iron Age settlement | NJ 210 585

In the mid-1990s, several coins of the Emperor Septimius Severus were found near Birnie, around a mile south of Elgin. Archaeologists from the National Museum of Scotland took a keen interest in the site, and over the next few years a programme of research, involving aerial photography, geophysics and excavation, revealed evidence of Neolithic, Bronze Age and medieval activity, including roundhouses and arrowheads. A number of Roman finds in the area, including coins and brooches, suggested prolonged contact with the Romans, although there was speculation that the coins were from a hoard that had been scattered by ploughing. Excavation of the site where the coins were found led to the discovery of a small round pot containing more coins, which was taken away for conservation. A second hoard was also found near by. Investigations of the site have indicated the presence of an Iron Age settlement, which was either trading with the Romans or receiving gifts from them. The coin hoards can now be seen in Elgin Museum.

Less than a mile to the southeast of the Iron Age settlement is a possible Roman site. Pottery found in the mid-19th century (and now in Elgin Museum) appears to date to the Roman period, although when exactly has not been confirmed. The site where the pottery was believed to have come from was investigated in the early 1980s, with subsequent excavation uncovering a V-shaped ditch with a slot in the bottom – typical of Roman defences. Aerial photography has indicated that there is a rectilinear enclosure of around 3.25 hectares, although there has been no evidence of Roman activity on the site beyond two fragments of pottery, which may not have come from Birnie.

Exploring

To get to the first site from Elgin, head south on the A941, crossing over the railway bridge. At the second roundabout, turn right and at the end of that road turn left and continue on the minor road for about three-quarters of a mile, following the road to the right where it splits. Take the left-hand road at Paddockhaugh, to find the Iron Age settlement is on the left.

To get to the second site, continue past the Iron Age site and take a right at the end of the road. When the road takes a sharp left, next to the distillery, the rectilinear enclosure is in the field on the right.

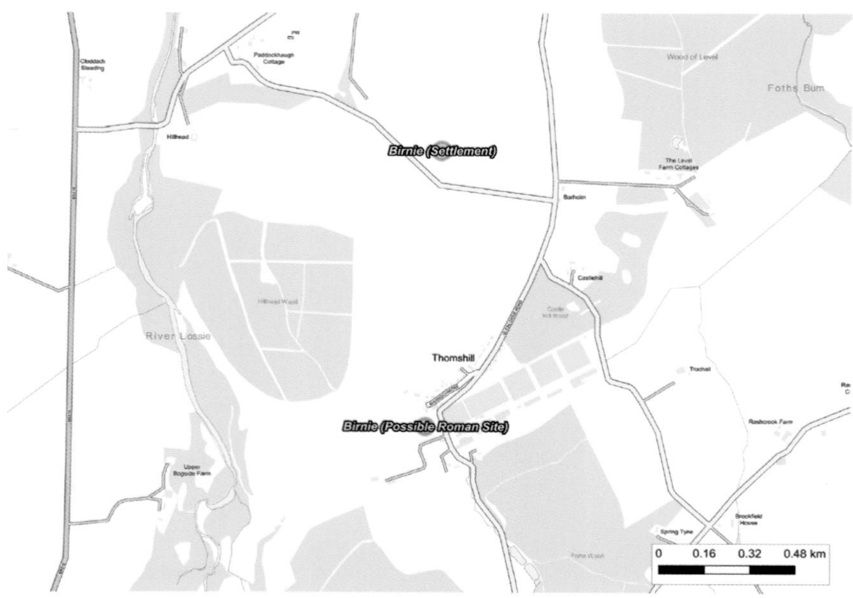

Looking across the River Spey towards Culbin Sands and Forest.

Culbin Sands/Forest

Possible Fortification | NH 902 575

Spread across the southern shore of the Moray Firth, Culbin Sands is a place of mystery, with occasional glimpses of an earlier time – a long-abandoned cottage, buried deep beneath the sands, with only the chimney poking above the surface. Originally fertile lands that were gradually covered over by the sands, particularly after one notable storm in 1694, the dunes became home to an extensive plantation in the 20th century when the Forestry Commission took over their care. Today, Culbin Forest is a renowned Site of Special Scientific Interest, notable for its unique ecosystem and wildlife, and a popular place to visit, with many tracks and paths which criss-cross the area.

The area is also known for a number of archaeological finds from across the Sands, including pre- and post-Roman items: Bronze Age axe heads, stone tools, querns, medieval coins, pottery and fishhooks. Roman finds that have come to light include coins from the reign of Hadrian and Antoninus Pius, with one found in 1898, dating to 21 BC. In addition to the coins, discoveries at Culbin Sands have included several brooches dated to the 2nd century, late 1st- to early 2nd-century glass bangles, and part of a glass

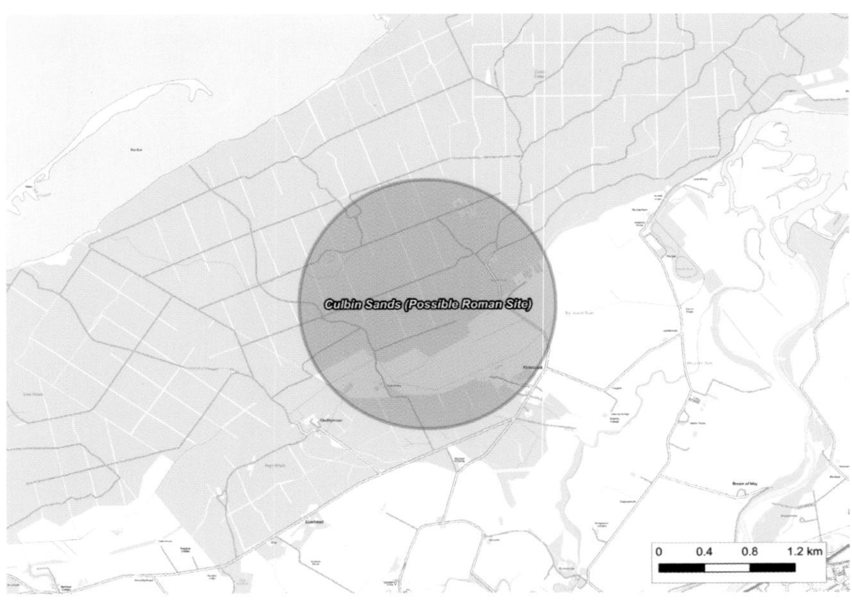

vessel that is speculated to date to the 1st century.

Although the area covered by the Sands is vast, the small number of finds hints that there may have been an Iron Age site in the vicinity, which was trading with the Empire, or that there was some sort of Roman settlement in the area. The latter might not be such a fanciful thought, given that the probably Roman sites of Birnie and Bellie are less than a day's march away. The eastern part of the Sands is on the edge of Findhorn Bay, into which the river of the same name flows, and many Roman sites were constructed in similar locations, such as the camp at Dun on Montrose Bay, Angus.

It will probably never be known for sure whether there is a Roman camp or fort underneath Culbin Sands, because of the forest on top of the site, but further surveys of the surrounding area may yet yield more clues.

Elgin Museum

1 High Street, Elgin, IV30 1EQ | Free Entry
www.elginmuseum.org.uk
Opening Times (seasonal) | Mon–Fri 10:00–17:00 | Saturday 11:00–16:00

Scotland's oldest independent museum is a treasure trove of archaeology, art and history from across Moray and the Highlands. While it has a limited number of artefacts from the Roman period on display, it does give an important reflection of the area during this period. The Birnie coin hoards are a definite highlight.

Muiryfold

Camp | NJ 489 520

Muiryfold is another camp identified from the air by St Joseph as part of the CUCAP programme of aerial photography. Identified in 1959, it was confirmed by excavation of the defensive ditches in the same year. The camp is built on a hill and has good views down both the Deveron and Isla valleys, although views to the northwest are restricted by the summit of the hill on which it sits. The camp is around 115 metres above sea level at its lowest point, rising to 145 metres at the highest point.

The site is presumed to date to the 1st century because of the style of the gates (*tituli*) that have been identified on the southern and western ramparts. The site is notable as being the penultimate known Roman site in Scotland and is curiously only just over one and a half miles away the camp at Auchinhove. This suggests that, if both sites were occupied at the same time, the army may have been split between the two.

Exploring

From Keith, head east on the A95, for around two

The site of the camp at Muiryfold.

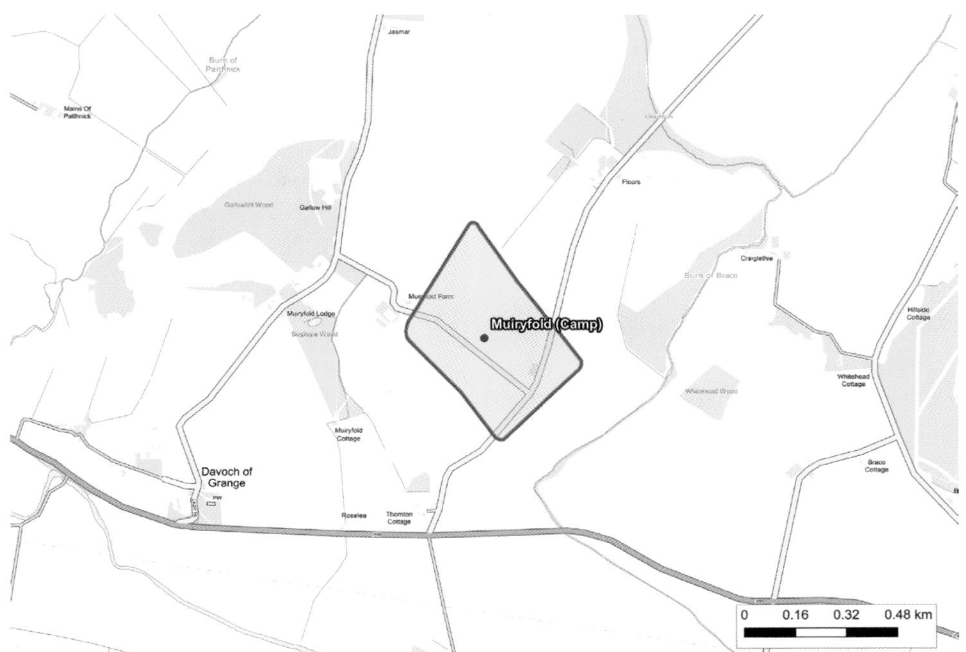

miles (passing the camp at Auchinhove at the turn-off to the B9018). After passing the church on the left, take the first minor road on the left at the farm of Thornton. After a quarter of a mile, take the first left and the camp will be mainly on the right of the road.

Tarryblake Wood

Possible Camp | NJ 52 49

Like the site at Fourman Hill, it has been speculated that there should be a Roman camp in the vicinity of Tarryblake Wood, because of the distance between Glenmailen and Auchinhove. Henderson-Stewart proposed this site, noting that it seemed to be an appropriate area, particularly as he hypothesized that the battle of Mons Graupius may have taken place near by. To date, there is no evidence in or around the wood of Roman activity.

Wester Alves

Possible Camp | NJ 111 629

Cropmarks have shown a rounded corner of a potential enclosure, although archaeologists have debated whether this belongs to drainage as the area has been heavily altered by agricultural practices, or whether it belongs to a Roman camp. The site has not yet been further investigated to confirm this.

Chapter 24

THE HIGHLANDS

Despite the size of the area covered by the Highlands, there is little evidence of Roman activity, with no known forts, fortlets or even camps. There are a few artefacts here and there, but these may have been traded with locals and are not themselves proof of the Roman army conquering the region.

Although the most northerly camp in the Roman Empire is probably at Bellie in Moray, the army knew there was much more to Scotland. According to Tacitus, the biographer of Agricola, the General had the fleet sail around Britain to prove it was an island, and the Roman writer Cassius Dio wrote that the Emperor Septimius Severus spent time this far north:

> But Severus did not desist until he had approached the extremity of the island. Here he observed most accurately the variation of the sun's motion and the length of the days and the nights in summer and winter respectively. Having thus been conveyed through practically the whole of the hostile country (for he actually was conveyed in a covered litter most of the way, on account of his infirmity), he returned to the friendly portion, after he had forced the Britons to come to terms, on the condition that they should abandon a large part of their territory. (*Cass. Dio* 77, 13, 3–4)

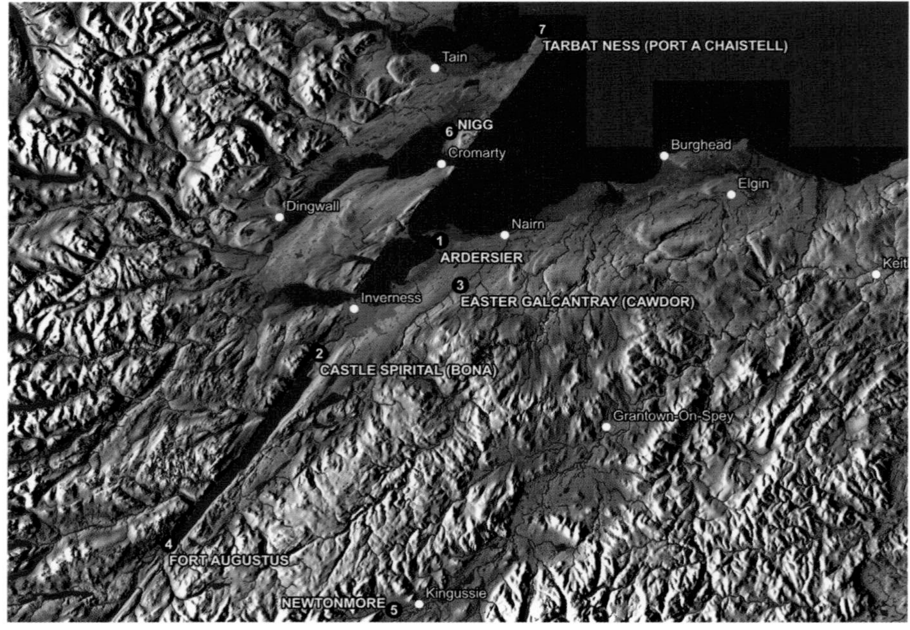

It is not clear where exactly 'the edge' was. Some archaeologists argue that it could be the Moray coast, although the Black Isle and Sutherland can be seen from there.

As in other parts of Scotland that are lacking in Roman activity, there have been some finds – from the usual coins to glass beads and brooches (including one found on Skye) – that show that the army had links to the local populations in the Highlands. There are even a couple of possible fortifications, suggesting that the Romans were a bit busier than some people think.

The site of a possible fort at the head of Loch Ness?

Ardersier

Sword & Spear | NH 78 55

William Roy notes that a sword and spearhead were dug up near the village of Ardersier in the middle of the 18th century. As always seems to be the case with artefacts found so long ago, the sword and spear have disappeared and it seems unlikely that it will ever be known whether the items were Roman, and where exactly they came from.

Castle Spirital – Loch Ness (Bona)

Fort (Possible) | NH 602 379

At the head of Loch Ness, on a peninsula between the river and Loch Dochfour, a small fort (sometimes called Bona) was recorded in the 19th century as being rectangular with rounded corners, surrounded by a rampart. A second account by the Rev. Grant noted two forts, one of which was square and protected by the river on one side, and one on the loch on the other. The bank and ditch remains of a second camp are apparently located in the next field.

From these descriptions there are two possibilities: that this is the site of a lost, small Roman camp (with an annexe in the next field), or that the camp may actually have been a medieval moated homestead (which would also typically have been rectangular and surrounded by a ditch).

Next to the site are the remains of the medieval Castle Spirital, today nothing more than a raised lump in the ground.

The alleged camp survived until the construction of the Caledonian Canal in the 19th century, which led to the creation of the Abban Water, causing part of the site to be flooded.

The remains of Castle Spirital.

Key Dates

1822: Grant notes a Roman fort between Loch Ness and Loch Dochfour

1845: *The New Statistical Account of Scotland* reports that the remains of a small Roman encampment can be seen at the head of Loch Ness

Exploring

The site can be visited by heading south from Inverness on the A82. Park by the village of Lochend and take the path that runs behind the houses (on the Inverness side) and down to Bona lighthouse. A path (overgrown in places) runs alongside the canal. Heading away from Loch Ness, Castle Spirital is a small raised mound among a clump of trees towards the end of the spur where the Abban Water and the Caledonian Canal meet.

Easter Galcantray (Cawdor)

Camp/Fort (Possible) | NH 810 483

Some (Wikipedia, for example) say that there is a Roman fort at Cawdor, but the archaeological evidence says something different.

Easter Galcantray was discovered in 1978 when Barri Jones flew over the site and spotted two crop-marks that appeared to form the southern defences of a possible camp, with a gap or entrance at one end. In the mid-1980s, Jones began a series of excavations at the site, recording two sections of the ditch on the surviving sides of the camp. Even though a river runs through the centre of the site, there was no sign of defences on the other side of the water. Jones noted that the ditches were consistent with the abandonment of a single-period timber fort, while radiocarbon dating from the site gave a range of dates for occupation of the camp (2270–3100 BC, AD 80–130 and 13th to 14th century). Later excavations found evidence of a cobbled road surface and a series of postholes, with one set over the entrance, implying that the gateway may have had a timber tower. There were relatively few finds – a glass bead (which could date from before the Romans to as late as the medieval period) and a fragment of pottery, which Jones noted was similar to material found at the Roman legionary fortress of Inchtuthil.

Despite the limited finds, and the bead, which is not conclusively Roman, Jones interpreted the site as a Roman camp. According to the radiocarbon dates, it may well have been occupied during the Roman

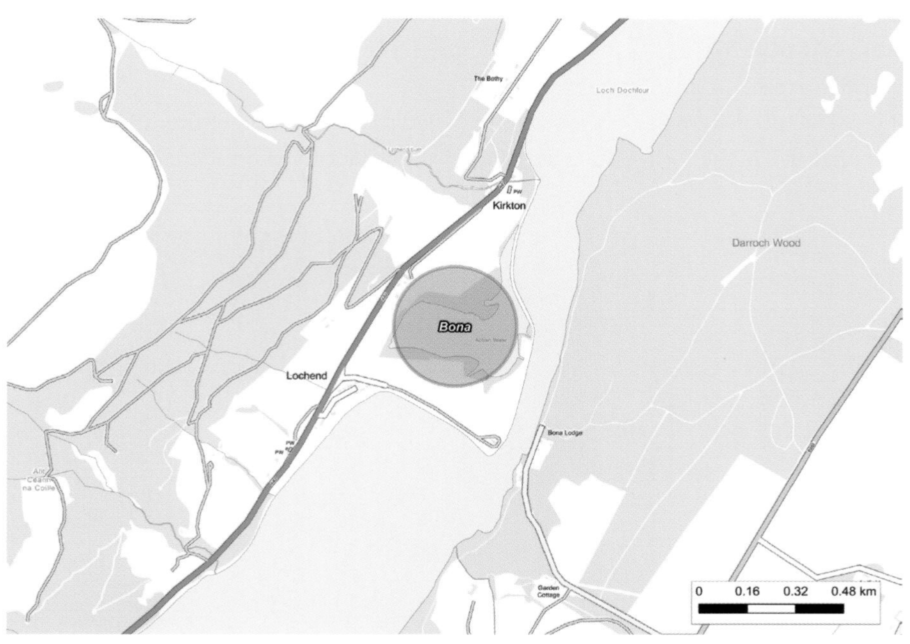

period, but not necessarily by the army. A closer look at the ditches reveals them to be irregular in shape, with one end being particularly bulbous – a distinctly non-Roman feature. There was no sign of a rampart either.

Archaeologists have long debated whether this is a Roman camp. The lack of finds, the mixed radiocarbon dates (which have been disputed by some scholars), the irregular shape of the ditch, and the lack of defences on the northern and eastern sides have now led to a general consensus that it is not. More recently, some archaeologists have argued that the camp was built by Vikings to stay in over the winter. Given that the nearby farm is called 'Holme Rose' (*holme* meaning 'small island' in Norse), it seems that the site at East Galcantray may be more Norse than Roman.

Exploring

Located about a mile to the southwest of the village of Cawdor, the site is next to the minor road, and almost opposite the farm of Easter Galcantray.

Easter Galcantray – apparently the site of a Roman fort.

Fort Augustus

Coin Hoard & Sculpture | NH 381 091

It might be known as Fort Augustus, but the village took the name from the 18th-century fort built in response to the 1715 Jacobite uprising, rather than any Roman site. The fort itself no longer exists, the last vestiges having been absorbed into the Benedictine Abbey during its construction in 1876. However, it is not true to say that there are no connections with the Romans in the village.

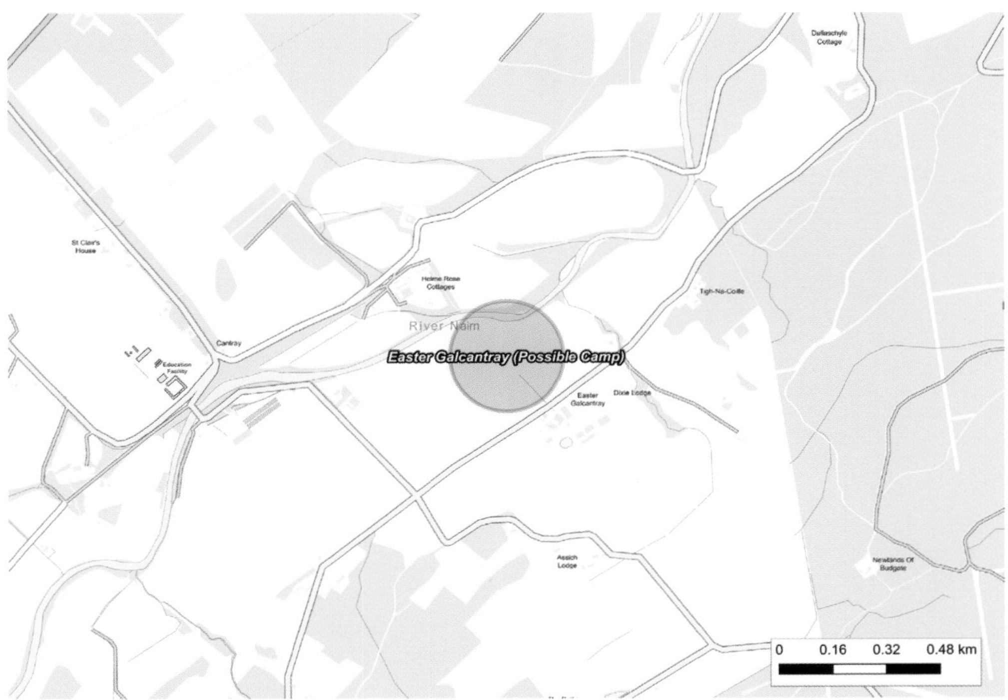

The view from Fort Augustus Abbey up Loch Ness.

No longer a Benedictine community, the abbey is still home to a Roman carving, which sticks out of a wall (above a door) within the entrance passage. It is not difficult to miss, as the wall is whitewashed. The carving is of the three-fold group of mother goddesses and is likely to date from the 1st or 2nd century. It is quite far from home, having originally been located at Hailes House, Colinton, to the south of Edinburgh. The stone itself seems likely to have come from one of the forts near Edinburgh (Cramond or Inveresk), and was moved to the abbey in 1925.

In 1767, long before the abbey was built, a coin hoard was discovered when repairs to the fort were being undertaken. Workers digging a trench uncovered a blue urn containing 300 coins, which were apparently all of the Emperor Diocletian (284–305). To be honest, it is unlikely that all the coins were from the same period but, in any case, as they have long since vanished, it is difficult to check the accuracy of the account.

As with any find, the uncovering of the hoard does not mean that there was a Roman fort or camp in the area, but it does show that the Romans were in touch with the locals, and it has been suggested that there may have been a Roman trading post in the area. Certainly, the end of the loch would have been strategically important. When the abbey closed, in the late 1990s, and was converted to flats, archaeologists were on hand to see if anything interesting might be uncovered. They found no evidence of Roman activity, although they were only watching the areas being redeveloped rather than opening up trenches. As is the case with many other possible sites in Scotland, more conclusive investigations will have to be undertaken to confirm whether or not the Romans were at Fort Augustus.

Exploring

The former monastery has been redeveloped as private accommodation although the abbey and its grounds can still be visited. The abbey is signposted from the centre of the village.

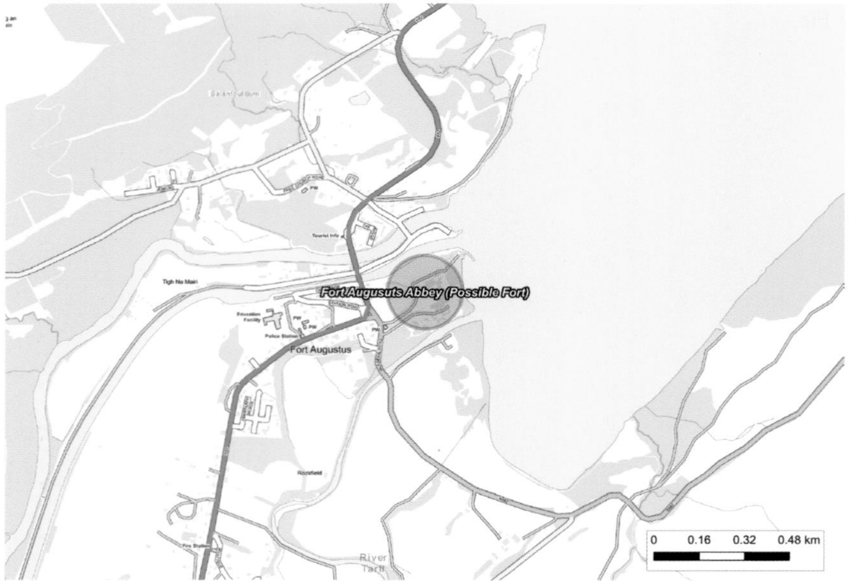

Newtonmore

Camp (Possible) | NN 713 990

As early as 1792, *The Old Statistical Account of Scotland* recorded a Roman camp here, with the village of Newtonmore (then called Benchar) sitting within the rampart. Around 1834, parts of the ditches were said to still be visible. The old accounts also note that an urn and a Roman tripod were found near the village, although it may actually have been a medieval kettle stand.

In 2003, an archaeological investigation took place in advance of a modern development being constructed in the area of the alleged camp. Pottery and some signs of pre-Roman activity were found, but there were no indications that the army had ever settled in the area.

Nigg

Coin & Inscribed Stone | NH 805 716

Traditionally, the Cromarty Firth has always been a safe anchorage for ships sheltering from the harsh North Sea. The Vikings were certainly active in the area, while during both world wars the Firth was used as a major dock and refuelling depot; anti-aircraft batteries are still visible on the North and South Sutors, guarding the entrance to the Firth. Even today, the Firth of Forth is used to 'park' oil rigs being decommissioned, so it seems likely that the Roman fleet would have sought its sanctuary.

The tiny hamlet of Nigg, at the foot of the North Sutor, seems an unlikely place for the Romans to have visited, but there have been two interesting finds. The first is a coin of Constantius II (AD 337–361), which was found during the Second World War when trenches were being dug. The coin was described as being worn and was deposited in the Hunterian Museum in Glasgow. No other coin finds were reported.

The second find was an inscribed stone, found in 1770 by a labourer. It was buried about 3 feet deep, and inscribed *R. IM. L* [*Romanii imperii limes*] ('The Roman Frontier'). William Roy, who wrote down the story, suggests that the marker may have been placed there by soldiers from the Fleet to mark the northernmost limits of the Empire. Sadly, the stone has long since disappeared. Roy also noted that there are two villages known as Nigg, this one and another to the south of the River Don, which was then opposite Aberdeen. He argues that the Cromarty Nigg seems like the better candidate for the stone, but also admits that there is a good case for it having been found at the other Nigg, as Roman artefacts have been found near there in the late 20th century.

Guided tours of the Second World War anti-aircraft defences on the South Sutor are sometimes available, and worth doing. The local Tourist Information office has details.

Looking from Cromarty towards the North Sutor guarding the entrance to the Cromarty Firth and Nigg Bay.

The site of the alleged fort at Tarbat Ness.

Tarbat Ness (Port a' Chaistell)

Fort & Harbour (Possible) | NH 930 870

In 1822, the Reverend Grant described a Roman station at Tarbat Ness. The site consisted of two Roman cairns, one 72 feet round and 5 or 6 feet high with a pyramid on top, and the other similar in height but half the circumference of the first. While Grant called them Roman, he does not explain why he came to this conclusion. Looking at the brief reference today, Grant seems to be describing a chambered cairn, of which there are many in the Highlands (such as Clava Cairns). Today, there are no traces of the Tarbat Ness examples.

Grant also mentions a second site near by, which he describes as a Roman 'military station and building' surrounded by two ditches, 12 feet wide, with a long rampart surrounding part of the site. Next to this was a square and a circular fortification with ramparts running southwards. By 1872, the site had been damaged by land reclamation and today there is no trace of any of the features on the ground. As there have been no Roman finds to date and the accounts are vague, it seems that the site at Tarbat Ness may not be Roman after all.

Exploring

The site is easily reached by car. The direct route is to head north on the A9, past Invergordon and then follow the signs to Portmahomack and then Tarbat Ness. The alternative route is to head to Cromarty on the Black Isle and then take the small car ferry (seasonal) over to Nigg and then drive northwards towards Portmahomack. There is plenty of parking at the Tarbat Ness lighthouse, and the sites are a short walk across fields, although there is usually livestock present.

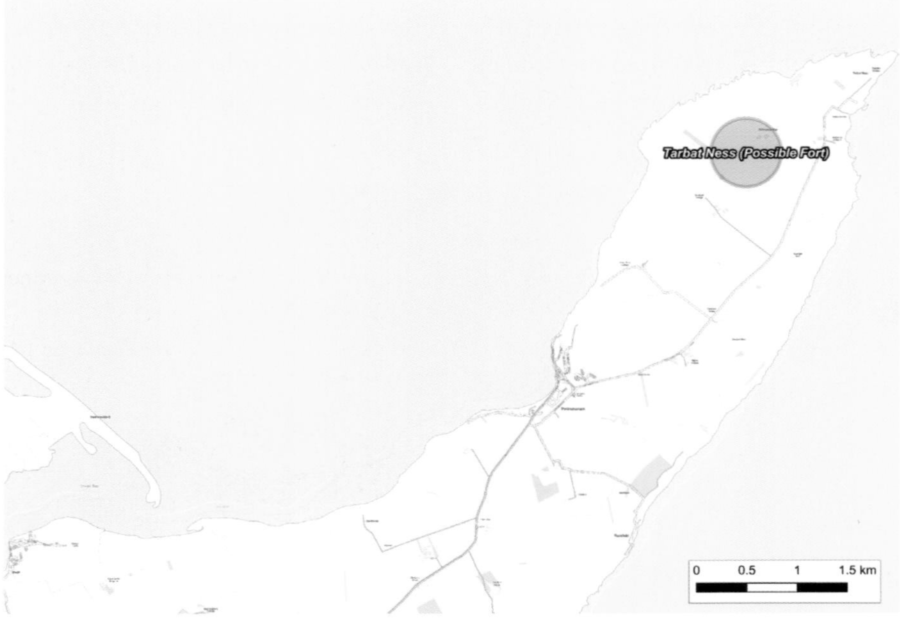

Appendix I: Abbreviations

Various abbreviations that occur in this book are detailed below. More information about the sources can be found in Appendix IV, 'Finding Out More'.

ADS Archaeological Data Service
CUCAP Cambridge University Collection of Aerial Photography
DES Discovery & Excavation in Scotland
HES Historic Environment Scotland
NSA *The New Statistical Account of Scotland*
OSA *The Old Statistical Account of Scotland*
PSAS Proceedings of the Society of Antiquaries of Scotland
RCAHMS The Royal Commission on Ancient and Historic Monuments of Scotland (now merged with Historic Scotland to form Historic Environment Scotland)

Appendix II: Glossary

This brief glossary of archaeological terms and occasional Latin terms should help to interpret the sites discussed here.

Aedes Sometimes known as the *sacellum*, this is the room within the *principia* where the regimental standards and statues of the imperial cult (the worship of the Emperor and his family) were kept. It was also the treasury of the fort, with many sites having a vaulted chamber underneath which housed the soldiers' pay and any booty from raids.

Alae Horse-riding auxiliary soldiers or cavalry.

Amphora Roman storage jars, usually used for storing olive oil, *garum* (fish paste) or wine. Fragments of *amphora* are often found on Roman sites and can often be dated.

Annexe An enclosed area that is protected by a single rampart and ditch, and attached to the defences of a fortification. An annexe can be found attached to a fort, a camp, and occasionally a fortlet.

Artefacts Objects or remains that have an archaeological significance.

Auxilia Paid mercenaries who were recruited from around the Empire and grouped into detachments that garrisoned forts.

Ballista A weapon used by the army to fire stone balls at the enemy.

Berm The space between a rampart and ditch.

Clavicula The endpoint of a rampart and ditch, which is curved.

Cohort A unit of soldiers.

Cohortes Auxiliary infantry soldiers.

Cropmark Patches of dark or light growth in crops or grass that are different from the surrounding area. Caused by features under the ground, they can often show the outline of the walls of buildings, or the internal layout of forts.

Culvert A drainage channel.

Dendrochronology The scientific method of dating tree rings to give a date of when the tree was felled.

Ditch A defensive feature surrounding a fortification that is constructed next to a rampart. Usually forts, fortlets and sometimes towers have at least three ditches surrounding them.

Earthworks These are 'lumps and bumps' or features in the ground that were created by human activity in the past. In Roman archaeology in Scotland, these are usually the remains of ramparts or walls that are no longer standing to their original height.

Epigraphy The study of inscriptions or epigraphs.

Finds *See* Artefacts.

Hillfort A generic term used to describe settlements enclosed by a rampart, built and occupied by the indigenous population. Hillforts are not just limited to hills; they can also be located on headlands (promontory forts) and in other locations.

Horrea A granary building usually constructed from stone to keep the grain dry. They have a unique outline and are constructed within forts.

Hypocaust An underfloor heating system used in Roman bath houses and certain domestic buildings. Within a fort they are found in the *praetorium*. The floor is built on raised pillars of stone or brick (*pillae*) and air is passed from a furnace among them, to heat the underfloor space.

In situ Term used to describe an archaeological feature when it has been found in its original location.

***Intervallum* road** The road that runs around the inside of the ramparts of a fort.

Mansio The Roman equivalent of a hotel for travelling officials.

Parchmarks *See* Cropmarks.

Porta decumana The rear gate of a fort or camp.

Porta praetoria The front gate of a fort or camp.

Praetorium The building in a fort where the commanding officer and his family lived.

Principia The headquarters building in the middle of a fort.

Promontory forts *See* Hillforts.

Ramparts A bank of earth surrounding a fortification, made up of soil dug out when creating an adjacent ditch. Smaller sites usually have one or two ramparts and ditch, but larger sites can have as many as four or five.

Samian The most recognizable Roman pottery, originating in France. It is a distinctive shade of red.

Slingshot Projectile weapons usually made out of stone or metal (often lead), which were launched at the enemy using a sling, emitting a high-pitched sound. Soldiers would often inscribe curses on the slingshot.

Stratigraphy The study of the layers or order in which archaeological remains are found in the ground, based on the concept that, the deeper the finds, the older they are. There can be exceptions to this; for example, finds at the bottom of a pit or well may not necessarily be as old as those in the undisturbed ground next to them.

Titulus A small bank of earth placed in front of the entrance to a camp as a defensive measure aimed at slowing down anyone trying to get to the interior.

Trial trenching A small excavation intended to confirm the origins of a site.

Via principalis The street in a fort or camp that leads from the *porta praetoria* to the *principia*.

Vicus A Roman settlement immediately outside of a fort.

Watching brief A procedure that is put into place when developers are building on a potential archaeological site. The archaeologist is on hand to record any features or artefacts that are dug up during the construction work.

Wattle and daub An early construction material for walls. Wooden branches are weaved together and a mud or clay mixture is plastered on to the wall.

Appendix III: Found Something Roman?

If you have found an object that you think might be Roman, there are a number of things you should do: note the place where the object was found as accurately as possible (preferably using a map or GPS unit); handle it carefully, to minimize any damage, and do not clean it; take photos of the object and where you found it; and try to avoid the temptation of poking around in the ground as this could damage any further objects. Next, contact the Treasure Trove Panel (https://treasuretrovescotland.co.uk), who can advise on what to do.

Sometimes people have objects lying around the house that they have inherited or found in the garden. You can contact the Treasure Trove Panel for advice on these, or alternatively contact your council's archaeology officer, or your local museum, who should be able to give you advice.

It is important to understand that it is illegal to dig or to metal-detect on a site that is a scheduled monument; details of these can be found on Canmore. Failing to declare found objects can be a criminal offence, so it is always best to check with the Treasure Trove Panel if you find something. Further information on metal detecting and scheduled monuments has been produced by HES and can be found through their website: www.historicenvironment.scot/

Appendix IV: Finding Out More

Organizations

If you want to learn more about Roman Scotland, and the latest archaeological developments, there are a number of groups that you can join. Alternatively, you can subscribe to various publications with articles on Roman Scotland, such as *Current Archaeology* and *History Scotland Magazine*. Many of the societies and organizations listed below also publish their own journals and magazines.

Archaeology Scotland An educational charity and membership organization that organizes Scottish Archaeology Month and produces *Discovery & Excavation in Scotland*, an annual summary of archaeological discoveries and finds from around the country.

Society of Antiquaries of Scotland National membership organization promoting Scotland's archaeology and history. It produces the annual

Proceedings of the Society of Antiquaries of Scotland as well as other publications.

Historic Environment Scotland Keepers of many of Scotland's monuments, as well as the National Register of Ancient Monuments and the online database of sites, Canmore.

National Trust for Scotland The NTS manages a number of Roman sites, particularly along the Antonine Wall.

The Roman Society The Roman Society is an academic-focused organization that promotes the study of the Romans and the Empire. Its two journals are *Britannia*, which covers British Roman studies (including an annual list of Scottish discoveries), and the *Journal of Roman Studies*, which has a pan-Empire focus.

Local Societies

There are a number of local societies across Scotland who undertake research into Roman remains and archaeology:

Dumfries and Galloway Natural History and Antiquarian Society
Edinburgh Archaeological Field Society
North of Scotland Archaeological Society
Perth and Kinross Heritage Trust

More information can be found either by consulting a local museum or Archaeology Scotland.

Further Reading

General

There have been a number of good books written about Roman Scotland, many of which are no longer in print, although they can easily be bought online. The antiquarian titles that are no longer in print can often be consulted in libraries and most are also available online, accessible at www.archive.org.

The books and sources detailed in this chapter focus on different aspects of the Romans in Scotland. For a good, general history of the Romans, from the Republic to the Empire, try *The Romans for Dummies* by Guy de la Bédoyère. The same author has also produced a general guide to Roman Britain, *Roman Britain: A New History*, which is worth reading to learn about why the Romans invaded Britain, and what life was like for citizens in the rest of Britain when the army headed northwards.

Modern

Breeze, D.J., 1983. *Roman Forts in Britain*, Aylesbury: Shire Publications
Breeze, D. ed., 1979. *Roman Scotland: Some Recent Excavations*, Edinburgh: Inspectorate of Ancient Monuments
Breeze, D.J., 2017. *The Roman Army*, London: Bloomsbury
Crawford, O.G.S., 2011. *Topography of Roman Scotland North of the Antonine Wall*, Cambridge: Cambridge University Press
de la Bédoyère, G., 2013. *Roman Britain: A New History*, London: Thames & Hudson
de la Bédoyère, G., 2006. *The Romans for Dummies*, John Wiley & Sons
Frere, S.S., 1991. *Britannia: A History of Roman Britain*, London: Pimlico
Jones, R.H., 2011. *Roman Camps in Scotland*, Edinburgh: Society of Antiquaries of Scotland
Keppie, L., 2015. *The Legacy of Rome: Scotland's Roman Remains*, Edinburgh: Birlinn
Shirley, E., 2001. *Building a Roman Legionary Fortress*, Arcadia Publishing (SC)
Woolliscroft, D. & Hoffmann, B., 2006. *Rome's First Frontier: The Flavian Occupation of Northern Scotland*, Stroud: Tempus

Mons Graupius

Maxwell, G.S., 1990. *A Battle Lost: Romans and Caledonians at Mons Graupius*, Edinburgh: Edinburgh University Press

See also the relevant sections in the various modern texts detailed above.

The Antonine Wall

Breeze, D.J., 2015. *The Antonine Wall*, Edinburgh: Birlinn
Hanson, W.S. & Maxwell, G.S., 1986. *Rome's North-west Frontier: The Antonine Wall*, Edinburgh: Edinburgh University Press
Keppie, L., 1982. The Antonine Wall 1960–1980. *Britannia*, 13: 91–111
Keppie, L., 2012. *The Antiquarian Rediscovery of the Antonine Wall*, Edinburgh: Society of Antiquaries of Scotland
Robertson, A.S., 2001. *The Antonine Wall: A Handbook to the Roman Wall between Forth and Clyde and a Guide to its Surviving Remains*, revised and edited by L. Keppie, Glasgow: Glasgow Archaeological Society

Journal Articles

Hanson, W.S., 1980. Agricola on the Forth-Clyde isthmus. *Scottish Archaeological Forum*, 12: 55–68

Older

The Old Statistical Account of Scotland and *The New Statistical Account of Scotland* were a series of books published in the early 1830s, containing details of each parish in Scotland. As they were written before any widespread use of modern farming methods, they contain details of many Roman sites that have since been eroded or ploughed out of existence. The texts are quite hard to find these days, but copies tend to be hidden away in the Reference section of local libraries. Alternatively, copies can be found online at www.electricscotland.com/history/statistical

Horsley, J., 1732. *Britannia Romana or the Roman Antiquities of Britain*, London

Macdonald, G., 1911. *The Roman Wall in Scotland*, Glasgow: James Maclehose and Sons

Maitland, W., 1757. *History and Antiquities of Scotland*, London

Roy, W., 1793. *Military Antiquities of the Romans in North Britain*, London

Sibbald, R., 1707. *Historical Inquiries, Concerning the Roman Monuments and Antiquities in the North-part of Britain Called Scotland*, Edinburgh

Stuart, R., 1845. *Caledonia Romana: A Descriptive Account of the Roman Antiquities of Scotland*, Edinburgh: Bell & Bradfute

Classical

A number of key classical texts inform archaeologists about Roman activity in Scotland, the best-known being by Tacitus. Most of the books detailed above contain references to the classical texts.

Polybius, 2010. *The Histories*, B. McGing, ed., Oxford: Oxford University Press

Tacitus, 2009. *Agricola and Germania*, J. B. Rives, ed., London: Penguin

Journals and Key Texts

Archaeologia Scotica **(AS)** The original journal produced by the Society of Antiquaries of Scotland. Only a handful of volumes were ever produced before the PSAS became the Society's main journal. Digital copies are freely viewable through the ADS.

Britannia An annual publication of Roman research and reports. Published by the Society for the Promotion of Roman Studies.

Discovery & Excavation in Scotland **(DES)** An annual publication that details most archaeological discoveries in Scotland since the 1940s. Non-recent back copies can be viewed online through the ADS; more recent copies are available from Archaeology Scotland.

Glasgow Archaeological Journal **(GAJ)** Out-of-print journal of the Glasgow Archaeological Society. Some volumes are available online or in national collections, but usually not complete runs.

Journal of Roman Studies **(JRS)** An annual publication of Roman research and reports, published by the Society for the Promotion of Roman Studies.

The New Statistical Account of Scotland by the Ministers of the Respective Parishes under the Superintendence of a Committee of the Society for the Benefit of the Sons and Daughters of the Clergy (known as *The New Statistical Account* or NSA). Published 1834–45 (Edinburgh). A 15-volume archaeological and statistical record of the parishes of Scotland, often mentioning long-vanished Roman sites.

The Statistical Account of Scotland, Drawn Up from the Communications of the Ministers of the Different Parishes (known as *The Old Statistical Account of* Scotland, or *OSA*). Published 1791–99 (Edinburgh). This is the original series that inspired *The New Statistical Account of Scotland*.

Proceedings of the Society of Antiquaries of Scotland **(PSAS)** An annual publication containing archaeological reports and records. Back issues are available through ADS, with more recent editions available from the Society.

Scottish Archaeological Journal **(SAJ)** An academic publication on Scottish archaeology, which includes some reports on excavations

The Scottish Historical Review **(SHR)** Journal with occasional reports on archaeological activities.

Transactions of the Dumfriesshire and Galloway Natural History and Antiquarian Society **(TDGNHAS)** Journal of the D&G Society. The journal is available to members, but second-hand copies can be tracked down on the internet.

Websites

Archaeological Data Service (ADS) (archaeologydataservice.ac.uk) An online depository of archaeological reports and journals, such as DES and PSAS.

Canmore (canmore.org.uk) This is the national database of all historic monuments in Scotland. All of the sites featured in this book can be found on Canmore.

Appendix V: The Sites – Resources Used

This is an extensive, but not exhaustive, list of the main texts consulted in compiling this book. For more detailed bibliographic lists, it is always worth consulting the site entry on Canmore or searching online through Google Scholar.

For journals, the initials are given, followed by the volume number, year of publication and then page numbers

Aberdeen and Aberdeenshire

Kair House
DES (1959) 25; (2003) 13
JRS 41 (1951) 65; 48 (1958) 92–93; 55 (1965) 83; 63 (1973) 233

Kintore
DES (1996) 8–9; (2000) 10–11; (2001) 11; (2002) 10
JRS 59 (1969) 59
PSAS 7 (1886) 387–394; 116 (1987) 205–209; 130 (2000) 26–33
Cook, M. & Dunbar, L., 2008. *Rituals, Roundhouses and Romans: Excavations at Kintore, Aberdeenshire 2000–2006*, Loanhead: Scottish Trust for Archaeological Research

Logie Durno
Britannia 9 (1978) 271–287
JRS 67 (1977) 141–142
Frere, S.S. & St Joseph, J.K., 1983. *Roman Britain from the Air.* Cambridge University Press, pp. 30–31

Normandykes
JRS 48 (1958) 93; 59 (1969) 118
Chalmers, G., 1887. *Caledonia: Or a Historical and Topographical Account of North Britain*, Paisley: Alexander Gardner

Raedykes
AS 1 (1792) 565–569; 2 (1822) 300
JRS 51 (1961) 119–135
PSAS 50 (1916) 317–359; 73 (1938) 250–252

Ythan Wells (Glenmailen)
Britannia 1 (1970) 163–178
JRS 59 (1969) 104–128
PSAS 50 (1916) 317–359
Haverfield, F., 1914. *Roman Britain in 1913*, Oxford

Angus

Cardean
Britannia 7 (1976) 299; 33 (2002) 285
DES (2001) 14–15; (1974) 7
JRS 45 (1955) 87; 63 (1973) 63

Dun
DES (1990) 40; (1974) 8
JRS 63 (1973) 214–246
PSAS 123 (1993) 286–290

Inverquharity
Britannia 15 (1984) 274; 16 (1985) 263; 18 (1987) 15–16, 29
DES (1983) 32–33; (1984) 35; (2002) 13

Stracathro
Britannia 1 (1970) 171–175, 273
DES (1955) 5; (1969) 2
JRS 45 (1955) 87; 48 (1958) 92
Woolliscroft, D. & Hoffmann, B., 2012. *Geophysical Survey of Stracathro Roman Fort. See* canmore.org

Ayrshire

Ardrossan
Britannia 16 (1985) 35–39
DES (1984) 34–35; (2006) 57; (2007) 68
GAJ 4 (1976) 12
JRS 41 (1951) 61
Smith, J., 1895. *Prehistoric Man in Ayrshire*, London

Brigurd
DES (1966) 15–17; (1972) 14

Girvan Mains
Britannia 15 (1984) 274; 9 (1978) 397–401
DES (1993) 86; (1996) 97; (2009) 171

Loudon Hill
DES (1947) 5; (1954) 7–8
JRS 37 (1946) 165–182; 39 (1949) 96–115; 45 (1955) 82–91

Outerwards
Britannia 2 (1971) 248–249; 3 (1972) 248–249
DES (1970) 13–14
GAJ 4 (1976) 111–123

Dumfries and Galloway

Birrens
Britannia 1 (1970) 42, 274; 16 (1985) 326; 28 (1997) 410–411
DES (1964) 25; (1965) 16–17; (1966) 21; (1967) 21; (1969) 18; (1977) 41; (1996) 31; (1999) 24; (2014) 63
JRS 41 (1951) 57–58
PSAS 30 (1895–96) 81–199
TDGNHAS 11 (1894–95) 55–67; 41 (1962–63) 135–155

Burnswark
AS 1 (1792) 124–129
DES (1967) 23; (1968) 20; (1966) 21–22; (2008) 52; (2013) 61
PSAS 33 (1898) 198–249
TDGNHAS 11 (1894) 55–67; 13 (1927) 46–58; 53 (1977) 57–104

Carzield
DES (1948) 7; (1955) 10–11; (1956) 14; (1967) 21; (1968) 14; (1973) 23
JRS 41 (1951) 58
TDGNHAS 22 (1942) 156–163

Dalswinton
DES (2009) 59
JRS 45 (1955) 85–85; 48 (1958) 89; 51 (1961) 122; 55 (1965) 79; 63 (1973) 217; 67 (1977) 131–133
TDGNHAS 34 (1955) 9–21

Drumlanrig
Britannia 16 (1985) 267, 18 (1987) 19–20, 36 (2005) 401–02
DES (1004) 35

Durisdeer
Clarke, J. 1952. Bothwellhaugh. In S. N. Miller, ed. *The Roman Occupation of South-Western Scotland*. Glasgow, pp. 124–126

Gatehouse of Fleet
DES (1960) 29; (1961) 35
JRS 41 (1951) 57; 51 (1961) 161

Ewes Door
Britannia 28 (2997) 410

Fourmerkland
JRS 41 (1951) 60

Glenlochar
DES (1955) 18
TDGNHAS 30 (1953) 1–16
Stell, G., 1996. *Dumfries and Galloway, Exploring Scotland's Heritage*, Edinburgh: RCAHMS

Glenluce
Britannia 24 (1993) 281

Raeburnfoot
Britannia 40 (2009) 123–136
DES (1947) 3; (1959) 22; (1960) 25
TDGNHAS 14 (189–98) 17–27; 24 (1945–46) 152–155; 39 (1960–61) 24–49

Dunbartonshire

Auchendavy
Britannia 16 (1985) 35–39; 33 (2002) 287
DES (1984) 34–35; (2006) 57; (2007) 68
GAJ 4 (1976) 12, 103–107
JRS 41 (1951) 61

Bar Hill
Britannia 10 (1979) 274–276; 11 (1980) 353; 12 (1981) 320; 13 (1982) 95–110; 15 (1984) 276
DES (1978) 30; (1979) 40; (1980) 36–37; (1981) 40–41; (1995) 92; (2006) 58
GAJ 10 (1980) 11–13; 12 (1985) 33–41
MacDonald, G. & Park, A., 1906. *The Roman Forts on the Bar Hill, Dunbartonshire*, Glasgow
Robertson, A.S., Scott, M. & Keppie, L., 1975. *Bar Hill: A Roman Fort and its Finds*, Oxford

Bearsden
Britannia 7 (1975) 302–304; 8 (1977) 365–367; 9 (1978) 413; 10 (1979) 276–277; 11 (1980) 353
DES (1973) 63–64; (1974) 80; (1975) 20; (1976) 29; (1977) 12; (1978) 25–26; (1979) 33; (1980) 33; (1981) 35; (1982) 24; (1995) 69; (2002) 33; (2009) 64
Breeze, D.J., 2016. *Bearsden: The Story of a Roman Fort*, Oxford: Archaeopress Archaeology

New Kilpatrick Cemetery
Britannia 14 (1983) 288
DES (2008) 59

Old Kilpatrick
Britannia 20 (1989) 270; 26 (1995) 336
DES (1988) 44; (1994) 61
GAJ (1928)
JRS 12 (1922) 241–242; 14 (1924) 206
PSAS 58 (1924) 325

Edinburgh and the Lothians

Castle Greg
Britannia 20 (1989) 271; 41 (2010) 352
DES (2012) 182–183; (2013) 188; (2015) 194

Cramond
Britannia 5 (1974) 163–224; 7 (1976) 305–306; 8 (1977) 368–370; 10 (1979) 278–279; 13 (1982) 328–395; 14 (1983) 289; 19 (1988) 429; 29 (1998) 380; 32 (2001) 321
DES (1955) 20; (1956) 17; (1957) 20; (1958) 22; (1959) 26; (1975) 24; (1976) 31–32; (1977) 13–14; (1978) 15; (1979) 18; (1982) 16; (1992) 51–52; (1996) 38; (2000) 33; (2001) 39; (2005) 63; (2002) 47; (2003) 68–69; (2005) 63–64; (2006) 68–69; (2008) 71
Holmes, N., 2003. *Excavation of Roman Sites at Cramond, Edinburgh*, Edinburgh: Society of Antiquaries of Scotland

Crichton
Britannia 14 (1983) 180
PSAS 52 (1918) 212; 66 (1932) 352

Dalkeith
DES (1974) 47; (1995) 55

Cameron, K. et al., 2010. *Excavations on the Route of the Dalkeith Northern Bypass, 1994–95 and 2006*. Scottish Archaeological Internet Report. Available at: http://archaeologydataservice.ac.uk/archiveDS/archiveDownload?t=arch-310-1/dissemination/pdf/sair44.pdf [Accessed May 29, 2018]

Edinburgh
DES (1995) 54; (2008) 72–73
PSAS 52 (1918) 38–48, 258; 94 (1960–61) 151–152; 113 (1984) 434–444

Elginhaugh
Britannia 12 (1981) 321; 14 (1983) 172–17716 (1985) 264; 18 (1987) 312–313; 40 (2009) 365–368
DES (1987) 31–32; (2007) 128–129
Hanson, W.S., 2007. *A Roman Frontier in Scotland: Elginhaugh*, Stroud
Hanson, W.S., 2007. *Elginhaugh: A Flavian Fort and its Annexe*, London

Glencorse Mains
Britannia 40 (2009) 230
DES (2008) 121; (2012) 84

Gogar Green
Britannia 13 (1982) 340; 18 (1987) 38–39
DES (1984) 16

The Ingliston Milestone
Britannia 4 (1973) 336–337; 40 (2009) 229
DES (1972) 29
PSAS 101 (1968–1969) 290–291

Inveresk
Britannia 9 (1978) 416–418; 16 (1985) 265; 26 (1995) 337; 28 (1997) 410; 33 (2002) 289; 39 (2008) 276–277
DES (1947) 3–4; (1971) 29–30; (1977) 22–23; (1981) 24; (1993) 55–56; (1996) 37; (1997) 29; (1999) 29–30; (2001) 33
PSAS 110 (1978–80) 186–304; 114 (1984) 251–259; 118 (1988) 139–176, 177–179; 123 (1993) 315–318

Linlithgow Palace
Britannia 1 (1970) 224; 21 (1990) 312
PSAS 101 (1971) 137

Pathhead
Britannia 29 (1998) 380
DES (1998) 64; (2004) 83
JRS 48 (1958) 88; 51 (1961) 121; 59 (1969) 107; 63 (1973) 216

Falkirk

Arthur's O'on
Britannia 11 (1980) 343
GAJ 4 (1976) 33
PSAS 110 (1990) 353–360

Camelon
Britannia 10 (1979) 275
DES (1998) 37
PSAS 35 (1900–01) 329–350; 109 (1977–78) 151–165; 124 (1994) 307

Carriden
Britannia 39 (2007) 276; 40 (2008) 228–229
DES (1972) 45; (1994) 8; (1997) 577–594; (2006) 78; (2007) 92; (2008) 82–83
JRS 41 (1951) 190

Castlecary
Britannia 26 (1995) 333–334
DES (1974) 64; (1976) 77; (2006) 79
GAJ 4 (1976) 12
PSAS 37 (1902–03) 271–346

Kinneil
Britannia 10 (1979) 275; 12 (1981) 150–154, 319–320; 13 (1982) 97–98
DES (1979) 3; (1981) 6; (2011) 82
PSAS 126 (1996) 303–346

Mumrills
Britannia 13 (1982) 398–399; 28 (1997) 40833 (2002) 287
DES (1985) 79; (1996) 42; (2004) 61; (2010) 74; (2016) 79
PSAS 59 (1924–25) 194–195; 63 (1928–29) 396–575; 94 (1960–61) 151

Rough Castle
Britannia 27 (1996) 400; 28 (1997) 408;
DES (1957) 38; (1959) 37; (1961) 55; (1995) 12; 2001 (45–46); (2006) 79
PSAS 67 (1925) 285–287; 39 (1005) 442–499; 67 (1933) 243–247; 110 (1981) 230–285

Seabegs Wood
Britannia 9 (1978) 415–416; 12 (1981) 156–161
DES (1977) 36; (2003) 76

Watling Lodge
Britannia 6 (1975) 226–227
DES (1972) 58; (1986) 3–4; (2015) 85
PSAS 105 (1975) 166–175

Fife

Auchtermuchty
DES (1996) 45
JRS 55 (1965) 82; 59 (1969) 116

Bonnytown
JRS 555 (1965) 82; 59 (1969) 114

Chapel Farm (Lochore)
DES (1950) 9; (1951) 8

Edenwood
Britannia 10 (1979) 274;27 (1996) 398
DES (1978) 37; (1996) 47–48

Glasgow

Balmuildy
Britannia 13 (1982) 106–107; 30 (1999) 331
DES (1971) 28; (1999) 66; (2005) 74
GAJ 29 (2007) 113–154
SAJ 29.2 (1999) 113–154
SHR 20 (1923) 173–180
Miller, S.N., 1922. *The Roman Fort at Balmuildy on the Antonine Wall*, Glasgow

Summerston
Britannia 9 (1978)
DES (1977) 53

Yorkhill
PSAS 12 (1876–78) 257; 52 (1917–18) 236–237

Highland

Castle Spirital Loch Ness (Bona)
AS 2 (1822) 35

Easter Galcantray (or Cawdor or Holme Rose)
Britannia 17 (1986) 370; 18 (1987) 34, 309; 19 (1988) 425; 20 (1989) 265
DES (1984) 14; (1985) 27; (1986) 18; (1987) 27; (1988) 15; (1989) 29; (1990) 24
PSAS 131 (2001) 186–187

Fort Augustus
DES (2005) 78; (2006) 87
PSAS 52 (1917–18) 38–48
Robertson, A.S., 1978. The circulation of Roman coins in North Britain: The evidence of hoards and site-finds from Scotland. In R.A.G. Carson & C.M. Kraay, eds. *Scripta Nummaria Romana*. London, p. 209

Newtonmore
DES (2004) 76

Nigg
PSAS 94 (1960–61) 148

Tarbat Ness
AS 2 (1822) 39–40

Inverclyde

Devol Moor
DES (1991) 60; (1995) 80

Hillside Hill
DES (1963) 43

Lurg Moor
DES (1952) 11–12; (1955) 25–26; (1959) 28; (1976) 54

Lanarkshire

Bothwellhaugh
Britannia 6 (1975) 20–35; 26 (1995) 337
Davidson, J.M., 1952. Bothwellhaugh. In S.N. Miller, ed. *The Roman Occupation of South-Western Scotland*. Glasgow, pp. 172–187

Castledykes
Britannia 15 (1984) 57–60; 19 (1988) 429–430
DES (1984) 26; (1985) 40; (1986) 30
SAF (1975) 18–24
Robertson, A.S., 1952. Castledykes (Corbiehall). In *The Roman Occupation of South-Western Scotland*. Glasgow: Glasgow Archaeological Society, pp. 127–171
Robertson, A.S., 1964. *The Roman Fort at Castledykes*, Edinburgh

Crawford
Britannia 18 (1987) 40
GAJ 4 (1976) 28
PSAS 103 (1970–71) 115
St Joseph, J.K., 1952. From Beattock to Carlops. In S.N. Miller, ed. *The Roman Occupation of South-Western Scotland*. Glasgow, pp. 113–114

Croy Hill
Britannia 7 (1976) 301–302; !976) 28; (1977) 12; (1978) 27; 8 (1977) 364–365; 10 (1979) 276; 27 (1996) 168–170
DES (1967) 24–25; (2004) 92; (2009) 127; (2000) 62
Hanson, W.S., 1979. Croy Hill. In D. Breeze, ed. *Roman Scotland: Some Recent Excavations*. Edinburgh: Inspectorate of Ancient Monuments

Little Clyde
DES (1992) 67; (2005) 134; (2006) 160; (2007) 185–186
JRS 14 (1924) 207

Mollins
Britannia 6 (1975) 35; 7 (1976) 304–305; 8 (1977) 369–370; 9 (1978) 416; 10 (1979) 278; 26 (1995) 336–337
DES (1975) 21; (1993) 93
Hanson, W.S. & Maxwell, G.S., 1980. An Agricolan Praesidium on the Forth–Clyde isthmus (Mollins, Strathclyde). *Britannia*, 11: 43–49

Motherwell
DES (1991) 70

Redshaw Burn
Britannia 32 (2001) 322
DES (2000) 86
GAJ 4 (1976) 1–6

Wandel
Britannia 2 (1971) 249
GAJ 4 (1976) 6

Moray

Auchinhove
DES (1974) 5
JRS 41 (1951) 65; 51 (1961) 123

Bellie
Britannia 17 (1986) 370
DES (1984) 12
JRS 59 (1969) 113–114

Birnie
Britannia 17 (1986) 370; 18 (1987) 34; 32 (2001) 319; 33 (2002) 284; 1 (2010) 346
DES (1969) 34; (1984) 13; (1985) 19; (1986) 11; (1988) 34; (1990) 21; (1999) 63; (2000) 58–59; (2001) 67–68; (2002) 81; (2003) 96; (2004) 84–85; (2005) 93–94; (2006) 109; (2007) 131; (2008) 122–123; (2009) 122; (2010) 108–109; (2011) 122
PSAS 131 (2001)

Culbin Sands
Britannia 1 (1970) 9
PSAS 66 (1932) 391; 68 (1934) 29; 84 (1952) 141; 88 (1956) 208, 218; 103 (1974) 231–232

Muiryfold
JRS 51 (1961) 123; 59 (1969) 118

Perth and Kinross

Ardoch
Britannia 1 (1970) 163–171; 2 (1971) 248; 9 (1978) 410; 15 (1984) 217–221; 16 (1985) 326; 26 (1995) 344; 28 (1997) 405–406
DES (1956) 6; (1973) 41; (1986) 40–41; (1993) 99; (1996) 81; (1997) 62; (1999) 70; (2002) 90–91; (2017) 139
PSAS 32 (1898) 399–476; 102 (1973) 122–128; 123 (1993) 291–313
Archaeological Journal 121 (1964) 196

Bertha
Britannia 5 (1974) 402; 40 (2009) 226–227
DES (1958) 30; (1999) 73; (2008) 155
JRS 49 (1959) 136–137
PSAS 116 (1986) 197

Blackhill
PSAS 38 (1903) 82–87

Cargill
Britannia 13 (1982) 335–336; 18 (1987) 16
DES (2005) 104; (2006) 129; (1965) 30; (2003) 104
JRS 33 (1943) 47; 48 (1958) 91; 56 (1966) 198

Carpow
Britannia 5 (1974) 290–291; 7 (1976) 299; 8 (1977) 356–425; 11 (1980) 351; 18 (1987) 27
DES (1964) 42–43; (1967) 42–44; (1968) 29–32; (1976) 42–43; (1979) 77; (1992) 76
PSAS 96 (1963) 184–207; 129 (1999) 481–575

Dalginross
Britannia 39 (208) 274
DES (1990) 44; (2006) 131
GAJ 4 (1976) 25
JRS 51 (1962) 162; 55 (1965) 81; 59 (1969) 109
PSAS 139 (2009) 273–274

Dunning
Britannia 20 (1989) 269–270; 26 (1995) 51–62
DES (1974) 52; (1988) 27; (1993) 27, 102; (1998) 376; (2009) 149; (2013) 151–152; (2014) 162–163
JRS 63 (1973) 218–219

Fendoch
DES (1984) 43; (2004) 105–106
JRS 28 (1938) 169
PSAS 70 (1935) 110–154; 73 (1938) 110–154

Glenbank
Britannia 18 (1987) 16–17
DES (1984) 4; (1998) 73; (1999) 70
PSAS 139 (2009) 273–274

Gourdie, Steeds Stalls
Britannia 18 (1987) 27
DES (1959) 27
JRS 33 (1943) 47–49; 41 (1951) 64

Inchtuthil
Britannia 18 (1987) 27
DES (1952) 10–11; (1955) 21; (1956) 19; (1957) 23; (1958) 29–30; (1959) 27–28; (2009) 145; (2010) 136–137; (2011) 46
JRS 43 (1953) 104; 44 (1954) 84; 45 (1955) 122–123; 46 (1956) 122; 47 (1956) 198–199; 48 (1958) 91; 49 (1959) 103–104; 50 (1959) 213; 51 (1961) 123, 160; 55 (1965) 82–83
PSAS 36 (1901) 182–242; 121 (1991) 27–44
Pitts, L.F. & St Joseph, J.K., 1985. *Inchtuthil: The Roman Legionary Fortress*, London: Society for the Promotion of Roman Studies

Kaims Castle
GAJ 4 (1976) 22
PSAS 35 (1900) 18–21

Strageath
Britannia 2 (1971) 248; 5 (1974) 402; 6 (1975) 225–226; 7 (1976) 300; 8 (1978) 361–363; 9 (1978) 410; 11 (1980) 351–352; 12 (1981) 319; 13 (1982) 336–337; 14 (1983) 284–287; 15 (1984) 275–276; 16 (1985) 263–264; 17 (1986) 371; 18 (1987) 309–310; 39 (2007) 274; 40 (2008) 227
JRS 41 (1951) 63; 48 (1958) 90
Frere, S.S. & Wilkes, J.J., 1989. *Strageath: Excavations within the Roman Fort 1973–1986*, London

Renfrewshire

Barochan Hill
Britannia 4 (1973) 275; 16 (1985) 265–267; 17 (1986) 311–313
DES (1972) 49; (1979) 40; (1984) 34; (1985) 49; (1986) 39; (1993) 91

Paisley
NSA Vol. 7 (Renfrew) 168

Whitemoss (Bishopton)
Britannia 48 (1958) 90
DES (1949) 10; (1952) 12–13; (1953) 14–15; (1954) 12–13; (1957) 25–27
JRS 40(1950) 93–94; 43 (1953) 105–106; 44 (1954) 86; 45 (1955) 123
PSAS 83 (1948) 28–32

Scottish Borders

Cappuck
DES (1949) 11; (1974) 61
GAJ 4 (1976) 6
PSAS 46 (1910) 446–483; 85 (1950) 138–145

Easter Happrew
Britannia 28 (1997) 412
DES (1955) 21; (1999) 79–80
PSAS 90 (1956) 93–101

Lyne
DES (1974) 49; (2017) 172
JRS 41 (1951) 57
PSAS 35 (1900) 154–186; 95 (1961) 208–218

Newstead
Britannia 19 (1988) 431; 22 (1991) 232; 25 (1994) 261; 26 (1995) 339–341; 28 (1997) 412; 29 (1998) 381; 33 (2002) 290
DES (1991) 7; (1992) 7; (1993) 7; (1994) 5; (1996) 89–90; (2005) 125
JRS 39 (1949) 99; 48 (1958) 87–88
PSAS 1 (1851) 28–33; 58 (1923) 309–324; 84 (1949) 1–38; 121 (1991) 215–222; 129 (1999) 373–391; 130 (2000) 457–467
Hunter, F. & Keppie, L.J.F. eds., 2015. *A Roman Frontier Post and its People: Newstead 1911–2011*, Edinburgh: NMSE Publishing

Oakwood
DES (1949) 11
PSAS 80 (1945) 103–117; 86 (1951) 202–205

St Leonard's Hill
Britannia 32 (2001) 332l 33 (2002) 290
GAJ 4 (1976) 6
DES (2000) 77; (2002) 101
JRS 48 (1958) 88; 51 (1961) 121; 55 (1965) 78; 59 (1969) 118

Stirling

Bochastle
DES (1948) 9–10; (1949) 10; (1953) 13–14; (1974) 52; (1998) 93; (2006) 164–165
JRS 59 (1969) 109
Anderson, W.A., Taylor, C. & Sommerville, A., 1956. The Roman fort at Bochastle, by Callander. *Transactions of the Glasgow Archaeological Society* (New Series), 14: 35–63

Craigarnhall
DES (1974) 51
JRS 67 (1977) 135; 68 (1973) 217–218

Doune
Britannia 15 (1984) 217–223, 275; 16 (1985) 264; 18 (1987) 17; 31 (2000) 381; 40 (2009) 227
DES (1984) 4; (1999) 87; (2010) 167
Masser, P., 2008. *Doune Roman Fort: Evidence from an Excavation on the Site of an Extension to Doune Primary School: Data Structure Report*
Masser, P., 2010. *Doune Roman Fort: Excavations to the East of Doune Primary School Carried Out in 2010: Data Structure Report*

Drumquhassle
Britannia 9 (1978) 411; 10 (1979) 275; 14 (1983) 168–172; 29 (1998) 379; 31 (2000) 381
DES (1978) 1; (2000) 89; (2004) 127–128
Masser, P. et al., 2010. Recent work at Drumquhassle Roman fort, Stirlingshire. *Scottish Archaeological Journal*, 24(2): 147–168

Dunblane
Britannia 27 (1996) 398
DES (1966) 37–38; (1967) 36; (1995) 14
GAJ 1 (1969) 35–36
JRS 59 (1969) 114

Malling
Britannia 9 (1978) 41–; 15 (1984) 275; 18 (1987) 29
DES (1974) 52; (2011) 179–180
JRS 59 (1969) 109–110; 63 (1973) 223–224
Wilson, D.R., 2005. Bias in air-reconnaissance. In K. Brophy & D.C. Cowley, eds., *From the Air*, Stroud: Tempus, pp. 64–72

Ochtertyre
Britannia 14 (1983) 288; 18 (1987) 39–40

Stirling
DES (1962) 88
PSAS 52 (1918) 245; 73 (1939) 244; 103 (1974) 127–128

Index